KAREN PONTOPPIDAN
KAREN PONTOPPIDAN
KAREN PONTOPPIDAN
KAREN PONTOPPIDAN
KAREN PONTOPPIDAN
KAREN PONTOPPIDAN
KAREN PONTOPPIDAN
KAREN PONTOPPIDAN

THE ONE WOMAN GROUP EXHIBITION

herausgegeben von / edited by Michael Buhrs und / and Ellen Maurer Zilioli

THE ONE WOMAN GROUP EXHIBITION

Es ist äußerst verlockend, die Situation in den Historischen Räumen der Villa Stuck für pseudoprovokante Gegenüberstellungen zu nutzen. Hier Franz von Stuck, der niederbayerische Künstlerfürst, der sein Selbstporträt über den Eingang des Empfangszimmers setzt und überhaupt die Selbstinszenierung in der von ihm geplanten Villa auf die Spitze treibt. Demgegenüber bieten sich verschiedene Möglichkeiten der ironischen Spiegelung an: a) Künstler*innen einer jungen Generation, die sich mit der Selbstvermarktungsindustrie unserer Zeit beschäftigen, oder b) Künstler*innen aus gänzlich anderen Kulturkreisen, die das westliche, bis heute durchaus weiterexistierende Hierarchiemodell des 19. Jahrhunderts untersuchen.

Zielführender ist jedoch die Methode c): die Einladung an eine Künstlerin, die auf subtile Weise Identitäten und Rollenklischees ins Wanken bringt, das eigene Tun hinterfragt (und damit den Output ihres Metiers überhaupt) und der es gelingt, auf Basis derartiger Unsicherheiten dennoch ein selbstbewusstes, vielfältiges und beeindruckendes Œuvre zu entwickeln, das sie zu einer der progressivsten Figuren des Autor*innenschmucks macht.

Ich bin äußerst glücklich darüber, dass mit Karen Pontoppidan eine international renommierte Künstlerin und unermüdliche Vermittlerin ihres Faches (aktuell als Leiterin der Klasse für Schmuck und Gerät an der Akademie der Bildenden Künste München) gerade nicht in die Rolle der Provokateurin schlüpft, sondern gemeinsam mit der Kuratorin der Ausstellung, Dr. Ellen Maurer Zilioli, einen intelligenten Parcours entwickelt, der vieles infrage stellt – unter anderem die Autorschaft der Objekte – und zumindest auf manches höchst pointierte Antworten gibt. Anderes wird bewusst offen und unbeantwortet gelassen ... Beiden, der Künstlerin und der Kuratorin, gilt mein herzlicher Dank!

Ein großer Dank gilt ebenso den Leihgeber*innen der Ausstellung aus Amsterdam, Apeldoorn, Dallas, München und Pforzheim für die Bereitstellung der Arbeiten. Ich danke des Weiteren der Projektkoordinatorin Sara Kühner, der Restauratorin Susanne Eid sowie den Teams sowohl vom Museum Villa Stuck als auch von Karen Pontoppidan für den reibungslosen Aufbau der ONE WOMAN GROUP EXHIBITION.

Das vorliegende Buch ergänzt die Ausstellung in wunderbarer Art und Weise durch die Texte von Dr. Ellen Maurer Zilioli und Dr. Maria Muhle wie auch durch die Gestaltung von Susanne Dell. Mein weiterer Dank gilt der Übersetzerin Wendy Brouwer, den Lektorinnen Tina Rausch und Sarah Trenker, dem Fotografen der Installationsansichten aus dem Museum Villa Stuck, Jann Averwerser, sowie Uta Grosenick und Rebecca Wilton vom DISTANZ Verlag für die gute Zusammenarbeit.

Michael Buhrs
Direktor . Museum Villa Stuck . München

THE ONE WOMAN GROUP EXHIBITION

It is extremely tempting to use the location of the Historical Rooms at Villa Stuck for pseudo-provocative juxtapositions. Here, where Franz von Stuck, the artist prince from Lower Bavaria, placed his self-portrait over the entrance to the reception room and took self-staging to the extreme by designing a villa for himself. Then again, there are also manifold possibilities for ironic reflection of a) a new generation of artists engaged with today's industry of self-marketing, or b) artists from completely different cultures who are investigating the still extant Western hierarchical model of the nineteenth century.

Closer to hitting the mark, however, is c) the invitation of an artist who subtly unhinges identities and stereotypes, questions her own actions (and in doing so even the work of her own profession) and nevertheless successfully develops such a self-confident, diverse and impressive oeuvre based on these instabilities that she has become one of the most progressive figures in auteur jewelry.

I am absolutely delighted that Karen Pontoppidan, an internationally renowned artist and relentless arbiter of her discipline (currently head of the jewelry and devices class at the Munich Academy of Fine Arts), has not slipped into the role of provocateur but rather, together with exhibition curator Dr. Ellen Maurer Zilioli, has developed an intelligent show that questions many things—including the authorship of objects—and provides highly pointed answers, at least to some of them; others will very consciously remain open and unanswered ... My sincere thanks go to both the artist and the curator.

A big thank you also goes to lenders from Amsterdam, Apeldoorn, Dallas, Munich, and Pforzheim for providing works for this exhibition. Furthermore, I thank the project coordinator Sara Kühner, restorer Susanne Eid, and the teams behind Museum Villa Stuck and Karen Pontoppidan for the smooth installation of THE ONE WOMAN GROUP EXHIBITION.

This book complements the exhibition superbly with texts by Dr. Ellen Maurer Zilioli and Dr. Maria Muhle and its graphic design by Susanne Dell. Further thanks extend to translator Wendy Brouwer, copy editors Tina Rausch and Sarah Trenker, and the photographer of the installation views at the Museum Villa Stuck, Jann Averwerser, as well as Uta Grosenick and Rebecca Wilton from DISTANZ publishing house, for the good teamwork.

Michael Buhrs
Director . Museum Villa Stuck . Munich

Schönheit unter Vorbehalt

Meine erste reale Begegnung mit den Arbeiten der Künstlerin Karen Pontoppidan war im Jahr 2004 in der Hnoss Gallery in Göteborg, jener legendären Plattform für zeitgenössischen Schmuck, die sich mehr als ein Jahrzehnt hartnäckig einsetzte, dem schwedischen Publikum die internationale Avantgarde näherzubringen. Ich erinnere mich gut an die Rauheit der Stücke. Den Formen, Kanten und Oberflächen war eine gewisse Robustheit eigen, die einen interessanten Kontrast bildete zu den präzise gearbeiteten Details der eingravierten Symbolik, welche viele der Broschen und Ringe zierte. Sie drückten Selbstbewusstsein aus und unterschieden sich von den meisten Stücken, die ich bislang gesehen hatte. Ich erinnere mich an den Kommentar eines Schmuckkünstlers in der Galerie: »Ich wäre nicht in der Lage, etwas so Grobes anzufertigen, selbst wenn ich es wollte.« Als Rezensent für die schwedische Zeitschrift *Form* schrieb ich damals über jene Ausstellung, dass sich hier »Schönheit unter Vorbehalt« manifestiere.

Heute ist Karen Pontoppidans Œuvre eine wichtige und weltbekannte Komponente der zeitgenössischen Schmuckkunst. Ihr Werk besteht allerdings nicht aus einer kontinuierlichen und kohärenten Aneinanderreihung von Objekten; vielmehr resultiert ihre projektorientierte Arbeitsweise in einer Ansammlung separater, deutlich unterschiedlicher Objektgruppen. Betrachtet man diese in der Retrospektive, so kann die Entwicklung ihrer Arbeit als eine Geschichte von Brüchen und Veränderungen gesehen werden. Dies wiederum stellt die vor allem auch in der Kunstwandwerksszene stark vertretene traditionelle Ansicht infrage, dass künstlerische Arbeit etwas ist, was sich langsam entwickelt und bei der der nächste Schritt logisch auf den vorhergehenden folgt. Und dennoch gibt es da etwas, das alles zusammenhält – eine bestimmte Einstellung, eine unterschwellige Unlust zu gefallen –, was wiederum jenes oben erwähnte künstlerische Selbstbewusstsein widerzuspiegeln scheint.

Auch als Pädagogin leistete Karen Pontoppidan einen wichtigen Beitrag in ihrem künstlerischen Schaffensbereich. Bevor sie ihre aktuelle Stelle an der Akademie der Bildenden Künste München antrat, war sie neun Jahre lang (2006–2015) als Professorin am Ädellab (dt. Edel-Labor), dem Fachbereich für Schmuck und Metallverarbeitung an der Konstfack University of Arts, Crafts and Design in Stockholm, tätig.
Für das RIAN Design Museum ist es eine große Freude, die Künstlerin wieder zurück in Schweden begrüßen zu dürfen, da die Wanderausstellung zu ihrer Retrospektive auch an der schwedischen Westküste gastiert.

Love Jönsson
Direktor . RIAN Design Museum . Falkenberg

Beauty with Reservations

My first real-life encounter with the work of Karen Pontoppidan took place in 2004 at the Hnoss gallery in Gothenburg, that legendary platform for contemporary jewelry that for more than a decade relentlessly introduced the Swedish audience to the international avant-garde.

I remember the roughness of the pieces. Shapes, edges and surfaces had a certain sturdiness that stood out against the fine details of the engraved imagery that adorned many of the brooches and rings. They expressed self-confidence, and were different from much of what I had seen. "I couldn't make something so crude even if I wanted to," I remember one jewelry artist commenting in the gallery. As a reviewer for Sweden's *Form* magazine, I wrote about the exhibition that it manifested "beauty with reservations."

Today, Karen Pontoppidan's œuvre forms a strong and well-known part of contemporary jewelry. But rather than presenting a continuous and coherent stream of objects, her project-oriented way of working has resulted in an output made up of separate, distinctly different groups. Seen in retrospect, the development of her work can be read as a story of ruptures and changes. This challenges the traditional notion, particularly strong within the crafts community, of artistic work as something that develops slowly and where the next step is logically based on the previous. Still there is something that keeps it all together—a certain attitude, an underlying unwillingness to please, that might reflect the artistic self-confidence mentioned earlier.

As a pedagogue, Karen Pontoppidan has also made a significant contribution to her artistic field. Before taking up her current position at the Akademie der Bildenden Künste in Munich, she served for nine years (2006–2015) as professor in the Ädellab department for jewelry and metalwork at the Konstfack University of Arts, Crafts and Design in Stockholm.
For the RIAN Design Museum it is a great pleasure to welcome the artist back to Sweden as the touring version of her retrospective exhibition makes a stop on the Swedish west coast.

Love Jönsson
Director . RIAN Design Museum . Falkenberg

THE ONE WOMAN GROUP EXHIBITION

Schmuck + Identität

»The power of art is unlimited for social change.« (Adrian Piper)[1]

Karen Pontoppidan (geb. 1968 in Kerteminde / Dänemark) führt das Schmuck-Auditorium auf ungewohntes Gelände, indem sie ihre Tätigkeit im traditionellen Metier mit kritischen Überlegungen zu diversen gesellschaftlichen Problematiken verknüpft. Das ist nicht unbedingt das, was mit einem hübschen Kleinod gemeinhin assoziiert wird.

Pontoppidans Intentionen kreisen um unbequeme, konfliktreiche, um chronische kulturelle Dilemma, die sie in ihren Arbeiten auf witzige, ironische, sarkastische, provokante Weise sowohl kommentiert wie auch konterkariert und ihnen damit eine ästhetische Dimension verleiht. Mit diesem Anliegen steht sie im internationalen Panorama nicht allein, wenngleich eine ähnlich konzise, theoretisch unterfütterte Haltung in der Welt des zeitgenössischen Schmucks wohl eher selten anzutreffen sein dürfte. Vor allem gelingt es Pontoppidan, die spezifische »Münchner Geschichte« in diesem Bereich durch eine weitere, singuläre und konsequent die bisherigen Tendenzen erweiternde, individuelle Note zu bereichern. Die Akademie der Bildenden Künste München und ihre Schmuckklasse erhielt mit ihr als Professorin erneut eine starke, unbeugsame Persönlichkeit, welche der Disziplin ein markantes Gesicht schenkt, das von dauerhaftem Bestand und zukunftsweisender Bedeutung sein wird.

Auch wenn die Dinge auf den ersten Blick nicht so erscheinen, alles fing ganz harmlos an. Pontoppidan hat sich ihr Handwerk von der Pieke auf angeeignet und beherrscht dieses meisterlich. Vielleicht liegt darin bereits eine Reibungsenergie, die sie immer wieder zum Verlassen des gediegenen Umgangs mit ihrer Materie stimuliert, ein ganz besonderer Reiz, der sie zur Absage an herkömmliche Glaubenssätze im Schmuck lockt, zur Grenzüberschreitung und Verweigerung – dazu im Folgenden mehr.

Nach zweijährigem Praktikum in Kopenhagen und einer Ausbildung in Schwäbisch Gmünd wechselte Pontoppidan an die Akademie in München und studierte ab 1991 bei Prof. Otto Künzli. Es entstanden BLUMEN&BOLLER, dazwischen KAKTEEN, AUTOSCHMUCK und VASEN – eine Mischung aus unförmigen und doch liebevoll gestalteten, absurd wirkenden Gebilden in farbenfrohem Email. Getrieben von der Lust und Freude am »Unschönen«, am Banalen und vielleicht Ekligen, Abstoßenden, Regelverletzenden, weidet sich die Autorin an der überraschenden Bandbreite ihrer Kreationen von Ringen und Broschen. Sie zeugen vom Verrat am Prunkhaften, am Klunker, am Juwel. Pontoppidan setzt an Schönheit, Kostbarkeit, Geschmack gekettete Dogmen außer Kraft. BLUMEN&BOLLER begegnen uns zunächst scheinbar plump, hässlich und zuweilen gar obszön. Tatsächlich aber verfügen sie über eigene Qualitäten, zum Beispiel in den brillant behandelten Oberflächen – glänzend, matt, geätzt, durch Sandstrahlung oder Beigaben pointiert. Sie verletzen ein Tabu und entwickeln zugleich ihr eigenes prägnantes, fremdes, abweichendes Charisma.

Neben dieser Werkgruppe, die Pontoppidan einige Jahre beschäftigte, fertigte die Autorin überhäkelte Schmuckstücke und genähte Miniaturschatullen, um erneut auf die Diskrepanz zwischen biederer Niedlichkeit und Andersartigkeit in persiflierender Übertreibung hinzuweisen, ein Camouflage-Motiv, das – wenn wir so wollen – durchgängig im Werk präsent bleibt und sich letztlich auch in dieser Ausstellung manifestiert.

Damit ist Pontoppidan gleich zu Beginn ihrer künstlerischen Laufbahn aus der Reihe getanzt und hat den Regelverstoß als persönliches Leitmotiv etabliert. Ihr Interesse gilt der Abweichung, dem »Nicht-Aufgehen« (der Schmuckrechnung), also der Nicht-Erfüllung von Erwartungen an die Künstlerin, was sie unter anderen mit Jutta Koether verbindet[2] – und nicht nur das, wie noch zu sehen sein wird. Das Abdriften und Vermeiden vom Regulären, vom akademischen Maßstab gerät zur subversiven Haltung, zur künstlerischen Strategie.[3] Im Gegensatz zur unbewussten und wiederholenden Übernahme von Symbolen und Zeichen im Rahmen bestehender Festschreibungen und Hierarchien setzt Pontoppidan auf das Widerstandspotenzial als kreatives Instrument, das die Identität ihrer Disziplin mit der Identität ihrer Urheberin in Beziehung setzt und diese Relation gleichzeitig facettenreich inszeniert beziehungsweise beleuchtet – durch Parodie etwa, durch den Blick auf die Kehrseite des dekorativ Verträglichen, durch die Inthronisierung einer widerspenstigen Ästhetik. Pontoppidan vollzieht einen künstlerischen Schachzug, der automatisch Warnsignale, Störfaktoren, Antagonismus, Andersartigkeit mit sich führt.[4] Und schafft sich dadurch Frei-

THE ONE WOMAN GROUP EXHIBITION

Jewelry + Identity

"The power of art is unlimited for social change." (Adrian Piper)[1]

Karen Pontoppidan (b. 1968 in Kerteminde, Denmark) leads the jewelry auditorium into unfamiliar territory by combining her traditional line of work with critical reflections on various social problems. Not quite what one commonly associates with a pretty piece of jewelry. Pontoppidan's intentions revolve around uncomfortable, conflictual, "chronic" cultural dilemmas that her work both comments on and contradicts in a witty, ironic, sarcastic, and provocative way, thus lending them an aesthetic dimension. She is not alone in her ambition in the international sphere, even though it would be difficult to find a similarly concise, theoretically underpinned position in the world of contemporary jewelry. Most notably, Pontoppidan succeeds in enriching this arena's unique "Munich history" with another singular, individual style that constantly expands on previous trends. With her as a professor, the Academy of Applied Arts and its jewelry class gained yet another strong, unrelenting personality who has endowed the discipline with a marked sense of vision that will be of lasting tenure and groundbreaking significance.

Everything began very innocuously, even though it may not seem so now. Karen Pontoppidan mastered her craft from the ground up. Perhaps early on a frictional energy already existed in it that drove her over and over again to abandon interacting with the material in a sedate way, a special allure that beckoned her to reject conventional tenets in jewelry, to overstep boundaries, to baulk—more on that later.

After a two-year work placement in Copenhagen and training in Schwäbisch Gmünd, Pontoppidan transferred to the Academy in Munich, studying from 1991 under Prof. Otto Künzli. There BLUMEN&BOLLER were created, interposed with KAKTEEN, AUTOSCHMUCK, and VASEN—a mixture of shapeless yet lovingly created, absurd-looking objects in colorful enamel. Driven by her passion for and joy in "the unattractive," in the banal, and perhaps the loathsome, the repulsive, and the breaking of rules, the artist revels in the surprising spectrum of her ring and brooch creations. They bespeak the perfidiousness of that which is showy, of "bling," of jewels; Pontoppidan renders invalid the dogmas associated with beauty, preciousness, taste. At first BLUMEN&BOLLER appear ungainly, ugly, and on occasion vulgar. Yet they possess, in fact, their own distinct qualities, for example in the superbly treated surfaces—glossy, matt, etched, which are emphasized by sandblasting or add-ons. They violate a taboo and at once develop their own incisive, unfamiliar, aberrant charm.

Alongside this group of works, which occupied Pontoppidan for several years, the author produced jewelry pieces covered with crochet and sewn miniature caskets, in order to point out once again in a satirizing overstatement the discrepancy between simple prettiness and otherness—a camouflage motif, which—if you will—remains present throughout the work and ultimately also manifests itself in this exhibition.

Right from the beginning of her artistic career, Pontoppidan was thus already "marching to a different tune" and had established violating the rules as her personal leitmotif. Actually it is the discrepancy, the misconception (of the jewelry), i.e. the non-fulfilment of expectations toward the artist that interests her, which, incidentally, links her to Jutta Koether, among others—and not only that.[2] Allowing leeway, avoiding what is mainstream, the academic standard, turns into a subversive stance, an artistic strategy.[3] Contrary to the unconscious and repetitive adoption of symbols and signs within existing definitions and hierarchies, Pontoppidan focuses on the potential of resistance as a creative vehicle that brings together the identity of her discipline with the identity of its creator and simultaneously stages and examines this relationship in multifaceted ways—through parody, for example, by viewing the flipside of what is decoratively agreeable, by empowering an unruly aesthetic. Pontoppidan executes an artistic gambit that by default brings with it warning signals, confounding factors, antagonism, and otherness.[4] And in doing so creates free spaces: "It is precisely here where transformation processes of identity take place."[5] Jewelry is "derailed," presenting alternative suggestions to beauty, to the norm.

räume: »Exakt hier ist der Ort, an dem Transformationsprozesse von Identitäten stattfinden.«[5] Der Schmuck »entgleist« und unterbreitet alternative Vorschläge zur Schönheit, zur Norm.
Wir kennen das Mitdenken des Gegenteils – etwa bei Otto Künzli und seinem proklamierten »Think the Opposite« – oder die generelle Proklamierung einer offenen experimentellen Aussage im zeitgenössischen Kunsthandwerk. Doch wird in diesem Fall der Diskurs ergänzt durch die Rückkoppelung von Ästhetik, Rezeption und Geschlecht, nach der Konditionierung von Wahrnehmung und Identität: Pontoppidan bewegt sich über die Jahre zunehmend in die Richtung einer gedankenvollen, hintergründigen, aufmüpfigen Stilvielfalt, die mit den expressiven BLUMEN&BOLLER einen bravourösen Auftakt nimmt und bereits hier die Notwendigkeit einer »veränderte(n) Erkenntnisbereitschaft« bezeugt, die sich einer »anderen Schönheit« zu öffnen vermag, welche Irregularität, Bruch und Irritation berücksichtigt.[6]

Nach BLUMEN&BOLLER wendet sich Pontoppidan mit ihrer bislang umfangreichsten Werkgruppe O.T. erneut einer prinzipiellen Fragestellung zu: der Bild- und Schmuckwürdigkeit. Die Zeichnung spielt dabei eine zentrale Rolle. Schon immer galt sie der Goldschmiedin als Refugium, als Notiz, als Medium zur Sammlung von Ideen, als experimentelles Stadium, als Mittel der Recherche. Sie rückt nun bei den Broschen und Ringen von O.T. als Gravur und Akzentuierung ins Blickfeld. Pontoppidan spürt Motive auf, die eher dem weiblichen Lebenszusammenhang, dem häuslichen Alltag entspringen, wie Klobrille, Pantoffeln, Socken, Bügeleisen oder auch Innereien und Körperteile. Es kann aber auch ein Sumoringer sein, eine Straßenwalze oder ein perlengeschmücktes Pissoir. Farbe tritt zurück. Die gesamte Atmosphäre der Objekte wird durch neutrale, gekratzte, leicht gesprenkelte oder milchig weiß charakterisierte Oberflächen und Farbigkeit beherrscht. Ab 2002 kommen Tier-, später Menschendarstellungen hinzu. Deren groteske Platzierung auf Silber, deren flüchtig wirkendes Auftauchen, deren bewusst durch Emailflecken, Niello oder Oxidation verschmutzten und damit malerisch akzentuierten Fonds, ihre unregelmäßigen, ihre offenkundig gewollt stümperhaft ausgeführten Konturen, die gezielt schlampige Anfertigung, die Applikation vager Verweise auf das Schmückende, die Perlenkette etwa, die Kette an sich, die teilweise wie Überbleibsel beiläufig die Broschenbilder umkränzen und ergänzen – all das sprengt die Doktrin des konventionell Schönen und Zulässigen.

Die Zeichnung fungiert dabei als Verbündete, als Instrument der Kritik, der unangemessenen Einmischung, des gekonnt trotzigen Einwandes, dabei keinerlei Anspruch auf Fingerfertigkeit oder Perfektion erhebend, im Gegenteil eine unbedarfte Naivität vorgaukelnd – was übrigens erneut zu Jutta Koether führt, von der gesagt wird, dass sie eine »Art des Zeichnens erfunden« habe, »die ›schlecht‹ genug ist, um die Arbeit einer höchst geübten Künstlerin zu sein«.[7] Nicht zufällig sind es zahlreiche Künstlerinnen, die sich auf dem Feld der Zeichnung engagieren und dadurch zu einer Verschiebung der klassischen Parameter in den Kunstgattungen beigetragen haben. Vor diesem Hintergrund »contemporary fine art drawing frequently overlap[s] with the critical concerns of feminism« und beinhaltet die Option »to instantiate non-hierarchical relationships, articulated in and across difference«[8] – Aspekte, auf die wir uns bei Pontoppidan berufen dürfen. Sie überschreitet die Schwelle zur künstlerischen Aktion. Sie attackiert und unterwandert das Dekorative, das Hübsche, das Idealisierende und Vervollkommnende, kurz: die Erwartung an die Schmuckoptik.

Mit den FAMILYPORTRAITS ereignet sich eine weitere Wende im Werk. Erbstücke aus Zinn liefern das Rohmaterial für diesen Zyklus. Reflektionen zur Familiengeschichte, zu Sinn und Tragweite verwandtschaftlicher Systeme, zu deren Eingriff und Auswirkung auf Identität und subjektives Empfinden bewegen die Künstlerin dazu, die Umrisse fiktiver Porträts auf unterschiedlich zugeschnittenen Zinnplatten durch Gravur einzubetten. Von der eher flachen Gestalt der O.T. wechselt Pontoppidan zu einer gebauten körperlichen Statur, deren vernähte, unregelmäßige Scheiben sich zu labilen Gebilden vereinen. Gesichter und Profile heben sich diskret von der matten, manchmal geschwärzten und vereinzelt farblich gefassten Fläche ab. Die gedrungenen oder gestreckten, offenen oder geschlossenen Gehäuse verraten einmal mehr die symptomatische Handschrift der Autorin, denn scheinbar ungelenk, unbeholfen, beliebig fügen sich die Glieder zu seltsamen Machwerken, die als Anhänger gedacht sind und auch als solche funktionieren. Die Porträts befinden sich gestreut ebenso auf der Außenseite wie auf der Innenseite, exponiert oder im Bauch der Konstruktionen ver- und geborgen. Fragil und doch massiv umschreibt die Haut dieser an Blüten, Früchte, Säcke, Körper, Schatullen gemahnenden, technoid und organisch zugleich wirkenden Objekte einen Raum, der doch nichts wirklich enthalten kann. Dieser beherbergt und versinnbildlicht jedoch im übertragenen Sinne das Anliegen der Künstlerin, ihre Sensibilität für unbequeme Sujets in Korrespondenz zur instabilen Konstellation ihrer

We are already familiar with thinking to the contrary—for example when Otto Künzli expounded his "Think the Opposite"—or the general proclamation of an overtly experimental statement in contemporary "arts and crafts." Yet in this case, the discourse is supplemented by a feedback of aesthetic, reception, and gender according to the conditioning of perception and identity. Meaning that over the years, Pontoppidan has moved more and more toward a thoughtful, profound, defiant range of styles, one which was set in motion in a masterful way with the expressive BLUMEN&BOLLER and which here already attested to the need for a "modified willingness for enlightenment," one that may open itself up to a "different beauty," one mindful of irregularity, disruption, and irritation.[6]

With the most extensive group of works to date after BLUMEN&BOLLER, Pontoppidan turns once again to a fundamental question—the worth of image and jewelry—with O.T. in which drawing plays a central role. For the goldsmith, it has always been a refuge, a memorandum, a medium to collate ideas, an experimental arena, a means of research. Now it comes to the fore in the brooches and rings of O.T. as engraving, an accent. Pontoppidan traces motifs that emanate more from the female life nexus, the everyday domestic realm, such as toilet seats, slippers, cars, socks, irons, but also entrails and body parts. In fact, it could just as well be a sumo wrestler, street roller, or a urinal decorated with cut pearls. Color takes a back seat here; the objects' overall feel is dominated by neutral, scratched, lightly dappled, or milky white surfaces and colors. From 2002 on, representations of animals and humans were added. Their grotesque application onto silver, their fleeting materialization, their versos deliberately "dirtied" with flecks of enamel as well as niello and oxidation and thus a painterly accent, their irregular, intentionally and overtly amateurish contours, the deliberate "shoddy" production, the application of vague references to the decorative, the pearl necklace for example, the necklace per se, which in part casually festoons and supplements the brooches' images like leftovers—all this blows apart the doctrines of conventional beauty, of what is acceptable.

Yet, at the same time, drawing functions as an ally, as an instrument of criticism, of inappropriate interference, of skilled, defiant dissent, and with it demands neither dexterity nor perfection yet masquerades as inexperienced naiveté—which, incidentally, brings us back again to Jutta Koether, of whom it was once said that she "invented a kind of drawing that is 'bad' enough to be the work of a highly skilled artist."[7] It is no coincidence that there are many women artists especially who engage in drawing and have thus contributed to a shift in the classical parameters of this genre. Against this backdrop, "contemporary fine art drawing frequently overlap[s] with the critical concerns of feminism" and implies the option "to instantiate non-hierarchical relationships, articulated in and across difference,"[8] aspects that we may appeal to in Pontoppidan. She crosses the threshold of artistic action. She attacks and subverts the decorative, the pretty, the idealizing and perfecting, in short: the expectation of jewelry's visual effect.

A further transition in her oeuvre takes place in her FAMILY PORTRAITS. Tin heirlooms provide the raw material for this cycle of works. Reflections on familial history, on the meaning and consequences of relational systems, on their encroachment and impact on identity and subjective sensibilities prompt the author to engrave the outlines of fictitious portraits onto tin plaques in differing shapes. The artist switches from the rather flat form of O.T. to a constructed, corpus-like form, whose stitched, irregular panels combine to form precarious creations. Faces and profiles stand out discretely from the matt, partly blackened and sporadically colored surfaces. The stocky or elongated, open or closed corpuses reveal once again the author's symptomatic signature style, for the elements resign themselves in a seemingly awkwardly, ungainly, arbitrary way to odd concoctions conceived as pendants, which do also function as such. The portraits are exposed or concealed and secure in the "belly" of the construction, on both the exterior and interior surfaces. Fragile and yet solid, the "skin" of these technoid and organic objects, reminiscent of blossoms, fruits, sacks, bodies, commemorative caskets, defines a space that cannot actually contain anything. In the metaphorical sense, however, it accommodates and epitomizes the objectives of the artist, her sensitivity toward uncomfortable subjects in correspondence with the unstable configuration of her works, with the respective sensitive and fluctuating fabric of familial relationships. And not forgetting the melancholic, poetic aspect, which is able to adapt to absence and time by means of imaginary picture albums and their implied allusions.

Werke, zur entsprechenden empfindlichen und veränderlichen Konsistenz familiärer Beziehungen. Nicht zu vergessen der melancholische, poetische Aspekt, der sich anhand imaginärer Bilderalben und ihrer implizierten Anspielung auf Absenz und Zeit einzustellen vermag.
Alle Werkgruppen der Autorin greifen Argumentationen auf, die Eigenständigkeit und Authentizität kontra gesellschaftlicher Norm und Konditionierung betreffen und dabei eine autonome Semiotik entwickeln durch rebellische, aufrührerische Physiognomie. Damit eignet sich Pontoppidan jene legendären »Leerstellen« an, veranschaulicht jene »Paradoxien«, jene noch undefinierten Posten in einer bestehenden symbolischen Ordnung, welche die Entstehung kontroverser Identitäten und die Aufhebung symbolischer Systeme garantieren – hier in Form einer alternierenden Ästhetik.[9]

Der Faden ist als weiblicher Identifikationsfaktor im Gepäck der Künstlerin fest verzurrt. Er besitzt eine hochgradig metaphorische Relevanz, verwebt er doch, bildlich gemeint, Gedanken überhaupt, garantiert den fortlaufenden Diskurs, den Bestand des Dialogs und sorgt für die Abwägung unterschiedlicher Argumente.[10] Die Linie der Zeichnung – wie bei O.T. – findet also eine logische Erweiterung in der Verwendung des Fadens, der über eine zusätzliche sozialkritische Verweiskette verfügt, wenn wir an die häusliche Produktion des Garns durch Frauen, an ihren Part in der Entwicklung der Textilindustrie, an deren Schlüsselrolle für die industrielle Revolution und so weiter denken. Am Anfang steht der Faden, an ihm hängen eine ganze Menge sozialhistorischer Gewichte.[11]
Und so zieht er sich auch durch Pontoppidans Werk, um komplexe Inhalte und Aussagen zu verflechten. Dezent und unauffällig verbandelt er die Sujets und Ideen. Zeichnung und Faden vermählen sich in einigen Arbeiten auf besonders nachdrückliche Weise, wenn Pontoppidan etwa mit Eisendraht in das Silber näht und ihre Darstellung leicht oxidieren lässt. Faden und Zeichnung verschmelzen im malerischen Schimmer.
Der Faden führt uns weiter zu HOME, einer Reihe von Anhängern, die, eng gekoppelt an FAMILYPORTRAITS, bereits parallel entworfen wurden. Anders als bei den Porträts, welche imaginäre Familienkonstruktionen suggerieren, deren Verformbarkeit, deren flüchtige, provisorische Konstellation ins Zentrum rücken, verdichtet sich in dieser Gruppe die Vorstellung der Wahlverwandtschaft, der Wahlfamilie, des selbst ausgesuchten sozialen Umfeldes, das doch im Laufe des Lebens die eigentliche Geborgenheit, die emotionale Behausung bietet und damit eine selbstständig ausgewählte Konstellation schafft. HOME erinnert an Schutz, Beheimatung, Zuflucht, Abschirmung und Hort – mit länglichen, hohen, kleinen, schmalen, weiß lackierten, verkratzten, geschwärzten oder in ihrem Naturzustand belassenen Häuschen aus Zinn, deren Flanken mit weißem, rotem, schwarzem, grauem Garn vernäht sind. Auf dem First befindet sich der Anschluss für die Transformation zum Halsschmuck.

Zinn wurde und wird bekanntermaßen unter anderem zum Glockenguss, für Kultgegenstände, Trophäen und Objekte zum Gedenken oder als Auszeichnung in Sport, Jagd und Wettstreit verwendet, so auch bei Pontoppidan. Er stammt von Eltern und Großeltern und ist mit familiärer Atmosphäre kontaminiert. Allein das Einschmelzen, seine Verwicklung in die Entstehung tiefsinniger Werkgruppen wie FAMILY PORTRAITS und HOME, symbolisiert einen Akt der Umkehrung von Wertesystemen, von Bedeutungsmustern. Darüber hinaus zelebriert die Künstlerin einmal mehr ihre Absage an die mit Preziosen verbundenen Kategorien von Ewigkeit und Bestand. Bei den Anhängern spielen Trägerin und Träger stets eine zusätzliche performative, interpretative Rolle. Sie nehmen teil an der Aufführung, der Zurschaustellung, an den Inhalten dieser Werke.

CANVAS_CONTEXT_CASH aus dem Zeitraum 2010 bis 2015 untersucht als Trilogie Beziehungen und Problemzonen zwischen den angewandten und den herkömmlich als freie bezeichneten Künsten. Bei CANVAS greift Pontoppidan das Element der Leinwand auf, welches sich als Referenzmaterial um schlichte Holzkörper legt. Sie scheinen sich an geometrischen Vorlagen zu orientieren, ohne aber einer klaren mathematischen Gestalt zu entsprechen. Dazu gesellen sich genietete oder genagelte ornamentale Applikationen. Sie setzen die Antithese zum Bild. Pop- und Op-Art, Jugendstil, Surrealismus, Farbfeldmalerei, Konzeptkunst, Assemblage sorgen unter anderem für Anregung und werden als Zitate fragmentarisch aufgerufen, eine freche Überlappung von »High« und »Low«, eine unterhaltsame Mischung zersprengter und aufgemischter Splitter und Verweise, die sich in einer neuen Einheit zusammenfinden. Und es geht noch weiter: Im Gegensatz zur Auseinandersetzung mit dem Instrumentenkanon und dem lockeren Aufheben einer vertrauten Allianz – wie eben von Leinwand und Holzrahmen bei CANVAS – ironisiert die Goldschmiedin mit CONTEXT eine gängige, ja modische künstlerische Attitüde, etwa die Studioproduktion ohne geringste Beteiligung des ideellen Urhebers. Kleine schachtelförmige Broschen aus nach innen gestülpter, bemalter Leinwand, von silbernen Heftklammern

All the author's groups of works seize on rationales of individuality and authenticity as opposed to societal norms and conditioning and thus develop an autonomous semiotics through a rebellious, insurgent external aspect. In doing so, Pontoppidan appropriates those legendary "empty spaces," exemplifies those "paradoxes," those still undefined positions in an existing symbolic order that guarantee the creation of controversial identities and the abolition of symbolic systems—here in the form of an alternating aesthetic.[9]

The thread is firmly bound in the artist's trappings as a factor of identification (female). Despite being of high metaphorical relevance, it actually "interweaves" thoughts, figuratively speaking, guarantees ongoing discourse, a continued dialogue; it ensures that differing arguments are taken into consideration.[10] The drawn line—as in O.T.—thus finds a logical extension in the use of the thread, which commands an additional sociocritical chain of reference when we think of the domestic production of yarn by women, of their part in the development of the textile industry, of their key role in the industrial revolution, and so on: the thread, on which so much sociohistorical weight hangs, is at the source of it all.[11] And thus it flows into Pontoppidan's work, in order to entwine complex subject matter and declarations. Understated and inconspicuous, it brings together subjects and ideas. Drawing and thread marry together in several works in a particularly emphatic way, for example when Pontoppidan sews silver with iron wire and allows the work to oxidize slightly. Thread and drawing meld in a painterly luster.

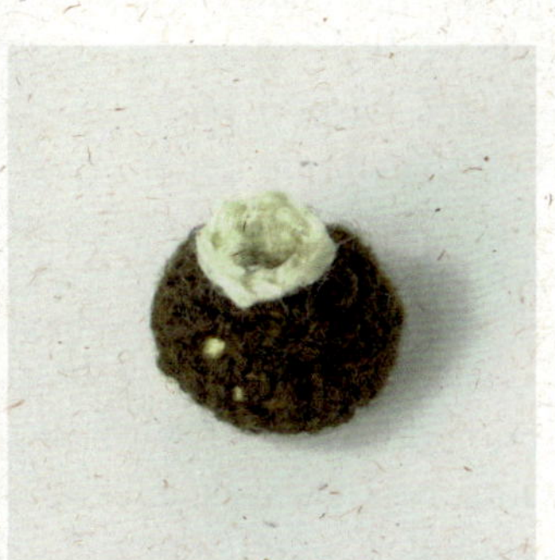

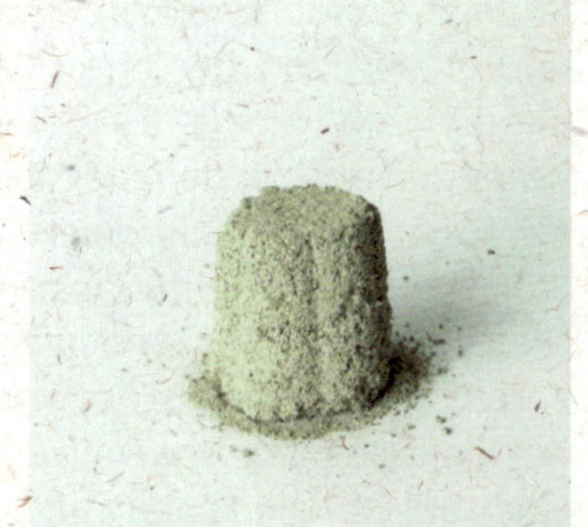

The thread leads us to HOME, a series of pendants that were designed in parallel with the closely linked FAMILYPORTRAITS. However, contrary to those—which suggest imaginary family constellations, whose plasticity, whose fleeting, tentative configurations shift to the fore—this group consolidates the concept of elective affinity, of elective family, of a self-determined social milieu, which over the course of one's life offers the real feeling of security, of emotional habitat, and in doing so gives rise to an independent, voluntary configuration. HOME evokes protection, providing a home, refuge, a shield, and shelter—with elongated, tall, small, narrow, and small dwellings painted white, scratched, burnished, or left in their natural state, whose sides are stitched with white, red, black, or grey yarn. And at the apex is the connector that transforms it into neck jewelry.

Tin was and is famously used for, among other things, bells, cultural artifacts, trophies, and commemorative objects, for accolades in sport, hunting, and competitions, and it is no different with Pontoppidan's tin. It comes from parents and grandparents and is tainted with a familial aura. The melting of it alone, its involvement in the creation of profound groups of works such as FAMILYPORTRAITS and HOME, represents an act of reversion in the system of values and of patterns of meaning. Once more the artist rejoices here too in her eschewal of eternity and permanence associated with precious items. With these pendants, the wearers always play an additional performative, interpretative role, taking part in the "performance," in the display, in the content of these works.

The trilogy CANVAS_CONTEXT_CASH, from 2010 to 2015, examines relationships and problematic areas between the applied and the conventionally defined free arts. With CANVAS, Pontoppidan picks up on the element of the canvas, which as reference material is wrapped around simple wooden frameworks. They appear to orient themselves on geometric templates, without, however, corresponding to a stringent mathematical form. Ornamental appliqués are then riveted or nailed to these, thus setting the antithesis to the image. Pop Art, Op Art, Art Nouveau, Surrealism, Color Field Painting, Conceptual Art, Assemblage, among others, cause quite a stir and are, when called upon intermittently as a quotation, an audacious overlapping of "high" and "low," an entertaining mix of scattered and stirred up fragments and references, which find themselves partnered in a new entity.

zusammengehalten, simulieren handwerkliches Engagement und handwerkliche Verpflichtung. In Wirklichkeit bemalten befreundete Künstlerkolleginnen die Leinwände, Goldschmiede und Studierende widmeten sich der Aufbringung einer funktionalen Broschur, Designer falteten die Kästchen. Allein die Signatur stammt von Pontoppidans Hand. Da es sich um die Vortäuschung manufakturähnlicher Produktionsbedingungen handelt, existieren exakt hundert Schatullen zu einem bescheidenen »Multiple«-Preis.

CASH führt uns schließlich zu einem Kernthema überhaupt: zum Geld. Nach verbreitetem Volksglauben bemisst sich die künstlerische Größe eines Werkes an seinem Preis. Pontoppidan persifliert diese kausale Beziehung und vernäht gewalzte und mit dicker Farbschicht bedeckte Silbermünzen zu unförmigen Knubbeln. Praktisch handelt es sich um Rohlinge, ihrer Ursprünge beraubt und auf das reine Material reduziert, das wiederum unter dem Farbmantel verschwindet wie unter einer tückischen Verkleidung. Die Autorin jongliert gerne mit dem Als-ob, mit der Vorspiegelung eines Status quo. Broschen verwandeln sich unter diesen Vorzeichen zu objekthaften Kunstwerken, die in Miniatur das Wandbild doubeln. Schwere und kompakte Anhänger mimen malerische Qualität. Nach längerem Gebrauch jedoch kann sich die Farbe abnutzen, das Innenleben freigeben und den merkantilen Diskurs durchschimmern lassen. In diesen Anhängern steckt also eine verzwickte Botschaft, die in erster Linie auf die Parodie abzielt, auf die ironische Enthüllung inhärenter Konfliktpotenziale in der Grauzone zwischen Kunst und Schmuck.

KNELL – The Gender Bell (2016–2018) bringt nun unmittelbar die Geschlechterdebatte ein. Das Äußere der Anhänger an zarten Gliederketten oder schlichter grauer Schnur orientiert sich in groben Zügen an realen Glocken. Pontoppidan manipuliert deren vertraute Silhouette und skizziert lediglich die Kontur. Zinn- und Feinsilberfolien, durch Heftklammern, Nähte oder Kleber collagiert, deuten den Körper mehr an, als dass sie ihn unmittelbar reproduzieren. Ausgefallene Klöppel – einmal die gegossene Miniausgabe einer Fruchtbarkeitsstatuette, das andere Mal ein Silberschlegel oder der Penisknochen eines Walrosses, ein Stück geschnitztes Hirschgeweih, ein mit Stoff verkleidetes oder vernageltes Knüppelchen, ein Schlangenknochen oder ein einfacher kleiner Zylinder – sorgen für einen wunderlichen Klang: kein lautes Läuten, eher ein leises Pochen, ein dezenter knarrender Ton. Bescheidene Ausstattung, schlichte Konzeption, befremdliche Aufmachung lenken geschickt das Augenmerk auf den gedankenvollen Bezugsrahmen, auf das spröde Naturell. Die Idee von Gehäuse, Körper und implizierter Appellfunktion vereinen sich in dieser Gestalt der Glocke. Die konstruierte, instabile Figur ist intendiert und korrespondiert zur Analyse von sozialer und geschlechtlicher Identität als labile, artifizielle und mobile Montage.[12] Das Organ der Glocke in unserem Fall verleiht dieser Diversität, dieser Vielfalt und Eigenheit von Identitäten, den jeweils spezifischen Tenor. KNELL bietet den Kontrapost zu klassischen symbolischen und realen Rangordnungen, imaginiert eine andere Stimmgewalt zwischen Intimität und Abgrenzung, weder melodisch noch spektakulär, eher dezent und entschieden.

Pontoppidan ist auf der Höhe der Zeit. Feministische Positionen in der Kunst begleiten uns bereits seit Langem. Von Anfang an galt deren Interesse der »Dekonstruktion, De-Kodierung der Wirklichkeit in Bild, Sprache, Geste, Verhalten« durch »Transformation, Montage, Kompilation, Verfremdung von Form und Material«.[13] Dass dies im Schmuckbereich passiert, ist nicht nur ein Novum, sondern fast ein Unikum – zumindest unter Berücksichtigung von Genderforschung.

Die Strategie der doppelbödigen Inszenierung, das Ausloten von Objektgrenzen, die ironische Unterwanderung herkömmlicher Konzepte gehören zum Repertoire dieser Ansätze. Ebenso die »Distanz«[14] – um überhaupt sehen und analysieren zu können. So durchläuft auch Pontoppidan einen beschwerlichen Weg bis zur finalen Realisierung ihrer Werke. Denn der Schmuck ist bis heute stärker als andere Gattungen an handwerkliche Prämissen gebunden. Selbst die gewagteste Autorin muss sich also zunächst von diesem Gepäck befreien, einen Teil ihrer Schulung hinter sich lassen, um in ihren Arbeiten inhaltlicher Aussage und gestalterischem Anspruch gerecht zu werden.

KNELL rückt darüber hinaus den Fokus der kritischen Auseinandersetzung auf das Bild des Korpus, des Gefäßes als Metapher, auf »die körperliche Präsenz in einer Gestik«[15] und erzählt von der Entwicklung des Körpers als Zeichen, die über sich hinaus als Anmerkung, als Kommentar visuell verweisen auf die dahinterstehende Botschaft. Das Verlassen stereotypischer, sanktionierter Ästhetik; das Einbauen von Störfaktoren, von Irritationen etwa durch das ungewöhnliche Material oder die Kombination von Nähen, Nieten, Kleben abseits goldschmiedischer Verfahren; der kalkulierte Wandel der Objekte im getragenen Zustand; die Titel, welche bereits eine sarkastische Hinterfragung andeuten; überhaupt Unförmigkeit und montiertes Gepräge – all diese Aspekte zeichnen Pontoppidans Arbeit aus und vernetzen ihre Vorgehensweise mit entsprechenden Tendenzen in der feministischen Kunst. Man könnte von »Abject Art« sprechen[16], was den Punkt allerdings nicht genau trifft. Zwar bricht Pontoppidan die Regeln und knüpft an Strömungen der »konzeptuellen Instal-

But that's not all. In contrast to engaging in the canon of instruments and the casual abolition of a familiar alliance as seen with the canvas and wooden framework in CANVAS, in CONTEXT the goldsmith presents an ironic take on prevalent, indeed fashionable artistic attitudes, such as production in an atelier yet without the spiritual creator taking part in the slightest way. Small carton-shaped brooches, made with the painted side of the canvas turned inward and held together with silver staples, feign artisanal engagement and a commitment to crafts. In reality fellow artist friends painted the canvases, goldsmiths and students devoted themselves to making the brooch function, and designers folded the tiny boxes. Yet the signature comes from Pontoppidan's hand alone. Since this is about imitating production techniques similar to those used in manufacturing, precisely one hundred of these tiny boxes are in existence at a modest "bulk" price.
CASH leads us then to a general central theme: money. According to widespread popular belief, the artistic greatness of an artwork is determined by its price. Pontoppidan satirizes this causal relationship by sewing ground-down silver coins covered in a thick layer of paint into unshapely agglomerations. On a practical level it is about blanks, divested of their origins and reduced to their pure material, which in turn disappears under a cloak of paint like a deceitful disguise. The artist takes delight in juggling with the "as if," with the affectation of a status quo. Under this presage, brooches are transformed into object-like artworks that, albeit in miniature, double as a picture on a wall. Heavy and compact pendants mimic painterly qualities. Yet the color can wear off after protracted use, with the interior surface liberating itself and hinting at the mercantile discourse within. Thus an intricate message is hidden in these pendants, one primarily aimed at parody and ironically exposing the inherent potential for conflict in the grey area between art and jewelry.

KNELL—The Gender Bell (2016–2018) now brings the gender debate directly to the table. The outward appearance of the pendants on delicate link chains or simple grey cord roughly nods to that of real bells; Pontoppidan manipulates their familiar silhouettes and merely sketches the outline. Tin leaf and fine-silver leaf "collaged" with staples, stitching, or adhesive hints at rather than directly reproduces the bodies. Eccentric bell clappers—a cast mini-edition of a fertility statue or a simple silver mallet, or the penis bone of a walrus, a piece of carved antler, a small cudgel clad or nailed with fabric, a snake bone, or a simple small cylinder—provide a curious chime: not a loud ring but rather a slight thud, a subtly creaking sound. Modest features, simple conception, and disconcerting design deftly guide the attention to contemplative frames of reference, to the object's intractable nature. The idea of casing, body, and the implied rallying appeal are brought together under the guise of the bell. This hypothetical, unstable representation is intentional, corresponding to the analysis of social and gender identity as a precarious, artificial, and mobile construct.[12] In our case, the organ of the bell accords this diversity, multiplicity, and singularity of identities their respective specific tone. KNELL provides the contrapposto to classical symbolic and real hierarchies and imagines a different vocal force between intimacy and boundary, neither melodic nor spectacular but rather understated and resolute.
Pontoppidan is in tune with the times. Feminist stances in art have long accompanied us. Right from the very beginning, their interest in "deconstruction, decoding reality in images, language, gesture, behavior" has taken effect through "transformation, montage, compilation, and the alienation of form and material."[13] That this takes place in jewelry is not only a novelty but is almost a rarity, at least when considering gender research.
The strategy of ambiguous staging, the exploration of the objects' limitations, and ironically infiltrating traditional concepts all belong to this repertoire of approaches. Likewise, the "distance"[14]—needed to be even able to see and analyze at all. And this is how Pontoppidan too traverses the arduous path to ultimately realizing her works. For jewelry is to this day more strongly linked to artisanal premises than any other genre. Even the most daring artists must therefore first free themselves from this baggage, leave part of their training behind, in order to do justice to the content and creative demand of their works.
KNELL, moreover, shifts the focus of critical examination to the image of the corpus, of the vessel as a metaphor, to "the physical presence within a gesture"[15] and tells of its development as a set of symbols that beyond annotation, beyond comment, visually refer to the message behind them. Abandoning the stereotypical, sanctioned aesthetic, incorporating confounding factors and irritations such as unusual materials or the combination of sewing, riveting, and gluing that are a far cry from goldsmithing processes, the calculated transformation of worn objects, the titles that already hint at sarcastic scrutiny, even the general shapelessness and assembled character—all of these aspects characterize Pontoppidan's work and connect her methods with corresponding tendencies in feminist art. One could speak of "Abject Art,"[16] though it admittedly falls short of the mark. In fact Pontoppidan breaks the rules and builds on the tides of "conceptual installation,"[17] yet she acts within the coordinates of the wearable

lation«[17] an. Trotzdem agiert die Autorin im Koordinatenfeld des tragbaren Schmuckobjekts, das Zeichencharakter, Hintergründigkeit, inhaltliche Aufladung erfährt, durchaus aber auch eine Zierde, eine Bereicherung darbieten kann – gerade durch den scharfen und boshaften Witz, durch kommunikative Effekte.
Wir können daher mit den Worten von Monika Leisch-Kiesl für die Werke Pontoppidans konstatieren, dass sie »schön« sind, gerade »weil es ihnen gelingt, die Komplexität gesellschaftlicher Zustände, politischer Strukturen und ideologischer Gewalt sowie die feinen Fäden, welche die Individuen mit diesen Systemen verweben, in einer Weise zu zeigen, die – ohne zu moralisieren – in eine Haltung sinnlicher und denkender Aufmerksamkeit führt«.[18]

Ein ähnliches Oszillieren zwischen Realität und Fake bieten die aktuellen Objektskulpturen KNELL II. Pontoppidan verlässt den Sektor des Schmuckes und dringt in die Domäne der Silberschmiede vor, eine Exkursion allerdings mit ketzerischen Absichten. Einfache Küchengeräte und häusliche Dinge – Bratpfanne, Gemüse- und Steakmesser, Bügeleisen, Saugglocke, Fleischhammer, Kochlöffel, Nudelholz, Nussknacker, Hammer, Schraubenzieher –, alles Elemente, die unter Umständen tatkräftige, wenn nicht sogar handgreifliche, energische Tätigkeiten nahelegen, werden in Feinsilber säuberlich abgeformt, hohl nachgebildet, respektlos montiert und verklebt. Wenn der Schmuck das männliche Publikum tendenziell ausblendet, so wird dieses auf dem nun vorliegenden Schauplatz automatisch mit angesprochen. Pontoppidan wählt daher vor allem Gegenstände von signalhafter Einprägsamkeit aus, die allgemein für die häusliche Situation Symbolkraft besitzen. Diese reflektiert wie keine andere die realen Verhältnisse der Geschlechterrollen und bietet daher das ideale Ambiente für eine blasphemische Beschwörung ihrer trivialen Utensilien, die – durch elegante Veredelung oberflächlich geadelt – in der banalen Verklebung patchworkartig zusammengesetzter Flecken das Ethos der Silberschmiedetradition jedoch konterkarieren: ein frecher Verrat, eine düpierende Herausforderung, eine Negation von dauerhaften Werten, von Sitte, Würde und sozialem Rang, die mit dem Handwerk bekanntermaßen assoziiert werden. Weil die Prüfung, die Durchdringung der Fragestellung weitere Aspekte fordert und eine breitere Bühne beansprucht. Das Motiv, die materielle Präsenz dieser Dinge geraten zur Metapher, dienen als ästhetischer »Austragungsort«[19] einer komplexen Verkettung von Gestalt, gesellschaftlicher Zuschreibung, von Affirmation und Konflikt. Pontoppidan trägt hier ein spannendes Manöver aus, wie sie überhaupt gerne in ihren Arbeiten Kodierungen aufhebt und dagegen andere – konträre, ungewohnte, diskursive – unterbreitet.

Auf solche Anliegen reagieren kann nur eine Position, die stets in Bewegung bleibt. Daher entziehen sich Werk und Autorin eher dem gängigen Zugriff, der Eindeutigkeit und klassifizierenden Zuordnung. Es geht Pontoppidan primär um die Anerkennung von Differenz, um die Option einer aufgeklärten Perspektive, einer modifizierten Annäherung an tradierte Sujets. Unter diesen Vorzeichen entstand auch die Idee zu THE ONE WOMAN GROUP EXHIBITION mit einem Seitenhieb auf aalglatte Kunstrezeption, die sich wiedererkennbare Handschriften wünscht und sperrigem Pluralismus eher verweigert. In den einzelnen Werkgruppen werden ebendas Rollenspiel, der Identitätswechsel, das schillernde Kaleidoskop der Subjektivität vorgestellt und durchkonjugiert. Damit bezieht sich Pontoppidan nicht nur auf den performativen Aspekt der Subjektkonstruktion im Gegensatz zur »dekonstruierbaren, verhandelbaren Größe«[20]. Sie bezieht sich ebenso auf die Relativität der Begrifflichkeiten Künstler und Kunst. Beide sollen sich dem kontroversen Prozess, der Vision von Wandelbarkeit und Authentizität stellen, welche die Diskussion bewegt. Radikal formuliert: »women must kill the aesthetic ideal through which they themselves have been ›killed‹ into art.«[21]

Wenn wir mit Judith Butler davon ausgehen, dass Geschlecht, Körperlichkeit, Identität durch Performativität hervorgerufen werden, durch »ständige Akte einer Wiederholung vorherrschender Normen«[22], dann können wir auf der Gegenseite konstatieren, dass eine Ermittlung, auch eine ästhetische Erkundung und Sondierung die Machtverhältnisse unterlaufen und Raum schaffen für diverse Erscheinungsformen.
Pontoppidans Engagement spiegelt diese Problematik. Sie umkreist in Form von Schmuckobjekten verwandte Argumente. Wenn wir ihre Arbeit im internationalen Umfeld verankern wollen, dann lässt sich ihre Position zum Beispiel mit denen von »Celebritys« wie Adrian Piper, Valie Export, Rosemarie Trockel, Cindy Sherman oder Jutta Koether vergleichen. Ein zentraler Beweggrund dieser Künstlerinnen besteht nicht nur in ihrer Hinterfragung von Postulaten, Mustern und Thesen, sondern ebenso in der Verabschiedung traditioneller Gattungspakete. Die Dekonstruktion und Metamorphose des Körpers, der Rollen- und Mediensprung als Ausdruck unabhängigen Agierens ohne Verpflichtung gegenüber etablierter Erwartungshaltung durch Öffentlichkeit, Kunstpublikum, Institutionen und andere Organe – eben darin liegt das Bestreben dieser Akteurinnen. Jutta Koether etwa bezeichnet ihr »performatives Engagement« in Sachen »Andersheit« als »ein Mittel der produktiven Verweigerung«, als »die Möglichkeit des Missverständnisses«[23].

jewelry object, which undergoes the semiotic character, subtleness, and charging of content but can by all means also adorn, enrich, precisely through the sharp and mischievous humor, through communicative effects.
We can therefore declare, using the words of Monika Leisch-Kiesl, that Pontoppidan's works are "beautiful," precisely "because they succeed in showing the complexity of social situations, political structures, and ideological violence as well as the fine threads that individuals weave together with these systems, in a way that—without moralizing—leads to a position of sensual and thoughtful mindfulness."[18]

The current object sculptures of KNELL II offer a similar commute between real and fake. Pontoppidan now leaves the jewelry sector and enters the realm of silversmithing, an excursion albeit with heretical intent. Simple kitchen utensils and domestic tools—a frying pan, paring and steak knives, an iron, plungers, a meat tenderizer, cooking spoon, rolling pin, nutcrackers, a hammer, screwdriver, toilet seat—all elements that might suggest under some circumstances energetic if not fierce activities, are neatly cast in fine silver, recreated, disrespectfully put together, and glued. If jewelry has a tendency to disregard the male audience, it will inherently be addressed in the current setting. Pontoppidan selects therefore mainly typically memorable objects that in general possess a symbolic power for the domestic realm. These reflect like no other the real relations of gender roles and thus offer the ideal stage for a blasphemous invocation of trivial utensils, which, superficially ennobled through their elegant refinement, contradict the ethos of the silversmithing tradition in the mundane assembly of the patchwork-like pieces—an insolent act of betrayal, deceptive provocation, a negation of long-lasting values, of customs, dignity, and social rank, traits famously known with craftsmanship. The examination and the pervasion of the questioning requires further aspects and calls for a wider stage. The motif and the material presence of these things become a metaphor and serve as an aesthetic "venue"[19] for a complex nexus of forms, social attribution, of affirmation and conflict. Here Pontoppidan performs an interesting "maneuver," as she delights in nullifying codes in her works—and presenting contrary, unfamiliar, discursive others.

Only a position that remains in flux can react to such concerns. Thus the work and artist are deprived of common access, of clarity, and of classification. For Pontoppidan it is primarily about recognizing difference, about the option of an "enlightened" perspective, of a modified approach to traditional subjects. It was with this in mind that the idea for the THE ONE WOMAN GROUP came about, with a sideswipe at a slick art reception that wishes for a recognizable signature yet rather rejects cumbersome pluralism. The role play, change of identities, the dazzling kaleidoscope of subjectivity are presented and conjugated in the individual groups of works. In so doing, Pontoppidan addresses not only the performative aspect of constructing subjects unlike the "deconstructible, negotiable dimension."[20] She also refers to the relativity of the concept of artist and art. They should both face the controversial process, the vision of mutability and authenticity that affect the discussions. Radically put: "Women must kill the aesthetic ideal through which they themselves have been 'killed' into art."[21]

If, with Judith Butler, we assume that gender, physicality, and identity are evoked by performativity, by "a constant act of repeating prevailing norms,"[22] then we can state, on the other side, that an exploration, also an aesthetic probing and investigation subverts the balance of power and creates space for diverse manifestations.
Pontoppidan's commitment reflects this difficulty, which revolves around related arguments in the form of jewelry objects. If we now wish to anchor her work in the international domain, her stance must, for example, be compared with that of "celebrities" such as Adrian Piper, Valie Export, Rosemarie Trockel, Cindy Sherman, and Jutta Koether. A central motivation of these artists consists in not only challenging theories, patterns, and theses but also the departure from traditional packaged genres. The deconstruction and metamorphosis of the body, the leap in roles and media as an expression of independent action without obligation to established expectations via the public, via the art audience, via institutions and other organs—it is in precisely these that the endeavor of these protagonists lies. Jutta Koether, for example, describes her "performative practices" with all things "otherness" as a "structural sense of disobedience," as "the potentials of misunderstandings."[23]

Seit Jahrzehnten liefert eine rege feministische Genderdiskussion den zeitgenössischen Bedürfnissen Nahrung, die auf dem aktuellsten Stand ebenjene Prämissen formulieren, wie sie auch von Pontoppidan in Gestalt von Schmuck thematisiert und gestreift werden. Zwar ist sie nicht im eigentlichen Sinne multimedial tätig, trotzdem aber mit ähnlichen Problemzonen beschäftigt, wie jenem »Raum zwischen künstlerischer Artikulation und rezeptiver Erwartung«, den Adrian Piper als Boden des Konflikts beschreibt.[24] Diese Ausstellung und ihre Statements bilden eine schöpferische Antwort und entfalten ein innovatives, facettenreiches Spektrum von möglichen Perspektiven auf Schmuck, Schmuckwahrnehmung und Standort seiner Urheberinnen und Urheber. Pontoppidan lädt mit ihrem Werk zum Umdenken ein, zum Verlassen des vertrauten Terrains und der eingeschliffenen Blickachsen – hin zu einer mobilen Wahrnehmung und Wertschätzung, die zu unserer gesellschaftlichen Situation passt und dieser entspricht. Es ist noch immer ein Aufbruch und kein Abschluss.

»Ich glaube nicht, dass eine Künstlerin Erklärungen abgeben sollte, wir sollten Kunst nicht auf diese Weise verstehen. Dennoch müssen die Dinge innerhalb einer Gesamtheit angesiedelt sein, die keine Zweifel über ihre Ausrichtung aufkommen lässt.«[25]
(Rosemarie Trockel im Gespräch mit Jutta Koether)

Ellen Maurer Zilioli

1 Adrian Piper. Käthe-Kollwitz-Preis 2018, Ausst.-Kat. Akademie der Künste, Berlin 2018, S. 3.

2 »Ich habe immer versucht, etwas herzustellen, was anders ist«, so die Künstlerin Jutta Koether. »Ich arbeite aktiv daran, Strukturen, in denen Künstlerinnen arbeiten und aufwachsen, zu untersuchen – und die Probleme zu finden«. Das »Nicht-Aufgehen« wird bei ihr zum Prinzip. Siehe: www.deutschlandfunk.de/feminismus-und-freiheit-in-der-kunst-fuer-ambivalenz-trotz.911.de.html?dram:article_id=418271, abgerufen am 16.1.2019.

3 Vgl. Julia Allerstorfer, »Performing Mimikry. Künstlerische Strategien der Transformation von Identität«, in: Ästhetische Kategorien. Perspektiven der Kunstwissenschaft und der Philosophie. Linzer Beiträge zur Kunstwissenschaft und Philosophie, Bd. 7, hrsg. von Monika Leisch-Kiesl, Max Gottschlich, Susanne Winder, Bielefeld 2017, S. 395–419, hier S. 410.

4 Vgl. ebd., S. 411–417.

5 Ebd., S. 417.

6 Monika Leisch-Kiesl, »Wenn Gegenwartskunst und die Kategorie des Schönen aufeinandertreffen«, in: Bielefeld 2017 (wie Anm. 3), S. 53–73, hier S. 60 ff.

7 Anne M. Wagner, »O Cologne!«, in: Jutta Koether. Tour de Madame, hrsg. von Suzanne Cotter, Achim Hochdörfer, Tonio Kröner, Ausst.-Kat. Museum Brandhorst München; Mudam Luxemburg 2018, S. 108–115, hier S. 110.

8 Marsha Meskimmon und Phil Sawdon, Drawing Difference. Connections between Gender and Drawing, London und New York 2016, S. 2.

9 Therese Frey Steffen, Gender, Stuttgart 2017, S. 65 ff.

10 Vgl. Der rote Faden. Gedanken Spinnen Muster Bilder, hrsg. von Vanessa von Gliszczyuski, Eva Ch. Raabe, Mona Suhrbier, Ausst.-Kat. Weltkulturen Museum, Frankfurt a. M. 2016, S. 11 mit Verweis auf André Leroi-Gourhan, Hand und Wort. Die Evolution von Technik, Sprache und Kunst, Frankfurt a. M. 2006.

11 Vgl. Maren Gebhardt, »Fäden der Moderne«, in: Frankfurt a. M. 2016 (wie Anm. 10), S. 195–201.

12 Vgl. Marie-Luise Angerer (Hrsg.), The Body of Gender. Körper, Geschlechter, Identitäten, Wien 1995, S. 11.

13 Silvia Eiblmayr, »Einleitung«, in: Kunst mit Eigen-Sinn. Aktuelle Kunst von Frauen, hrsg. von Silvia Eiblmayr, Valie Export, Monika Prischl-Maier, Ausst.-Kat. Museum Moderner Kunst / Museum des 20. Jahrhunderts, Wien 1985, S. 8/9, hier S. 8.

14 Eva Meyer, »Distanz. Eine kalkulierte Reserve«, in: Wien 1985 (wie Anm. 13), S. 13–18, hier S. 13.

15 Eiblmayr 1985 (wie Anm. 13), S. 9.

16 Vgl. Hanne Loreck, »Struktur als Körper. Abject Art, informe und Eva Hesses plastische Arbeiten«, in: Raum und Körper in den Künsten der Nachkriegszeit, hrsg. von der Akademie der Künste. Zusammengestellt von Angela Lammert. Symposium anlässlich der Ausstellung Germaine Richier, Berlin 1997, S. 67–82, hier S. 67; Loreck bezieht sich auf das Konzept »abjection" von Julia Kristeva.

17 Ebd., S. 70.

18 Monika Leisch-Kiesl 2017 (wie Anm. 6), S. 70.

19 Vgl. Angerer 1995 (wie Anm. 12), S. 17.

20 Frey Steffen 2017 (wie Anm. 9), S. 21.

21 Sandra M. Gilbert und Susan Gubar, The Madwoman in the Attic: the Woman writer and the Nineteenth-Century Literary Imagination, New York 1979, S. 17; hier zit. n. Frey Steffen 2017 (wie Anm. 9), S. 59.

22 Zit. n. Angerer 1995 (wie Anm. 12), S. 26.

23 Wagner 2018 (wie Anm. 7), S. 110, zit. n. Benjamin H. D. Buchloh »A Conversation with Jutta Koether«, in: October, Nr. 157, Sommer 2016, S. 15–23, hier S. 16.

24 Helmut Draxler, »Strukturen und Reaktionen. Adrian Pipers Transformation des Minimalismus«, in: Adrian Piper. Käthe-Kollwitz-Preis 2018 (wie Anm. 1), S. 19–37, hier S. 19.

25 Wagner 2018 (wie Anm. 7), S. 112/113, zit. n. Jutta Koether, »Interview with Rosemarie Trockel«, übers. v. John Lundon, in: Flash Art, Nr. 134, Mai 1987, S. 40–42.

For decades a lively feminist gender discussion has provided nourishment for contemporary needs that currently frame those very premises thematized and touched upon by Pontoppidan in the form of jewelry. Although she does not in fact work multimedially as such, she is nevertheless occupied with similar problem areas, such as that of "space between artistic articulation and receptive expectation," which Adrian Piper describes as the base of the conflict.[24] This exhibition and its statements form a creative response and unfold an innovative, multifaceted range of possible perspectives on jewelry, the perception of jewelry, and the standpoint of its creators. Pontoppidan's work is an invitation to change one's thinking, to leave familiar terrain and ingrained lines of sight—to a "mobile" perception and appreciation that fits and corresponds to our social situation. If anything, it is a departure, not an ending.

"I don't believe that an artist should give explanations; we mustn't understand art that way. However, things must be set within a tonality which doesn't leave any doubts about their direction."[25]
(Rosemarie Trockel in conversation with Jutta Koether)

Ellen Maurer Zilioli

Unless otherwise cited, all quotations in German were translated into English by the translator.

1 Cited in Adrian Piper, Käthe-Kollwitz-Preis 2018, exh. cat. Akademie der Bildenden Künste (Berlin, 2018), p. 3.
2 "I always tried to produce something different," thus the artist Jutta Koether. "I am actively working to investigate structures in which women artists work and grow–and to find the problems." "Misconception" becomes a principle for her. See www.deutschlandfunk.de/feminismus-und-freiheit-in-der-kunst-fuer-ambivalenz-trotz.911.de.html?dram:article_id=418271 (accessed January 16, 2018).
3 See Julia Allerstorfer, "Performing Mimikry: Künstlerische Strategien der Transformation von Identität," in Monika Leisch-Kiesl et al., eds., Ästhetische Kategorien: Perspektiven der Kunstwissenschaft und der Philosophie: Linzer Beiträge zur Kunstwissenschaft und Philosophie, vol. 7 (Bielefeld, 2017), pp. 395–419, here p. 410.
4 Ibid., pp. 411–17.
5 Ibid., p. 417.
6 Monika Leisch-Kiesl, "Wenn Gegenwartskunst und die Kategorie des Schönen aufeinander treffen," in Leisch-Kiesl et al. 2017 (see note 3), pp. 53–73, here pp. 60 ff.
7 Anne M. Wagner, "O Cologne!," in Achim Hochdörfer and Tonio Kröner, eds., Tour de Madame: Jutta Koether, exh. cat. Museum Brandhorst München and Mudam Luxemburg (Cologne, 2018), pp. 108–15, here p. 110.
8 Marsha Meskimmon and Phil Sawdon, Drawing Difference: Connections between Gender and Drawing (London and New York, 2016), p. 2.
9 Therese Frey Steffen, Gender (Stuttgart, 2017), pp. 65.
10 See Vanessa von Gliszczynski et al., eds., Der rote Faden: Gedanken Spinnen Muster Bilder, exh. cat. Weltkulturenmuseum, Frankfurt am Main (Bielefeld, 2016), p. 11 with reference to André Leroi-Gourhan, Hand und Wort: Die Evolution von Technik, Sprache und Wort (Frankfurt/Main, 2006).
11 See Maren Gebhardt, "Fäden der Moderne," in ibid., pp. 195–201.
12 See Marie-Luise Angerer, ed., The Body of Gender: Körper, Geschlechter, Identitäten (Vienna, 1995), p. 11.
13 Silvia Eiblmayr, Introduction in Silvia Eiblmayr et al., eds., Kunst mit Eigen-Sinn: Aktuelle Kunst von Frauen, exh. cat. Museum moderner Kunst and Museum des 20. Jahrhunderts (Vienna, 1985), pp. 8–9, p. 8.
14 Eva Meyer, "Distanz: Eine kalkulierte Reserve," in ibid., pp. 13–18, here p. 13.
15 Eiblmayr 1985 (see note 13), p. 9.
16 See Hanne Loreck, "Struktur als Körper: Abject Art, informe und Eva Hesses plastische Arbeiten," in Akademie der Künste, ed. Raum und Körper in den Künsten der Nachkriegszeit, compiled by Angela Lammert (Berlin, 1997), pp. 67–82, here p. 67. Symposium for the exhibition of Germaine Richier; Loreck refers to the concept of "abjection" by Julia Kristeva.
17 Ibid., p. 70.
18 Monika Leisch-Kiesl 2017 (see note 6), p. 70.
19 See Angerer 1995 (see note 12), p. 17.
20 Frey Steffen 2017 (see note 9), p. 21.
21 Sandra Gilbert and Susan Gubar, The Mad Woman in the Attic: The Woman Writer and the Nineteenth-Century Library Imagination (New York, 1979), p. 17; here cited in Frey Steffen 2017 (see note 9), p. 59.
22 Cited in Angerer 1995 (see note 12), p. 26.
23 Anne M. Wagner in exh. cat. 2018 (see note 7), pp. 108–15, here p. 110; cited in Benjamin H. D. Buchloh, "A Conversation with Jutta Koether," October 157 (Summer 2016), pp. 15–23, here p. 16. See also: www.mitpressjournals.org/doi/pdfplus/10.1162/OCTO_a_00257 (accessed January 16, 2019)
24 Helmut Draxler, "Strukturen und Reaktionen: Adrian Pipers Transformation des Minimalismus," in exh. cat. 2018 (see note 1), pp. 19–37, here p. 19.
25 Wagner 2018 (see note 7), pp. 108–15, here pp. 112–13.
Cited in Jutta Koether, "Interview with Rosemarie Trockel," transl. John Lundon, Flash Art 134 (May 1987), pp. 40–42.

»Ich als Wir«

Karen Pontoppidans THE ONE WOMAN GROUP EXHIBITION

Bereits Mitte der 1930er-Jahre stellt Walter Benjamin in seinem zentralen Text zur politischen Ästhetik des 20. Jahrhunderts den Begriff der »technischen Reproduktion« in den Mittelpunkt und setzt ihm die traditionellen – laut Benjamin »überkommenen« – Formen einer Ästhetik der Produktion und Produktivität entgegen, nämlich diejenigen von »Schöpfertum und Genialität, Ewigkeitswerte[n] und Geheimnis«. »Das Kunstwerk im Zeitalter technischer Reproduzierbarkeit«, dessen verworrene Editionsgeschichte als Symptom für die Verquickung ästhetischer und politischer Einsätze in den 1930er-Jahren steht, kann als eine Art Endpunkt für eine Geschichte der Wechselfälle und Verwerfungen eines Paradigmas der Mimesis oder Nachahmung sowie seines Gegensatzes – ebendem des Schöpfertums und Geniekults – gelesen werden. Oder, vielmehr, kann dieser Gegensatz, der weiterhin in der Reflexion und Praxis von Kunst insistiert, nach diesem Text, also im 20. und 21. Jahrhundert, nicht mehr ohne Rückgriff auf die Frage der (massenhaften) Reproduktion, des Technischen und der Zirkulationswege der technischen Reproduktionen gedacht werden. Denn dieser Text hat den großen Vorteil, das mimetische Anliegen, das heißt dasjenige der Nachahmung, Wiederholung oder Kopie, unter dem Decknamen der Technik oder der technischen Medien zu verhandeln und es damit aus den Debatten um einen malerischen Realismus im 19. Jahrhundert, auf den die Malerei im 20. Jahrhundert vehement mit ihrer eigenen Abstraktion reagiert, herauszulösen. Dadurch wird deutlich, dass der Einsatz dieser Debatte weniger die Gegenständlichkeit oder Ungegenständlichkeit des Dargestellten als vielmehr die Rolle ist, die dem Darstellenden – dem Künstler – eingeräumt wird: Der Subjektivität des künstlerischen Subjekts stellt Benjamin, so könnte man etwas salopp formulieren, zunächst die Objektivität der technischen Bildproduktionsmaschine (des Objektivs) entgegen. Eine derart technisch informierte reproduktive Ästhetik hinterfragt damit eine Instanz zugleich intentionaler, subjektiver und kritischer Autorschaft beziehungsweise stellt den Fragen nach künstlerischer Identität eine Wiederholungspraktik an die Seite, um diese so unter Druck zu setzen, zu problematisieren und zu dekonturieren.

Dies tut Benjamin gleich zu Beginn seines Texts, wenn er feststellt: »Das Kunstwerk ist grundsätzlich immer reproduzierbar gewesen. Was Menschen gemacht hatten, das konnte immer von Menschen nachgemacht werden. Solche Nachbildung wurde auch ausgeübt von Schülern zur Übung in der Kunst, von Meistern zur Verbreitung der Werke, endlich von gewinnlüsternen Dritten. Dem gegenüber ist die technische Reproduktion des Kunstwerks etwas Neues, das sich in der Geschichte intermittierend, in weit auseinanderliegenden Schüben, aber mit wachsender Intensität durchsetzt.«[1] Als derlei Techniken der Reproduktion nennt Benjamin den Guss, die Prägung, den Holzschnitt und Kupferstich, die Radierung und die Lithografie, den Druck und zuletzt die Fotografie, die »die Hand im Prozeß bildlicher Reproduktion zum ersten Mal von den wichtigsten künstlerischen Obliegenheiten entlastet«.[2] Die Beschleunigung des technischen Reproduktionsprozesses führt zuletzt zur Entwicklung des Tonfilms und damit zu einem neuen Standard, »auf dem sie nicht nur die Gesamtheit der überkommenen Kunstwerke zu ihrem Objekt zu machen und deren Wirkung den tiefsten Veränderungen zu unterwerfen begann, sondern sich einen eigenen Platz unter den künstlerischen Verfahrungsweisen eroberte. Für das Studium dieses Standards ist nichts aufschlußreicher, als wie seine beiden verschiedenen Manifestationen – Reproduktion des Kunstwerks und Filmkunst – auf die Kunst in ihrer überkommenen Gestalt zurückwirken.«[3]

Laut Benjamin ist es also die technische Reproduzierbarkeit des Kunstwerks, die Folgen haben soll für die Kunst als Ganzes, deren traditionelle – laut Benjamin »überkommene« – Formen sich vielmehr in den Begriffen einer Ästhetik der Produktion und Produktivität verstehen, nämlich denjenigen von »Schöpfertum und Genialität, Ewigkeitswerte[n] und Geheimnis«.[4] Nun ist diese These Benjamins zwar einerseits historisch und medial indiziert – zur Diskussion steht die technische Reproduktion um 1900 in ihrer »entwickeltsten« Form, der Filmkunst –, andererseits verweist sie darauf, dass nicht nur Reproduktion immer schon die Kunst bestimmt hat, sondern auch technische Reproduktion zu verschiedenen historischen Momenten, bei den Griechen, im Mittelalter et cetera, zum Tragen kommt. Während jedoch die manuelle Reproduktion weiterhin, so könnte man etwas überspitzt sa-

"I as We"

Karen Pontoppidan's THE ONE WOMAN GROUP EXHIBITION

Walter Benjamin, in his pivotal text from the mid-nineteen-thirties on the political aesthetic of the twentieth century, focused on the concept of "mechanical reproduction," contrasting it with traditional—and, according to Benjamin, "handed-down"—forms of aesthetic of production and productivity, namely that of "creativity and genius, everlasting value and secrecy." Benjamin's "Work of Art in the Age of Mechanical Reproduction," whose convoluted publishing history, in essence a symptom of the combination of aesthetic and political commitments in the nineteen-thirties, can be read as a kind of terminus for an account of the vicissitudes and rejections of a paradigm of mimesis or imitation and its opposite—that of creativity and the cult of the genius. Or rather, this opposition which continues to assert itself in the reflection and practice of art, can no longer, after this text, i.e. in the twentieth and twenty-first centuries, be considered without recourse to the question of (mass) reproduction, of the technical and the circulatory paths of mechanical reproduction. That is because Benjamin's text has the great advantage of negotiating mimetic concerns: that of imitation, repetition, or copy, under the pseudonym of technology or technical media, and thus of liberating it from the debates on painterly realism in the nineteenth century, to which painting in the twentieth century vehemently reacted with its own abstraction. Through this, it becomes clear that the point of this debate is not so much the objectivity or non-objectivity of what is represented but rather the role granted to the one representing—the artist: Benjamin initially counterposes the subjectivity of the artistic subject, so to speak, with the objectivity of the mechanical image-making machine (the lens). Such a technically informed reproductive aesthetic at the same time thereby challenges an agency of intentional, subjective, and critical authorship and sets reproductive practice against questions of artistic identity, in order to pressurize, problematize, and de-contour it.

Benjamin's text does this right from the outset, when he observes: "In principle, the work of art has always been reproducible. Objects made by humans could always be copied by humans. Replicas were made by pupils in practicing for their craft, by masters in disseminating their works, and, finally, by third parties in pursuit of profit. But the technological reproduction of artworks is something new. Having appeared intermittently in history, at widely spaced intervals, it is now being adopted with ever-increasing intensity."[1] Benjamin named such "techniques" of reproduction casting, embossing, woodcut and copperplate engraving, etching, lithography, printing and, finally, photography, which "for the first time ... freed the hand from the most important artistic tasks in the process of pictorial reproduction."[2] The acceleration of mechanical reproduction processes led ultimately to the development of talking film and thus to a new standard "that permitted it to reproduce all known works of art, profoundly modifying their effect, but it also had captured a place of its own among the artistic processes. In gauging this standard, we would do well to study the impact which its two different manifestations—the reproduction of artworks and the art of film—are having on art in its traditional form."[3]

According to Benjamin, it is thus the mechanical reproducibility of the artwork that should have consequences for art as a whole, whose traditional—and, according to Benjamin, "handed-down"—forms are understood more in terms of an aesthetic of production and productivity, namely those of "creativity and genius, everlasting value and secrecy."[4] On the one hand, Benjamin's thesis is indexed historically and medially—up for discussion here is the technical reproduction around 1900 in its "most developed" form, film art; on the other hand, however, it indicates that not only has reproduction determined art all along but that technical reproduction also came into effect at various times in history, with for example the Greeks, or in the Middle Ages. Yet whereas manual reproduction continues to hold on to a paradigm of creative aesthetics, insofar as the artistic gesture performed here preserves a uniqueness and, thus in the fabrication itself, another authenticity, a signature, the technical reproduction breaks with this paradigm, by replacing the manual gesture during the reproduction with the filtering gaze of the artist, who takes their pick from what already exists, reproduces, adopts, repeats, re-enacts, frames, and reframes it. That the artist remains involved in it is beyond dispute—not, however, in the sense of the classical imaginings of the creative genius but rather as a kind of medium or mediator of already existing realities.

gen, an einem Paradigma schöpferischer Ästhetik festhält – insofern die hier ausgeführte künstlerische Geste eine Einzigartigkeit und damit selbst in der Fälschung noch eine Echtheit, eine Signatur bewahrt –, bricht die technische Reproduktion mit diesem Paradigma, indem sie in der Reproduktion die händische Geste durch den filternden Blick des Künstlers ersetzt, der aus Bestehendem aussucht, es reproduziert, sich aneignet, wiederholt, nachstellt, framed und reframed. Dass daran der Künstler beteiligt bleibt, steht außer Frage – jedoch nicht im Sinne klassischer kreativer Genialitätsvorstellungen, sondern vielmehr als eine Art Medium oder Mediator bereits existierender Wirklichkeiten.

Anstatt nun jedoch diesen vielleicht nicht ganz so standhaften Gegensatz zwischen händischer und technischer Reproduktion weiterzuspinnen, könnte man vielmehr fragen, ob es nicht ungleich interessanter wäre, ihn dahingehend aufzulösen, dass auch schon die manuellen Kopien und Malübungen (wenn auch noch verlangsamte) technische Reproduktionen sind; dass man Technik also gerade als eine kulturelle Verfahrensweise, als eine Kulturtechnik, verstehen muss, die alles Re-Produzieren betrifft, insofern es ihr um eine Wiederholung eines bereits Dagewesenen – sei es Natur oder Kunst – geht, die ohne die Anrufung subjektiver Künstlerschaft im Sinne einer Veredelung oder reflexiven Aufladung, gar Vorstellungen von Genieästhetik operiert. Technik bedeutet in diesem Sinne also nicht, oder nicht ausschließlich, dass es zur Reproduktion nur dann kommt, wenn irgendwo durch Knopfdruck eine Maschine (sei sie auch noch so digital oder verschwindend klein, *infime*) ausgelöst wird. Als »technisch« muss man vielmehr jenes Moment in der Reproduktion verstehen, das eine klassisch-schöpferische Vorstellung von Ästhetik – und vom Kunst-Machen – und damit auch die Geschichte vom autonomen kreativen Subjekt als Garant für das Kunstwerden der Kunst unter Druck setzt.

In diesem Sinne wäre auch THE ONE WOMAN GROUP EXHIBITION der Künstlerin Pontoppidan zunächst vielleicht etwas kontraintuitiv als eine »technisch-ästhetische« Ausstellung zu bezeichnen: Denn gezeigt werden Schmuckarbeiten, also eine künstlerische Produktion, die traditionellerweise nicht nur eindeutig händische Züge trägt, die schon in der Bezeichnung von Schmuck*hand*werk deutlich werden, sondern die darüber hinaus auch noch weiblich kodiert ist und sich damit im semantischen Feld des Affekts, der Intuition, des Filigranen und zart Gearbeiteten wiederfindet.

»Technisch« bezieht sich also nicht so sehr, oder nicht ausschließlich, auf die Machart der Objekte (händisch, manuell oder maschinell, mechanisch) – obgleich es auch diese betrifft und die Schmuckarbeiten von Pontoppidan beide Produktionsweisen de facto miteinander verbinden. Vor allem aber meint technisch hier die Frage nach der spezifischen Form der Künstleridentität, die dieser Produktion und der damit verbundenen Ausstellungsweise entspricht. Eine solche Technisierung setzt eine doppelte Bewegung der Des-Identifizierung in Gang, die die Künstlerin hier vorführt und umsetzt: eine Des-Identifizierung von der gegenderten Vorstellung von Schmuck auf der einen Seite (= weiblich) sowie eine Des-Identifizierung von der ebenfalls gegenderten Vorstellung vom Künstler auf der anderen Seite (= männlich). Dabei werden diese Positionen jedoch nicht vertauscht, die Künstlerin tritt nicht an die Stelle des ehemals männlichen Geniekünstlers, den Kant als ein »Naturwesen« bestimmt hat, das in Gesellschaft lebt, der also in gewisser Weise selbst das Medium ist, vermittels dessen die Natur der Kunst ihre Regeln gibt. Der Emanzipation der Künstlerin als Frau und Schmuckkünstlerin liegt hier keine Anähnlichung an diese männliche Genievorstellung zugrunde, genauso wenig wie ihr die Demonstration zugrunde liege, die Schmuckkunst sei ebenfalls eine männliche, rationale, vernünftige, ästhetische Kunst und nicht »nur« eine weiblich kodierte, affektiv beladene.

Ein solches Modell der Emanzipation als Integration wird hier entschieden zurückgewiesen – ähnlich wie dies bereits jene Feministinnen der 1970er-Jahre vorgeführt hatten, die sich in der »Wages for Housework«-Debatte sowohl gegen eine Essentialisierung der Weiblichkeit dieser Arbeit gestellt haben, die auf eine andere Art weiblicher Gemeinschaft der Sorge hindeuten könnte, als auch dagegen, den Eintritt der (Haus-)Frauen in die männlich kodierte Lohnarbeit, die ausschließlich zu einer doppelten Belastung und Ausbeutung führen musste, als Emanzipation misszuverstehen. So ruft Silvia Federici dazu auf, die »Arbeit aus Liebe«, also jene familiäre, weiblich kodierte Reproduktionsarbeit, als Bestandteil einer kapitalistischen Arbeitsteilung zu thematisieren und ihr mit »Verweigerung« zu begegnen,[5] um sich so endgültig von einem Emanzipationsmodell zu verabschieden, das ausschließlich durch Integration zu denken ist, in diesem Fall durch Integration in die Lohnarbeit: Daraus folgt, dass Reproduktionsarbeit und Lohnarbeit zugleich abzulehnen sind, um so die damit einhergehenden Rollenverteilungen zu zerschlagen. Diese Argumentation gilt es zu extrapolieren für die allgemeine Frage nach Formen nicht-integrativer, nicht-modellorientierter, sondern vielmehr verqueerter, vervielfältigender Emanzipation, wie es in der Ausstellung von Pontoppidan vorgeführt wird.

But instead of spinning this perhaps not so entirely unwavering dichotomy between manual and technical reproduction further, one could ask whether it would not be more interesting to rather dispel it to the effect that manual copies and painting exercises as well are technical reproductions (albeit slowed down), that technology must therefore be understood precisely as a cultural method, as a cultural technique, which concerns all re-production insofar as it concerns duplicating something that already existed—be it nature or art—which operates without appealing to subjective artistry in the sense of refinement or reflexive inspiration, or even visions of the genius aesthetic. Thus technique in this sense does not, or not exclusively, mean that reproduction only occurs when a machine (be it digital or infinitesimally small) is triggered by pressing a button somewhere; it is more a matter of understanding "technical" as that moment in reproduction which puts pressure on a classical creative concept of aesthetics—and of making art—and with it also on the history of the autonomous creative subject as a guarantor of art becoming art.

In this sense, THE ONE WOMAN GROUP EXHIBITION by artist Karen Pontoppidan could be described as a "technically aesthetic exhibition" even though it would at first glance seem perhaps counterintuitive: for works of jewelry, an artistic oeuvre is displayed that traditionally not only bears distinctly manual characteristics already apparent in describing jewelry handicrafts but is, moreover, still coded as female and thus found again in the sematic field of emotion, intuition, the filigree and the delicately crafted.

"Technical" here is therefore not so much, or not exclusively, the making of the "objects" (by hand, manually or by machine, mechanically), even though it also concerns these—and the jewelry works by Karen Pontoppidan in fact bring together both methods of production; "technical" here means rather, above all, the question of the specific form of artist identity that corresponds to this oeuvre and its associated mode of display. A "mechanization" such as this thus initiates a double act of dis-identification, which the artist, Karen Pontoppidan, presents and implements here: on the one hand, dis-identifying with the gendered concept of jewelry (=female) and, on the other hand, dis-identifying with the likewise gendered concept of the artist (=male). In doing so, however, these positions are not interchanged; the woman artist does not take the place of the former male artist genius, whom Kant defined as a "creature of nature" that lives in society, which is, in a way, itself the medium through which nature informs art of its rules. There is no assimilation to this male notion of genius underlying the emancipation of the female artist as a woman and jewelry artist, just as there is no demonstration that jewelry art is likewise a male, rational, aesthetic art and not "only" a female coded, emotionally laden one.

Such a model of emancipation as integration is decisively rejected here, similarly to what had already been demonstrated by the feminists in the nineteen-seventies who in the wages-for-housework debate opposed not only an essentialization of the "feminality" of this work, which could point to another kind of female society of care, but also the misunderstanding that the inclusion of women (and housewives) into male-coded wage labor would result in emancipation, when in fact it would have had to lead exclusively to a double burden and exploitation. Thus Silvia Federici appeals for a thematization of the "work of love," that familial, female-coded reproductive work as a part of the capitalist division of labor and to confront it with "refusal,"[5] in order to irrevocably depart from a model of emancipation that can only be thought of exclusively through integration, in this case through the integration into wage labor. It thus follows that reproductive work and wage labor must be rejected simultaneously in order to shatter the concomitant division of roles. It is imperative to extrapolate from this argument the general issue of forms of non-integrative, non-model-oriented but rather queer, duplicating emancipation as presented in Karen Pontoppidan's exhibition.

The reason for this is that the movement of emancipation and that of her exhibition lie in rejecting this dichotomy in its entirety, this structural dualism that substantiates any hierarchic, normative, and normalizing distinction. Instead of adopting the (male) genius as a role model to which one should adapt, in other words, by establishing a mimetic relationship of assimilation "upward," Karen Pontoppidan's response to these many emancipatory and identitarian challenges is one of (Benjaminian) replication: in this way THE ONE WOMAN GROUP EXHIBITION presents copies of the artist as an artist, a kind of "technical" reproduction or even self-replication of an artistic identity, a duplicative appropriation, fragmentation, and creation of new artistic identities. These self-copies of artistic identities are grouped around thematic focal points, which in turn unravel, tear apart, and rearrange the artist's "œuvre," even her "lifetime œuvre," in order to make the "I as we"

Denn deren Emanzipationsbewegung und die ihrer Ausstellung liegen darin, diesen Gegensatz als Ganzen, diesen strukturellen Dualismus, der jedwede hierarchische, normative und normierende Unterscheidung begründet, zurückzuweisen. Anstatt das (männliche) Genie als Vorbildfunktion anzunehmen, an die es sich anzupassen gilt – also eine mimetische Beziehung der Anähnlichung »nach oben« zu etablieren –, ist Pontoppidans Antwort auf diese vielfachen emanzipativen und identitären Anforderungen eine der (benjaminschen) Vervielfältigung: So stellt THE ONE WOMAN GROUP EXHIBITION Kopien der Künstlerin als Künstlerin vor, eine Art technischer Reproduktion oder eben Selbstvervielfältigung einer künstlerischen Identität, eine vervielfachende Aneignung, Zersplitterung und Generierung neuer künstlerischer Identitäten. Gruppiert werden diese Selbstkopien künstlerischer Identitäten um thematische Schwerpunkte, die das »Werk«, gar das »Lebenswerk« der Künstlerin wiederum zerfasern, auseinanderreißen, umdisponieren, um so das »Ich als Wir« auch auf der Ebene der künstlerischen Produktion sicht- und denkbar zu machen: Denn auch dieses »Werk« ist nicht allein verständlich im bildungsroman(t)ischen Paradigma einer kontinuierlichen Fort- und Weiterentwicklung der künstlerischen Persönlichkeit im und durch ihr Werk, sondern zeigt vielmehr die Diskontinuitäten, Brüche, inselhaften Abschottungen einzelner Werkpartien auf. Die Ausstellung ordnet diese Werkgruppen thematisch, das heißt einer extern gesetzten Kategorisierung folgend, und bestätigt damit noch einmal den Bruch mit einem künstlerischen (Selbst-)Entwicklungsparadigma: nicht lediglich eine Künstleridentität, die umsetzt, verwirft, verbessert und zuletzt perfektioniert, sondern viele Identitätssplitter, -facetten, -schichtungen, die von einem thematischen Feld zum nächsten zu flanieren scheinen, geradeso als wären es kleine freundschaftliche Menschentrauben auf einem großen Fest, die abschweifen, sich neu zusammensetzen und wieder abdriften. THE ONE WOMAN GROUP EXHIBITION ist damit in gewisser Weise das Gegenteil der sprichwörtlichen »One Man Show«.

Künstlerische Wiedererkennbarkeit muss unter solch einem Verfahren der willfährigen Vervielfältigung und Reproduktion des eigenen Ichs als ein Wir leiden. Genauso leidet eine klar zuordenbare Autorschaft, die uns zugleich Aufschluss gibt, wie ein Werk in korrekter Weise durch Freilegung ihrer Intentionen zu lesen und zu reflektieren ist. Es leidet, vielleicht, wahrscheinlich – ein Marktwert, der mindestens genauso viel mit der Vermarktung der Kunst als Ware wie mit der Vermarktung der dazugehörigen Künstlerpersönlichkeit zu tun hat. Leiden muss ein einheitlicher künstlerischer Stil, eine klare künstlerische Form, eine eindeutige Künstler*innenbiografie. Leiden muss die Innovation zugunsten der Wiederholung, die Poiesis zugunsten der Mimesis, die Produktion zugunsten der Reproduktion – und gerade darin besteht die Herausforderung dieser paradoxen one woman Gruppenausstellung: zu zeigen, inwiefern eine solche Vervielfältigung, ein solcher Kopiervorgang des Selbst, eine solche (im oben entwickelten erweiterten Sinne technische) Reproduktion »zurückwirkt auf die Kunst als Ganzes« (Benjamin), auf die Idee von Künstleridentität als Ganzes, von Genie und Schöpfung, die hier grundlegend infrage gestellt und dekonstruiert werden, die sozusagen der Vervielfältigung geopfert werden – nicht, weil es anders nicht geht, sondern weil es anders nicht möglich ist. Weil jedwede Geste der künstlerischen, politischen, affektiven Emanzipation keine Anähnlichung nach oben sein kann (nicht sein darf), kein Austausch eines ausgelaufenen Modells durch eine neues Modell, sondern eine Vervielfältigung in der Horizontalen, eine massenweise Vervielfältigung, Neuordnung, Umgruppierung und Zirkulation, die die Modellfunktion als solche und die mit ihr verbundene Idee von Emanzipation als Integration infrage stellt.

Maria Muhle

1 Walter Benjamin, »Das Kunstwerk im Zeitalter seiner technischen Reproduzierbarkeit«, in: Gesammelte Schriften, Bd. I.2, Frankfurt a. M. 1980, S. 471–508, hier S. 474.
2 Ebd.
3 Ebd., S. 475.
4 Ebd., S. 473.
5 Vgl. Silvia Federici, »Die Reproduktion der Arbeitskraft im modernen Kapitalismus«, in: dies., Aufstand aus der Küche. Reproduktionsarbeit im globalen Kapitalismus und die unvollendete feministische Revolution, Münster 2015, S. 106–127. Vgl. auch die Einleitung zu diesem Band: Kitchen Politics – Queerfeministische Interventionen (Bini Adamczak, Mike Laufenberg, Felicita Reuschling, Sarah Speck, Susanne Schultz, Chris Tedjasukmana), »Einleitung oder: Anleitung zum Aufstand aus der Küche«, in: ebd., S. 6–20, hier S. 7, S. 14–17.

visible and conceivable also on the level of artistic production: for this "oeuvre" too is not just comprehensible in the coming-of-age paradigm of a continuous advancement and development of the artistic personality in and through "its" work but rather highlights the discontinuities, fragments, and isolated seclusion of individual work pieces. The exhibition arranges these groups of works according to themes—according to an externally established categorization, and in so doing confirms once again the break with an artistic paradigm of (self-) development: not an artist identity that transforms, discards, improves, and finally perfects but rather many slivers, facets, strata of identity, which appear to wander from one thematic field to the next, as if they were small friendly clusters of people at a party, wandering off, reassembling, and drifting off again. Hence THE ONE WOMAN GROUP EXHIBITION is, in a way, the opposite of the proverbial "one man show".

Artistic recognizability must suffer from such a process of compliant duplicity and reproduction of its own I as a we. Likewise a clearly attributable authorship suffers, which at the same time offers clues as to how a work is correctly to be read and reflected upon by exposing its intentions. It suffers, perhaps, probably, the market value that has at least as much to do with the commercialization of the art as a commodity as it does with the marketing of the artist personality pertaining to it. A consistent artistic "style," a stringent artistic form, an explicit artist biography must suffer. Innovation must suffer in favor of repetition, poiesis in favor of mimesis, production in favor of reproduction—and it is precisely therein that the challenge of this paradoxical one woman group exhibition lies: to show to what extent such a duplication, such a process of copying the self, such a (technical, in the expanded sense above) reproduction "impacts art as a whole" (Benjamin), the idea of the artist identity as a whole, of genius and creation, which here are fundamentally questioned and deconstructed, which are, so to speak, sacrificed to duplication—not because it cannot otherwise be done but because it is not possible any other way. Because any gesture of artistic, political, affective emancipation cannot (must not) be an assimilation upward or replacement of a discontinued model with a new model but rather a duplication in the horizontal, a mass duplication, realignment, rearrangement, and circulation, which questions the model function per se and the associated idea of emancipation as integration.

Maria Muhle

1 Walter Benjamin, "The Work of Art in the Age of Its Technical Reproducibility and Other Writings on Media," ed. Michael W. Jennings et al., transl. Edmund Jephcott et al. (Cambridge, MA, and London, 2008), p. 20.

2 Ibid.

3 Ibid., p. 21.

4 Ibid., p. 20.

5 See Silvia Federici, "Die Reproduktion der Arbeitskraft im modernen Kapitalismus," in id., Aufstand aus der Küche: Reproduktionsarbeit im globalen Kapitalismus und die unvollendete feministische Revolution (Münster, 2015), pp. 106–27. See also "Kitchen Politics – Queerfeministische Interventionen – Bini Adamczak, Mike Laufenberg, Felicita Reuschling, Sarah Speck, Chris Tedjasukmana (2012): "Einleitung oder: Anleitung zum Aufstand aus der Küche," in ibid., pp. 6–20, here p. 7, pp. 14–17.

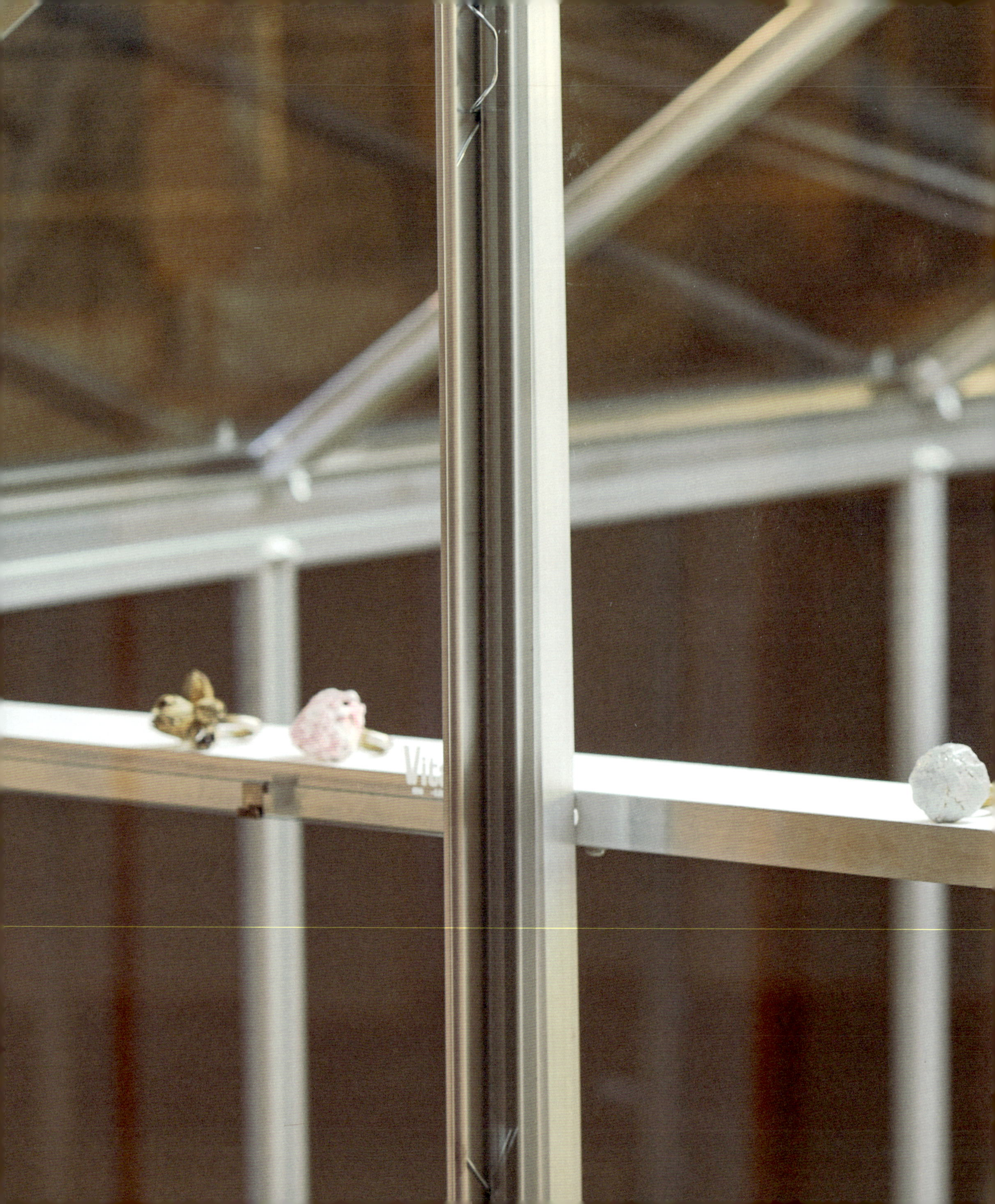

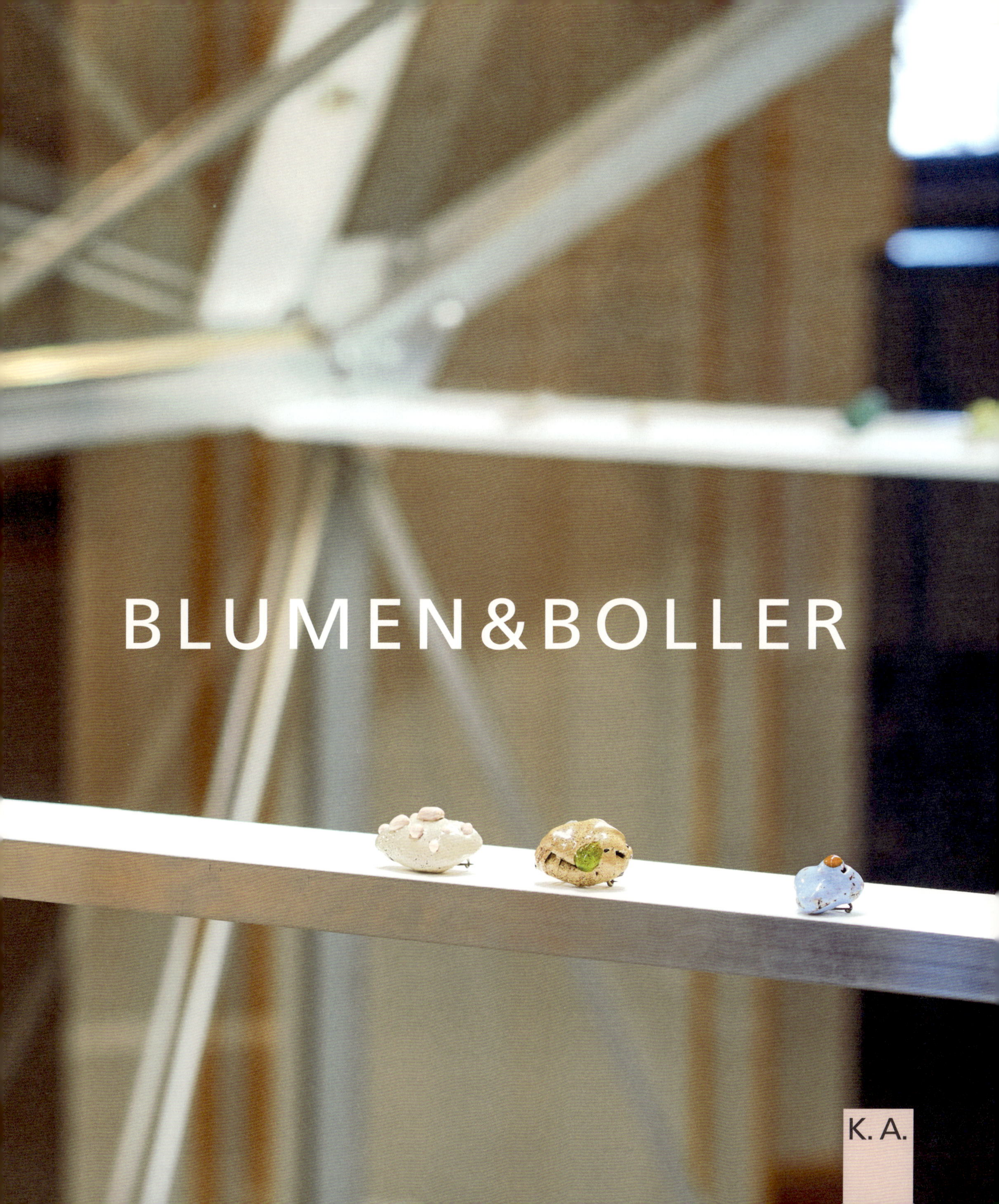
BLUMEN&BOLLER
K. A.

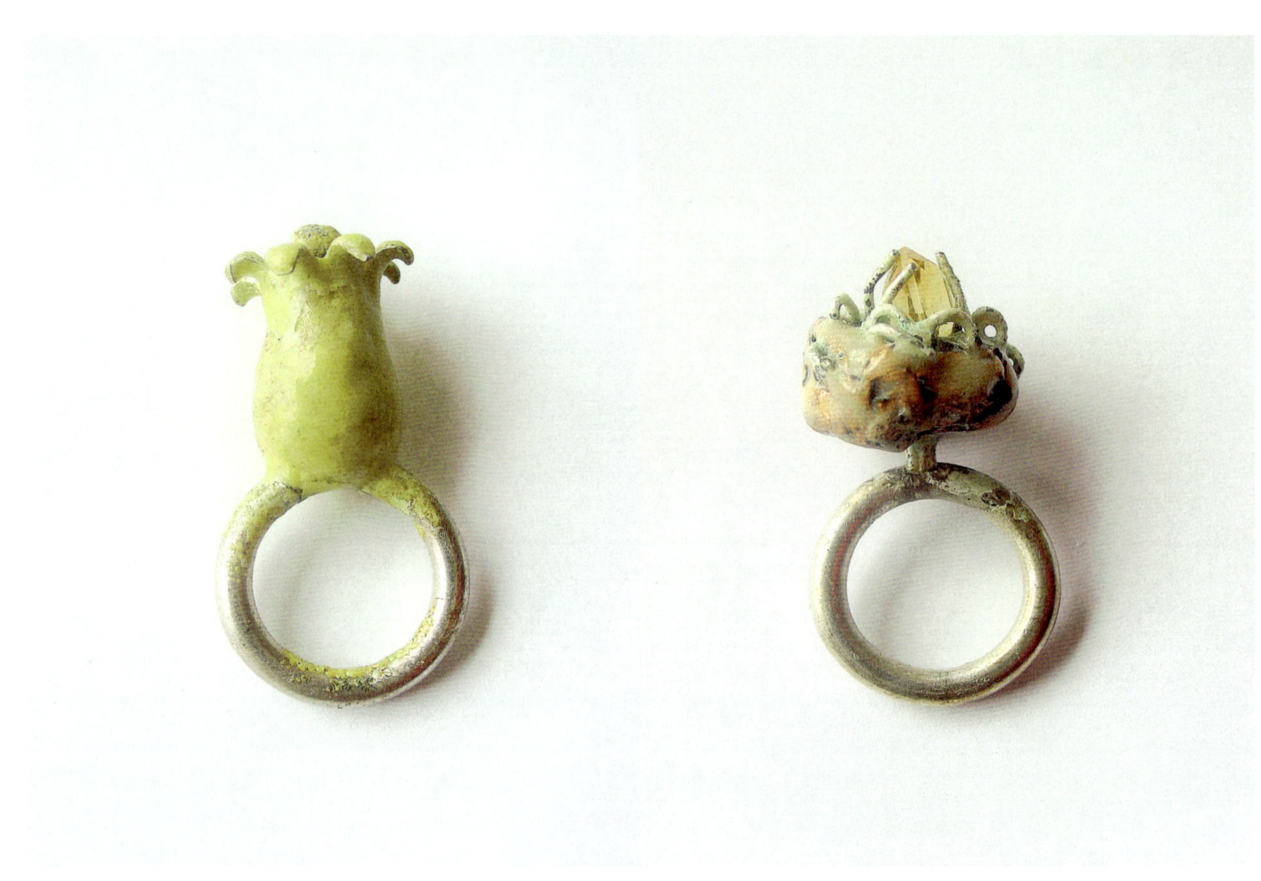

BLUMEN&BOLLER Ringe / rings 1994–1997 Silber / silver Kupfer / copper Emaille / enamel Citrin / citrine

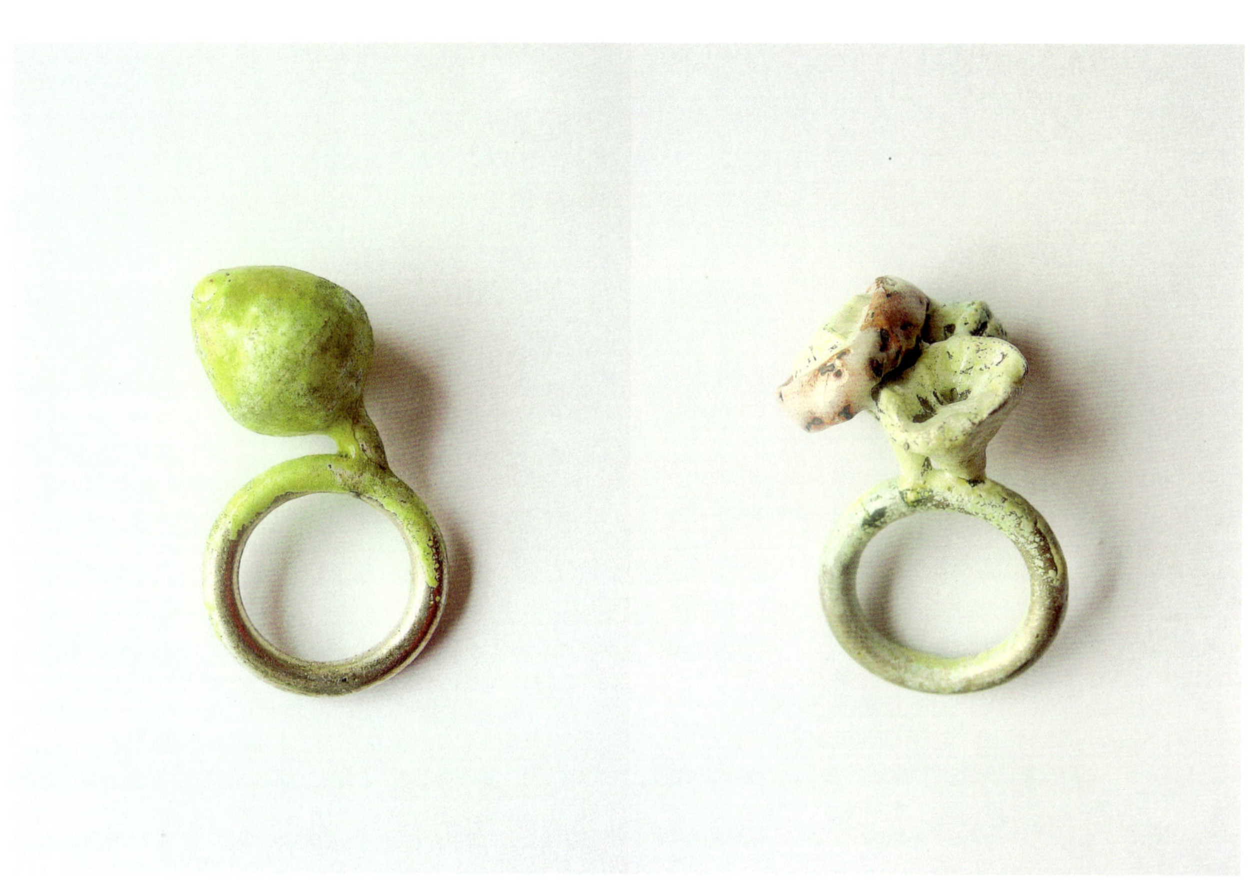

Stofflichkeit

Als Kind versenkte ich oft meine nackten Füße im frischen Kuhfladen auf den Feldern. Es faszinierte mich, wie die Konsistenz des Kuhmists diesen zwischen meinen Zehen hervorquellen ließ. Ich konnte die Körpertemperatur in der feuchten Mitte des Kuhfladens spüren – und auch das kühlere Gefühl auf meiner Haut näher an der Oberfläche. Zog ich einen Fuß aus dem Fladen heraus, war da dieser kurze Moment der Enttäuschung, seine perfekte Form für immer ruiniert zu haben. Doch wenn ich dann weglief, löste sich nach und nach dunkler Kuhmist von meinen Füßen und zeichnete so ein Bild meiner Bewegungen ins Gras. Dennoch war genug Mist an meinen Füßen, dass kleinere Blätter oder Staub an ihnen hängen blieben, die sie mit jedem Schritt größer und ausladender werden ließen, bis ich sie schließlich mit Wasser abwusch. Aus dem Wasserhahn in der Nähe der Weide kam unkontrolliert eiskaltes Wasser. Sobald man den Hahn aufdrehte, schoss es in alle Richtungen. Das war der zweite Teil dieses Abenteuers – das Abwaschen des grün-braunen Mists mit Wasser, das so kalt war, dass meine nackten Füße rot anliefen.[1]

K.A.

Materiality

When I was a child I would place my bare feet in the fresh cow dung on the meadow. I liked how its consistency would make the dung float up between my toes. I felt the body temperature in the center of the moist manure and the colder sensation on my skin at the surface. When I stepped out of the cow dung there was a short moment of sorrow for ruining its perfect shape, but as I ran away dark cow dung would spill from my feet onto the grass leaving a drawing of my movement. My feet would be covered still, and small leaves or dust would stick to the dung on my feet and make them grow bigger with every step until finally rinsed with water. The tap by the meadow released an uncontrolled stream of cold water, and as soon as it was turned on the water would spurt out in all directions. It was the second part of the sensation—rinsing the green-brown cow dung off with the icy water that would blush my naked feet.[1]

K.A.

BLUMEN&BOLLER Ring / ring 1995 Silber / silver Kupfer / copper Eisen / iron Emaille / enamel

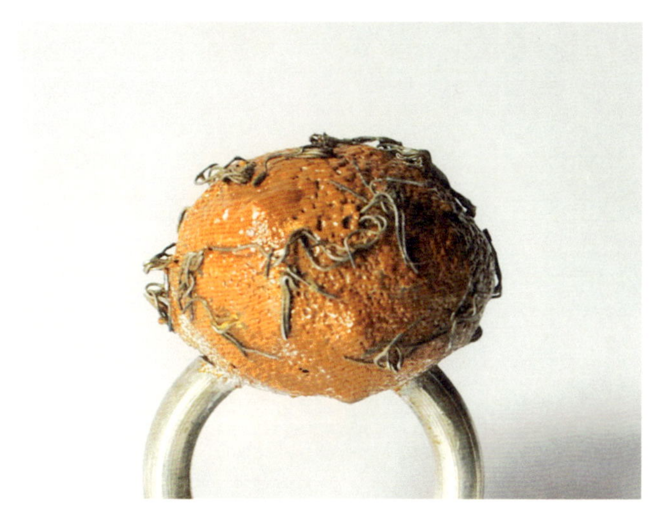

K. A.

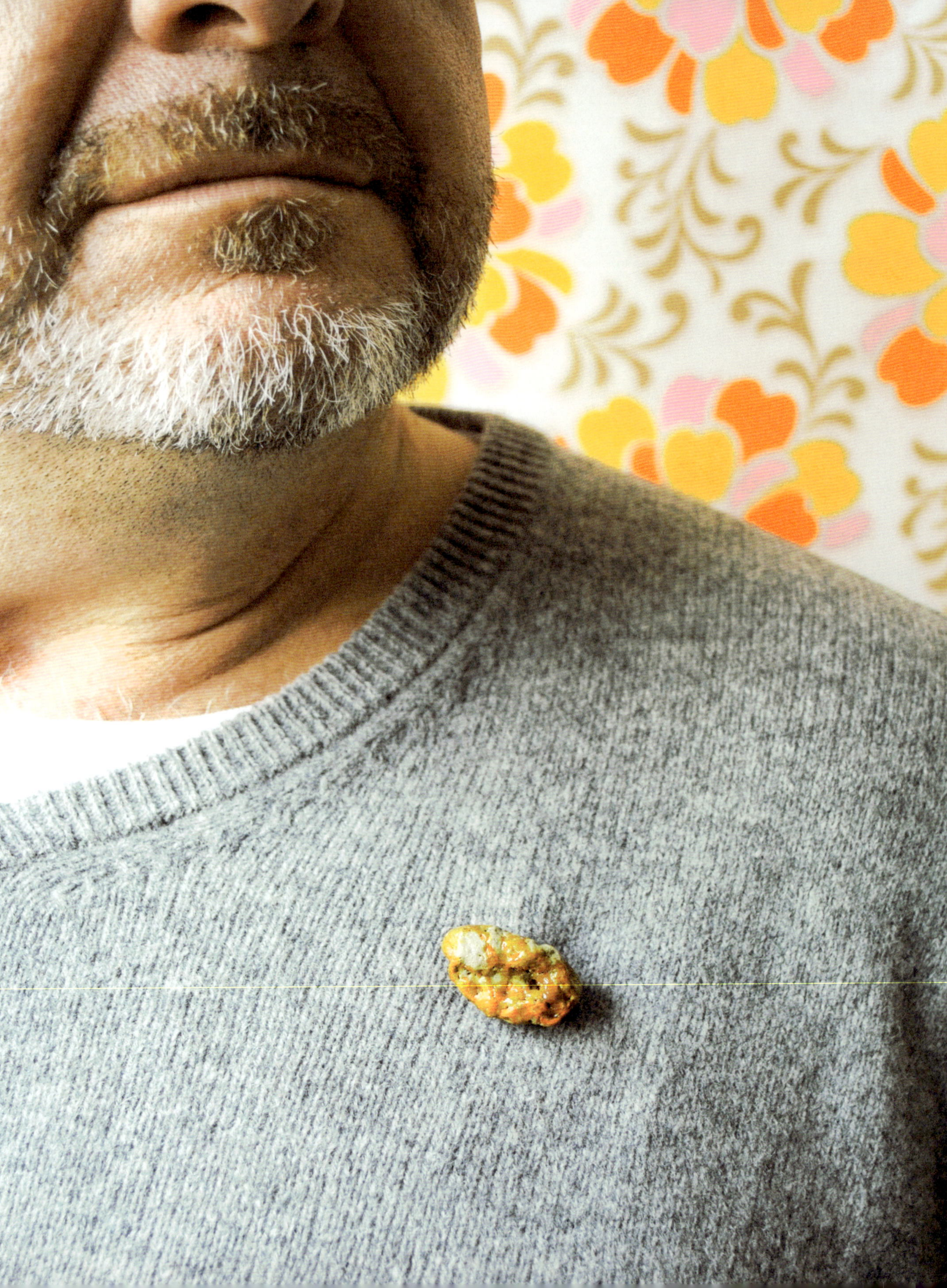

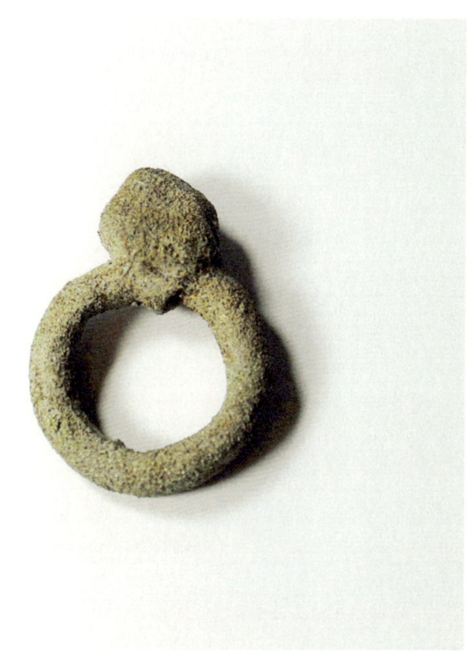

BLUMEN&BOLLER Brosche / brooch 1996 Silber / silver Kupfer / copper Emaille / enamel
BLUMEN&BOLLER Ring / ring 1997 Kupfer / copper Emaille / enamel Goldstaub / golddust

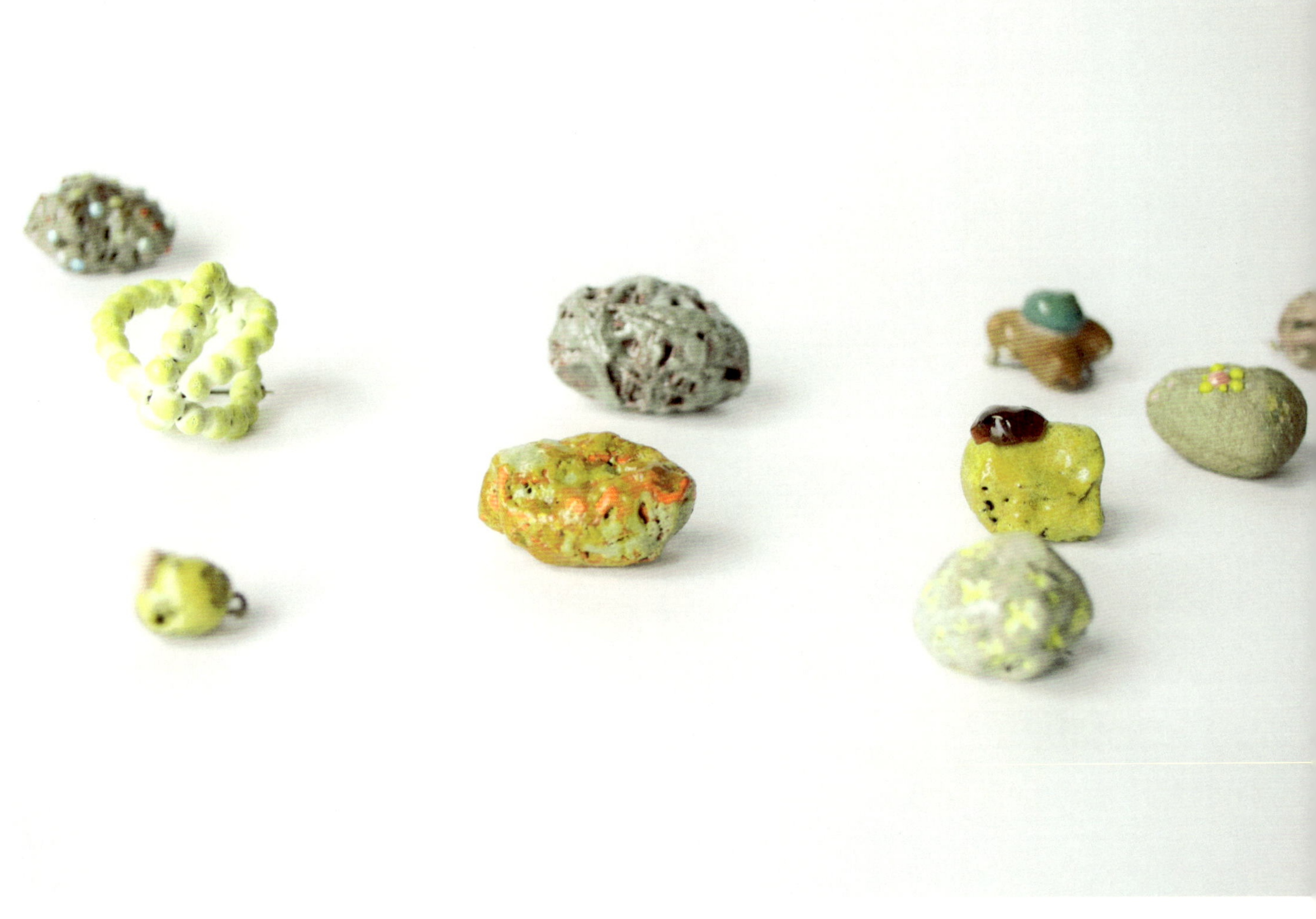

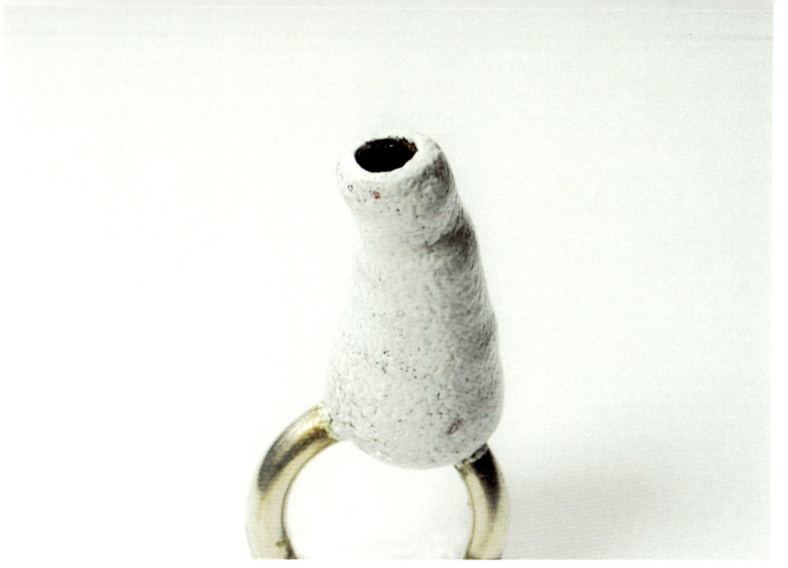

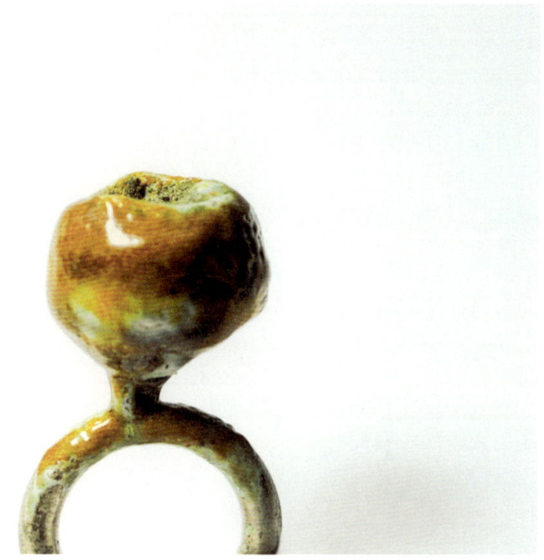

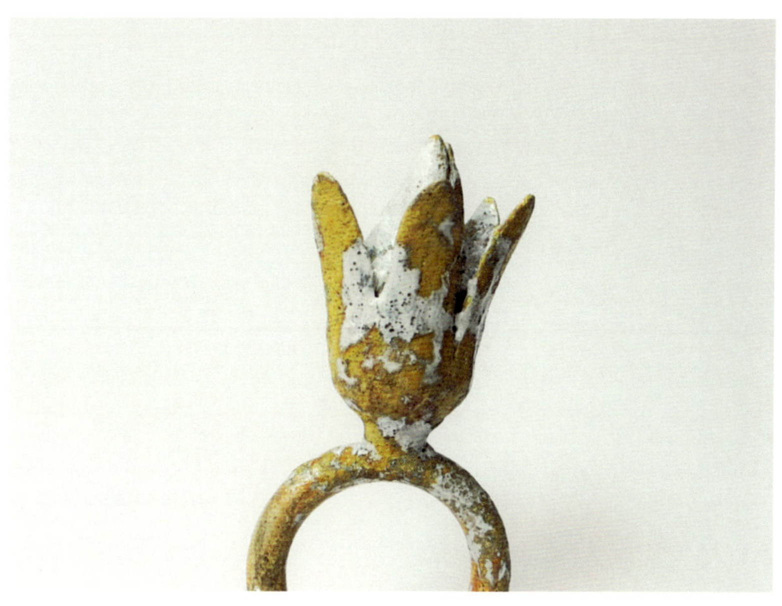

BLUMEN&BOLLER Broschen / brooches 1994–1996 Silber / silver Kupfer / copper Emaille / enamel
BLUMEN&BOLLER Ringe / rings 1995 + 1997 Silber / silver Kupfer / copper Emaille / enamel

»Boller« gibt es laut Duden nicht. Karen Pontoppidan bezeichnet damit kleine materialisierte Ansammlungen in Klumpen- oder Knödelform. Sie verbindet damit eine ganze Reihe von Bildern und Begriffen: »Warzen, Brustwarzen, Popel, Exkremente, Geschwüre etc. – alles natürliche Boller, die durch den menschlichen Organismus entstehen«. Schmuck steht immer in engem Bezug zum Körper. Hier ist dieses Verhältnis zusätzlich thematisiert. Allerdings scheinen die meisten der pontoppidanschen BOLLER seltsam und fremdartig, ja unheimlich aus sich heraus zu leuchten und zu glühen. Auch hier verbindet sich Faszination mit Schrecken, Menschliches mit Extraterrestrischem.[2]
Otto Künzli

According to the German dictionary Duden, the term "Boller" does not exist. Karen Pontoppidan, however, associates them with small assemblages in the form of clusters or dumpling shapes, with which she consolidates an entire series of images and concepts: "Warts, nipples, boogers, excrement, ulcers, etc.—all natural aggregations that are created by human organisms." Jewelry is always closely related to the body. Here this relationship is additionally thematized. Most of Pontoppidan's BOLLER (Lumps) look strangely and peculiarly, even uncannily as though they are lit up from inside and glowing. Here too fascination and dread, the human and extraterrestrial come together.[2]
Otto Künzli

BLUMEN&BOLLER Ringe / rings 1993–1994 Silber / silver Kupfer / copper Emaille / enamel

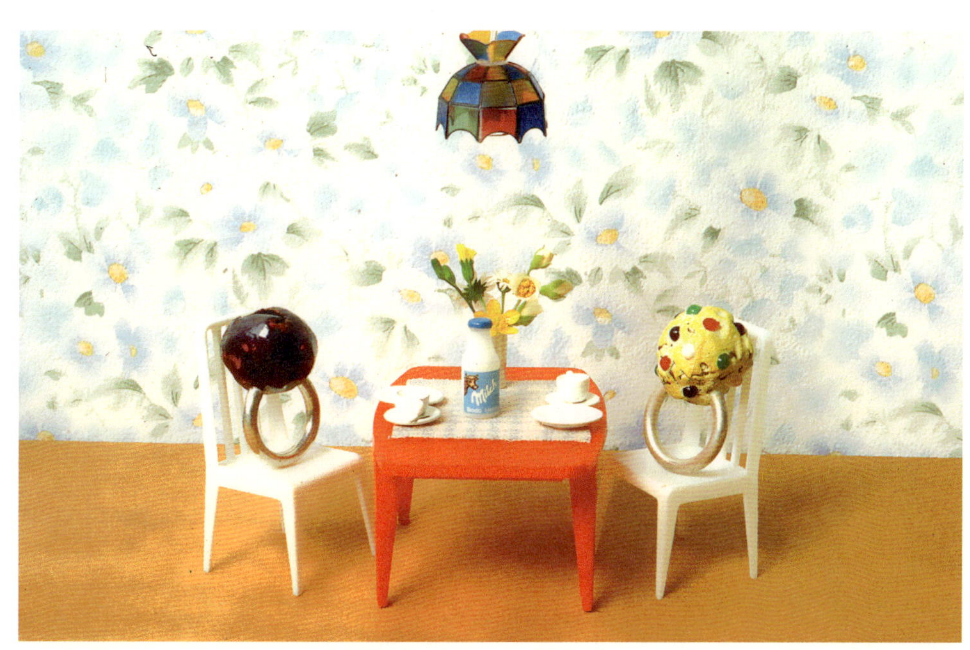

K. A.

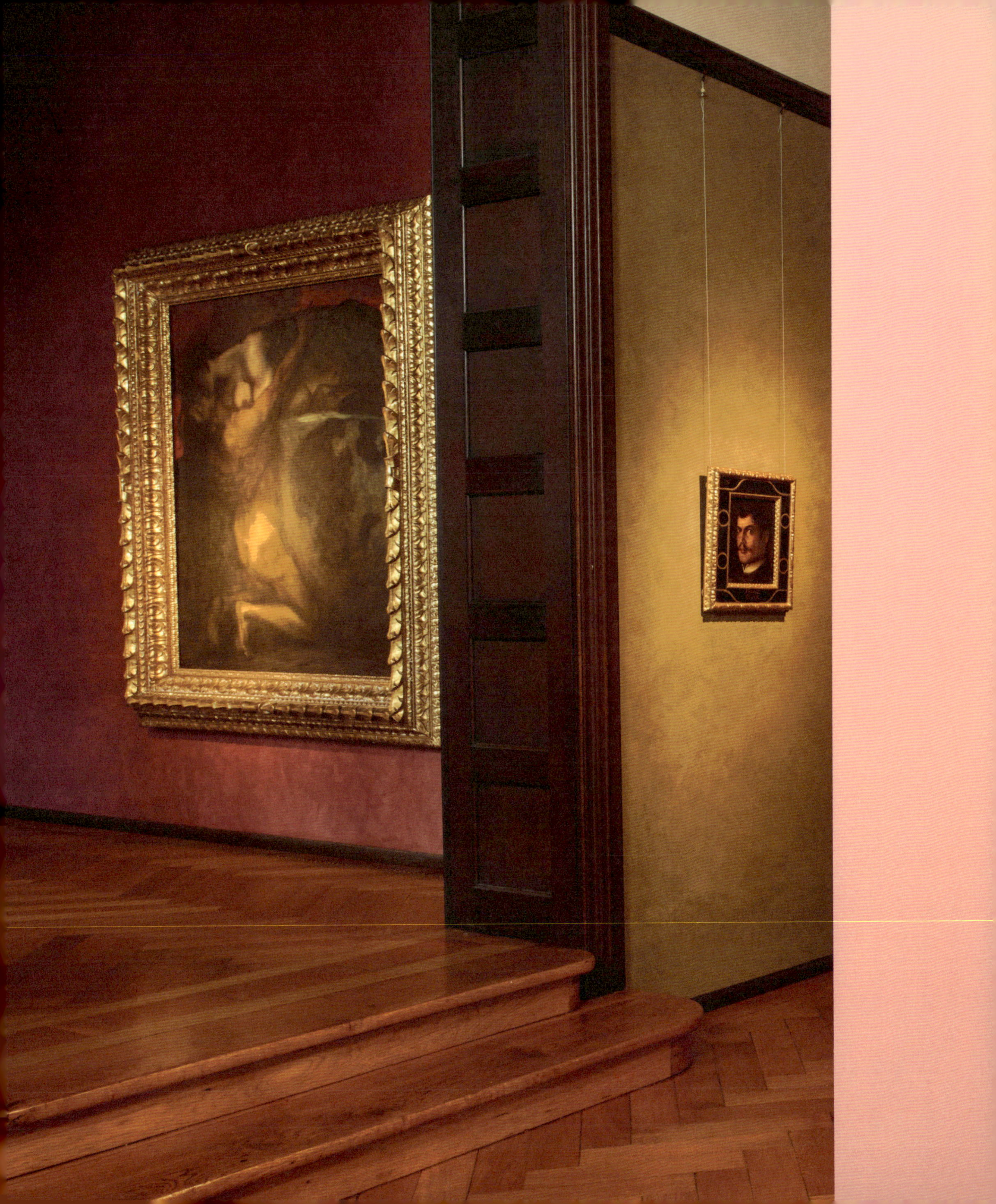

O.T.

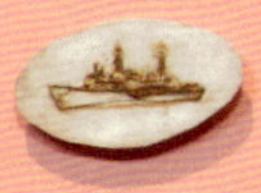

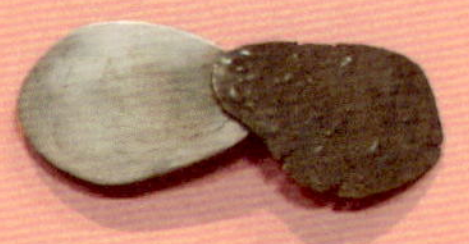

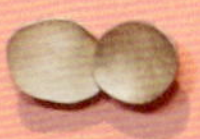

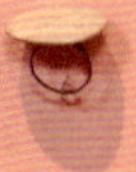

R. E.

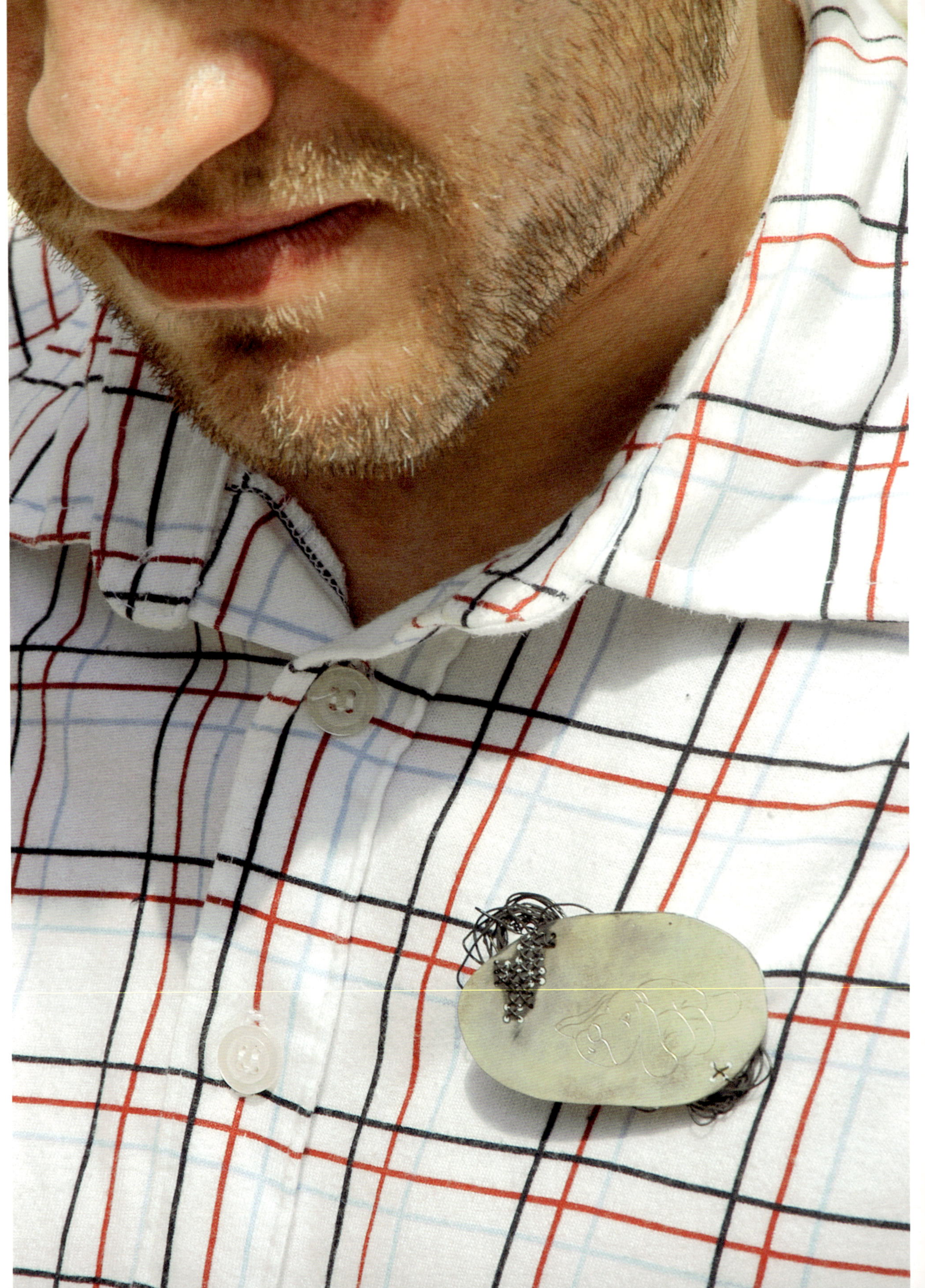

Der pontoppidansche Schmuck stellt Fragen. Antworten gibt er nicht. Wer ihn trägt, muss sich zu ihm bekennen. Distanz oder Indifferenz sind ebenso wenig möglich wie der Rückzug auf das Argument der »schönen« oder symbolisch aufgeladenen Form. Dem Schmuck tragenden Individuum bleibt wenig Spielraum für Ausweichmanöver. Es wird auf sich selber zurückgeworfen. Nach Karen Pontoppidans Auffassung ist Schmuck ein Medium, in dem jedes Thema hautnah und öffentlich zur Sprache gebracht werden kann, und die stärkste Kunstform überhaupt. Hierin liegt eine ungemein konsequente, aber nicht provokante oder dogmatisch auftretende Radikalität. Eine Umwertung der Werte, wie sie rigoroser nicht sein könnte.[3]
Barbara Maas

The pontoppidanian jewelry asks questions. It does not provide answers. Anyone who wears it must do so with conviction. Distance or indifference are just as out of the question as retreating behind the argument of the "beautiful" or symbolically charged form. Individuals wearing this jewelry have little scope for evasion. They are thrown back upon themselves. In Karen Pontoppidan's opinion, jewelry is a medium through which any subject can be expressed directly and publicly, and it is the most potent of all art forms. And this is her radicalism. Utterly uncompromising, but neither provocative nor dogmatic. A reevaluation of values that could hardly be more rigorous.[3]
Barbara Maas

O.T. Brosche / brooch 2005 Silber / silver Gold / gold Eisen / iron Emaille / enamel

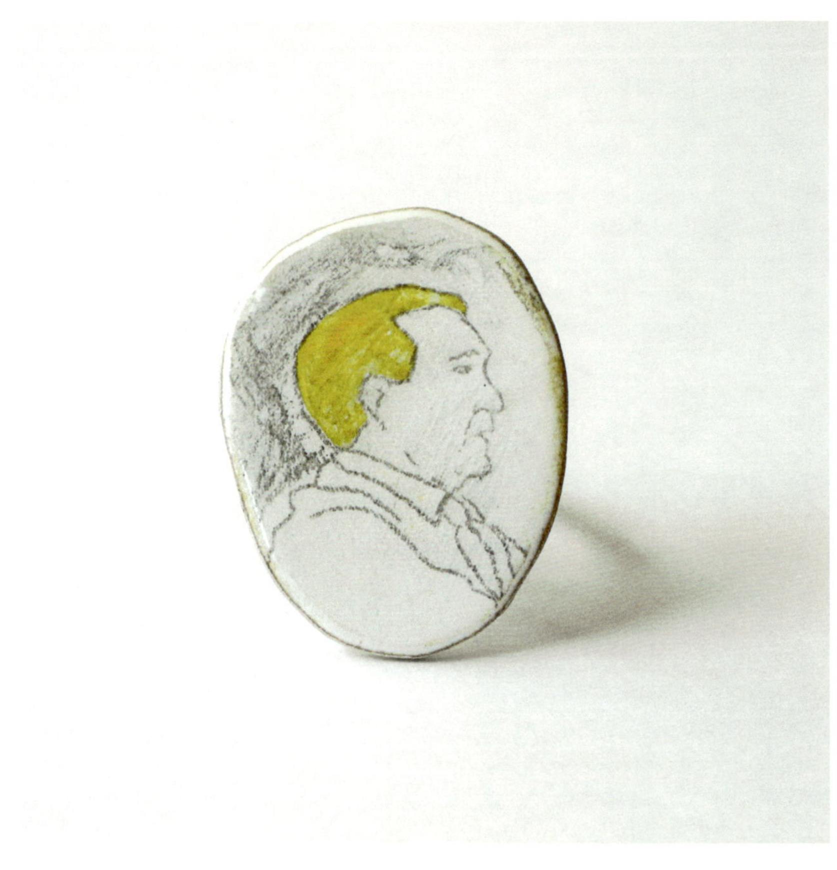

O.T. Ringe / rings 2006–2007 Silber / silver Gold / gold Emaille / enamel Niello / niello

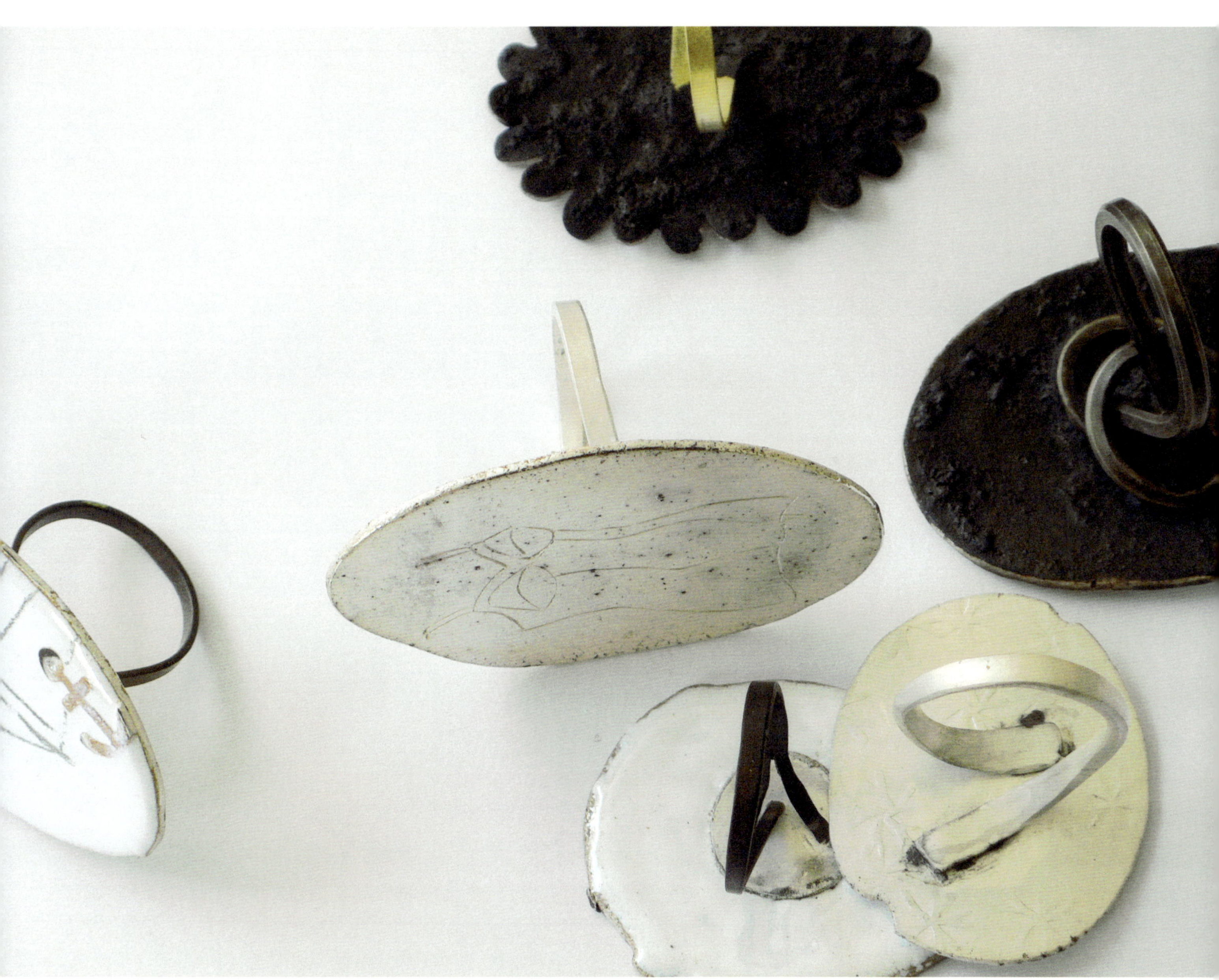

R. E.

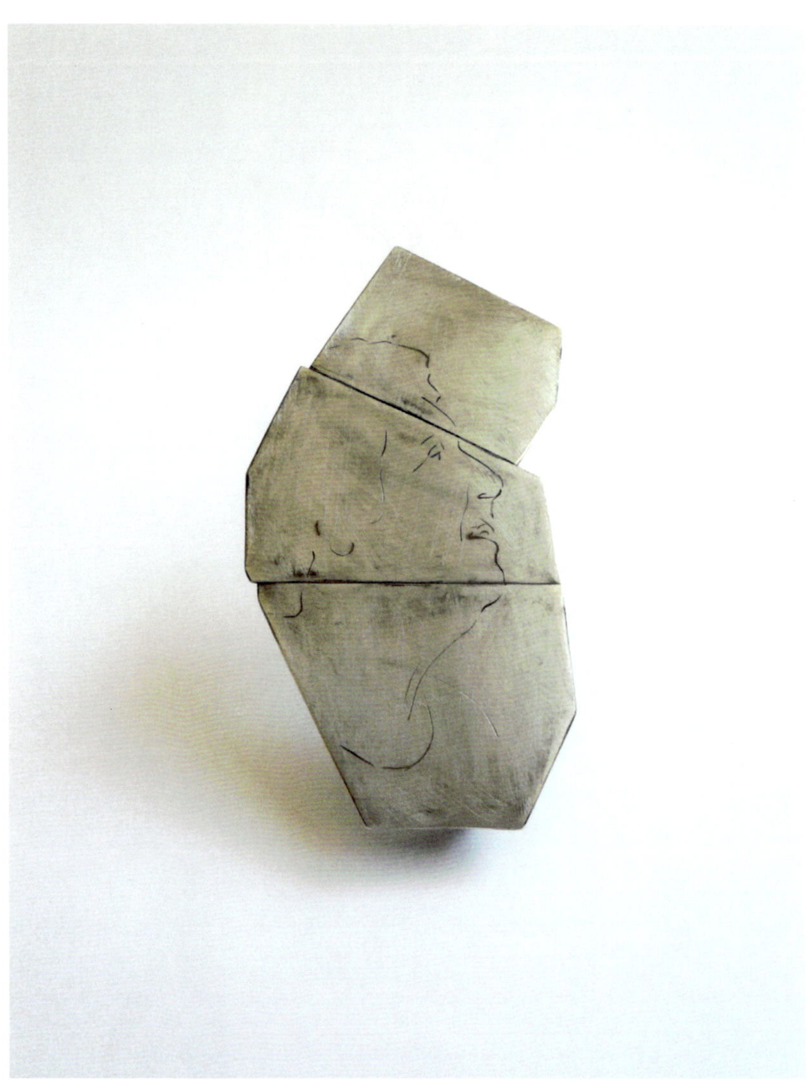

O.T. Brosche / brooch 2007 Silber / silver Niello / niello

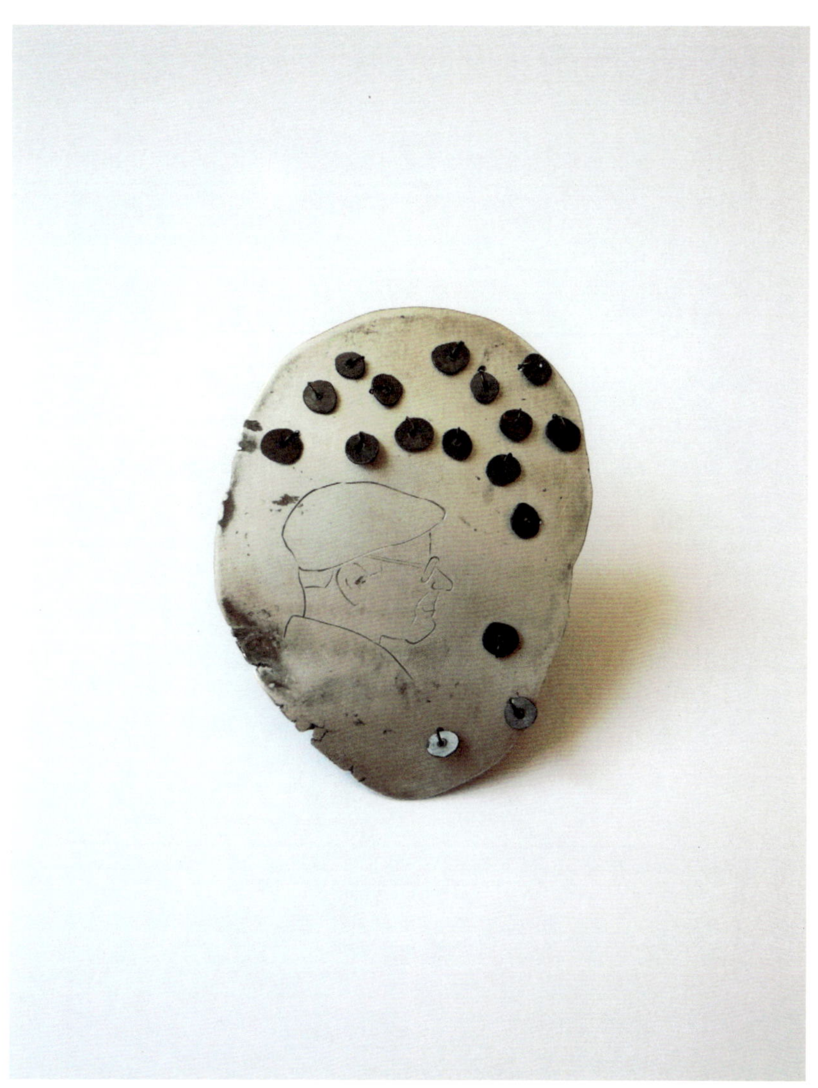

O.T. Brosche / brooch 2006 Silber / silver Niello / niello Eisen / iron Schrot / shot

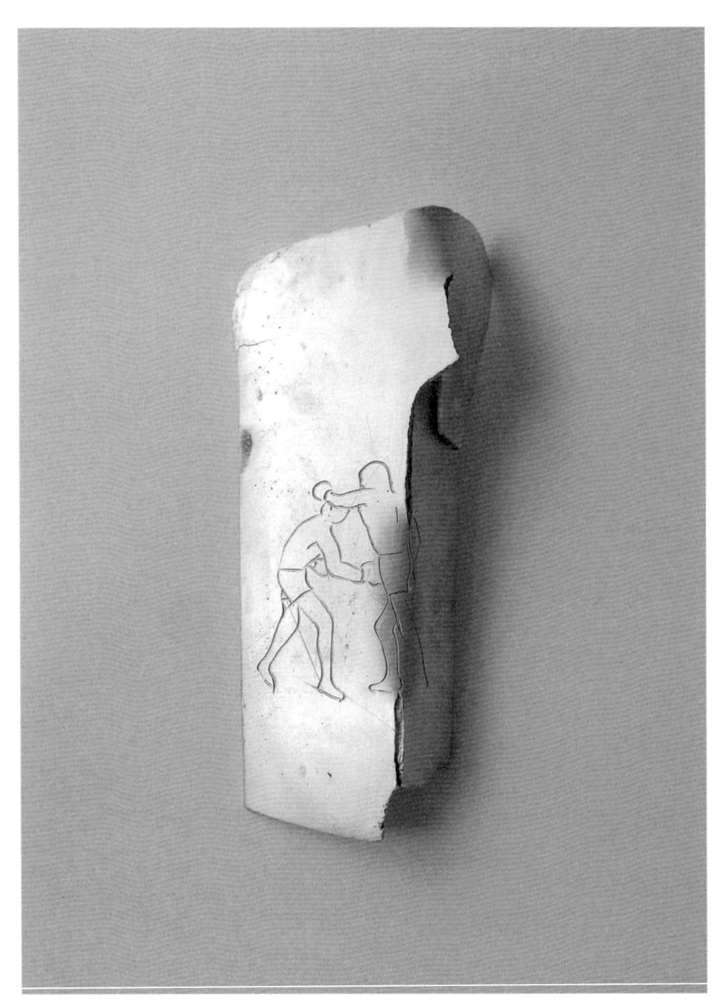

O.T. Broschen / brooches 2004–2006 Silber / silver Gold / gold Emaille / enamel

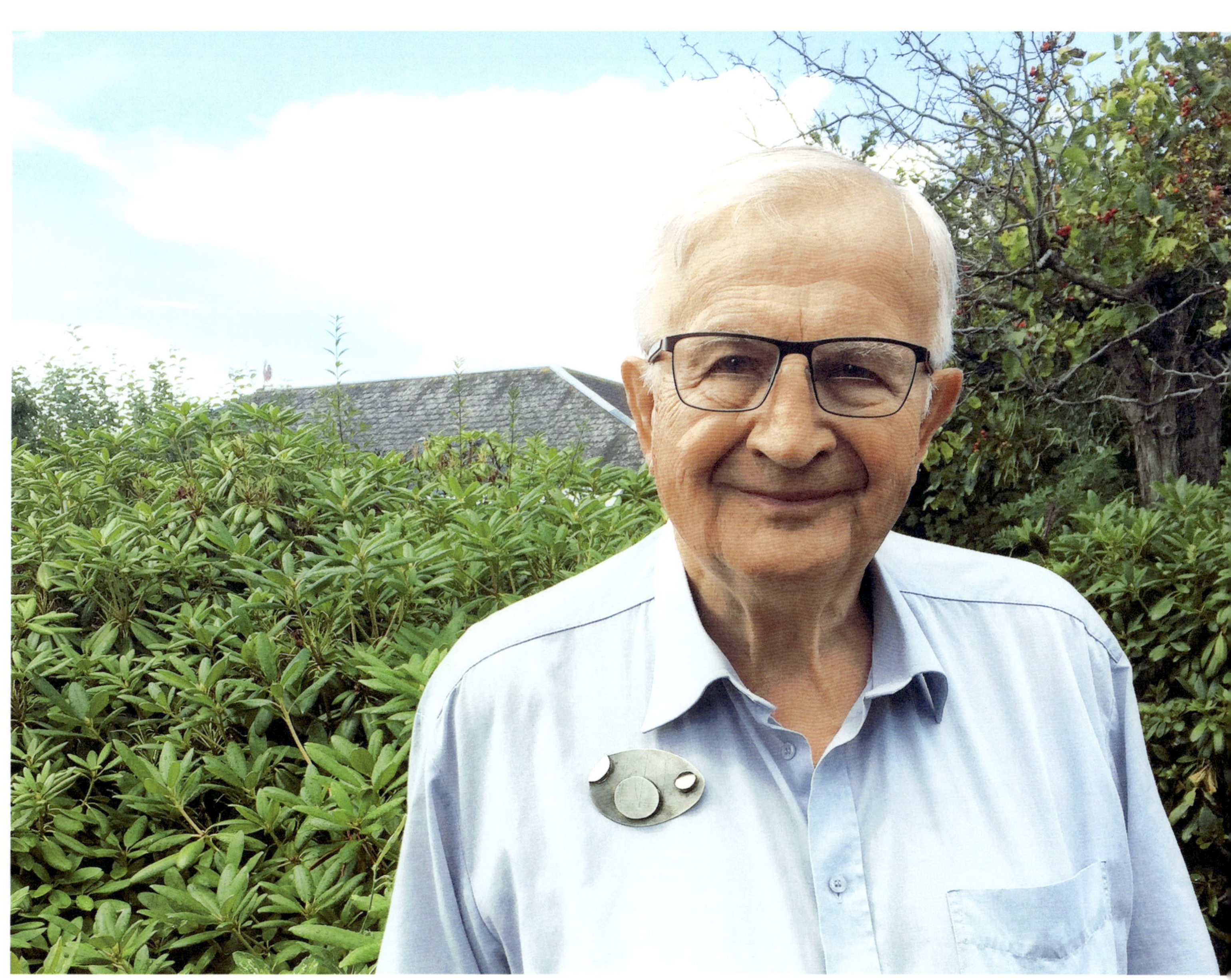

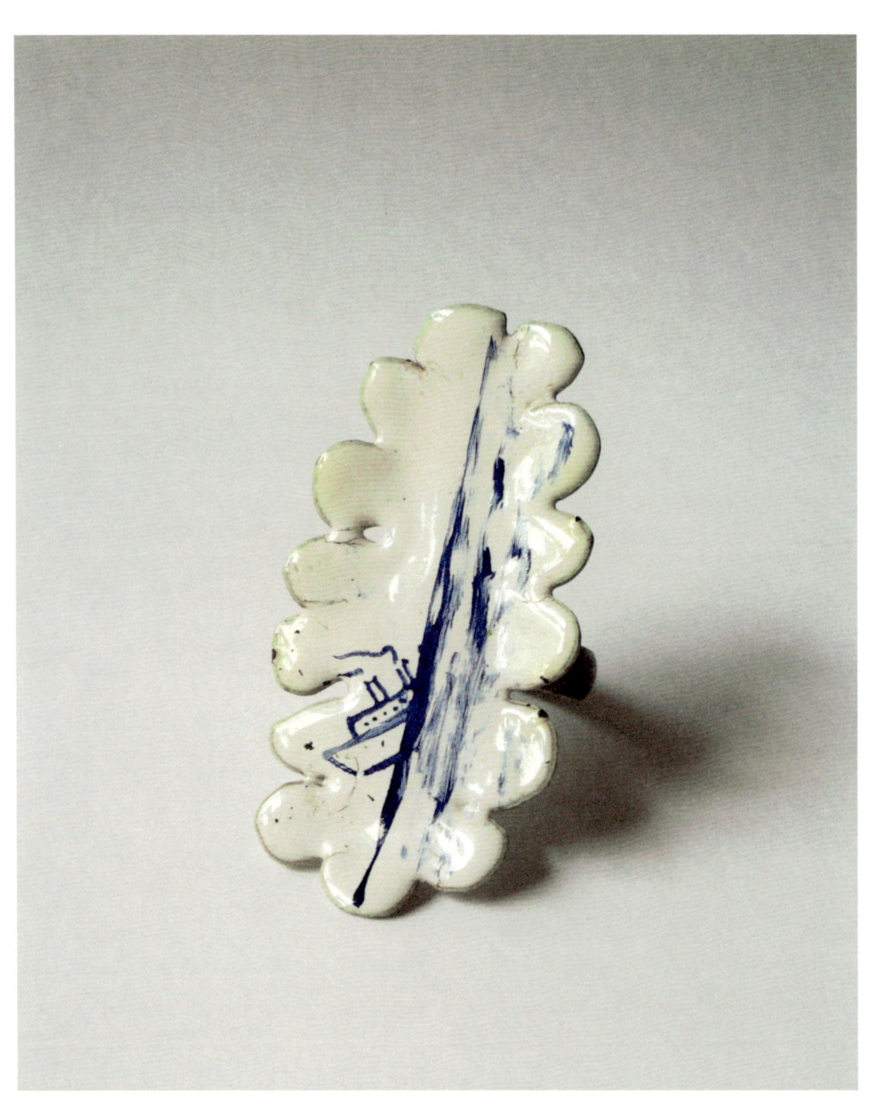

O.T. Ring / ring 2001 Silber / silver Emaille / enamel

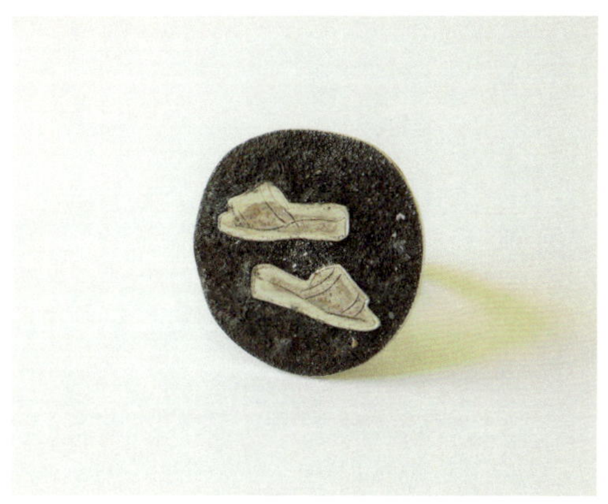

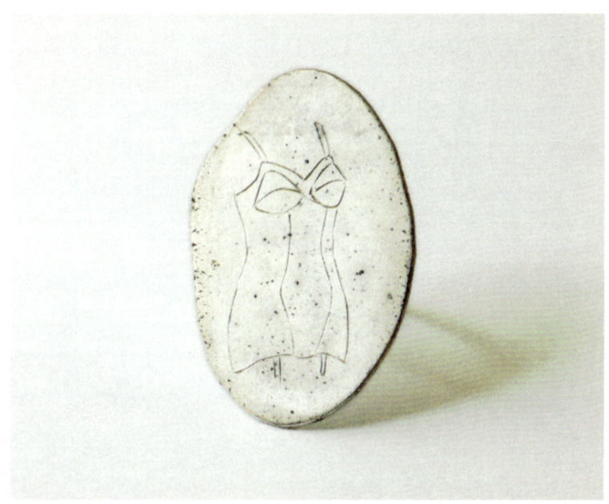

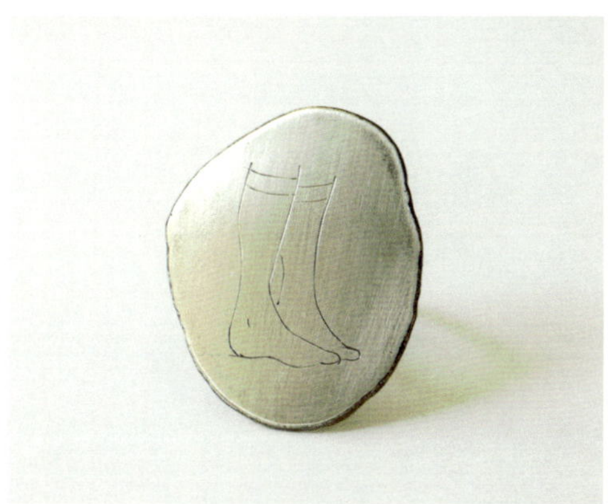

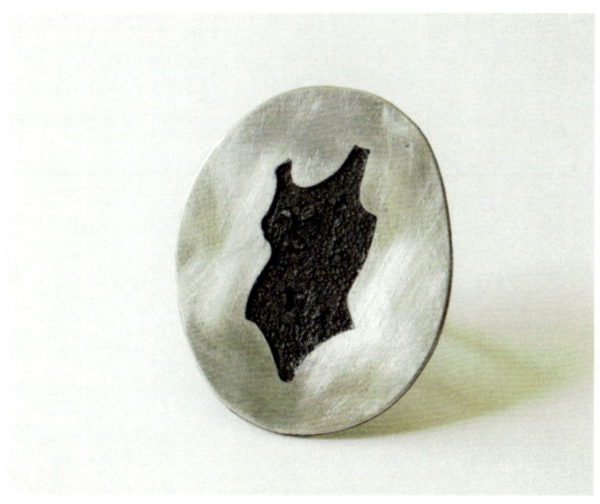

O.T. Ringe / rings 2006 Silber / silver Gold / gold
Niello / niello Emaille / enamel

Meine Arbeiten beleuchten nicht nur Schmucknormen, sie hinterfragen auch zum Teil die gesellschaftlichen Normen, die dem Schmücken zugrunde liegen. Wenn zum Beispiel eine Brosche ein perlengeschmücktes Pissoir zeigt, dann ist es auch ein Hinterfragen von Rollenverhalten in unserer Gesellschaft.[4]
R.E.

My works not only illuminate jewelry norms, they also question some of the social norms, which are the foundation of adornment. For example, when a brooch displays a pearl-framed pissoir, then it is also questioning role behavior in our society.[4]
R.E.

O.T. Brosche / brooch 2001 Silber / silver Gold / gold Emaille / enamel Perlen / pearls

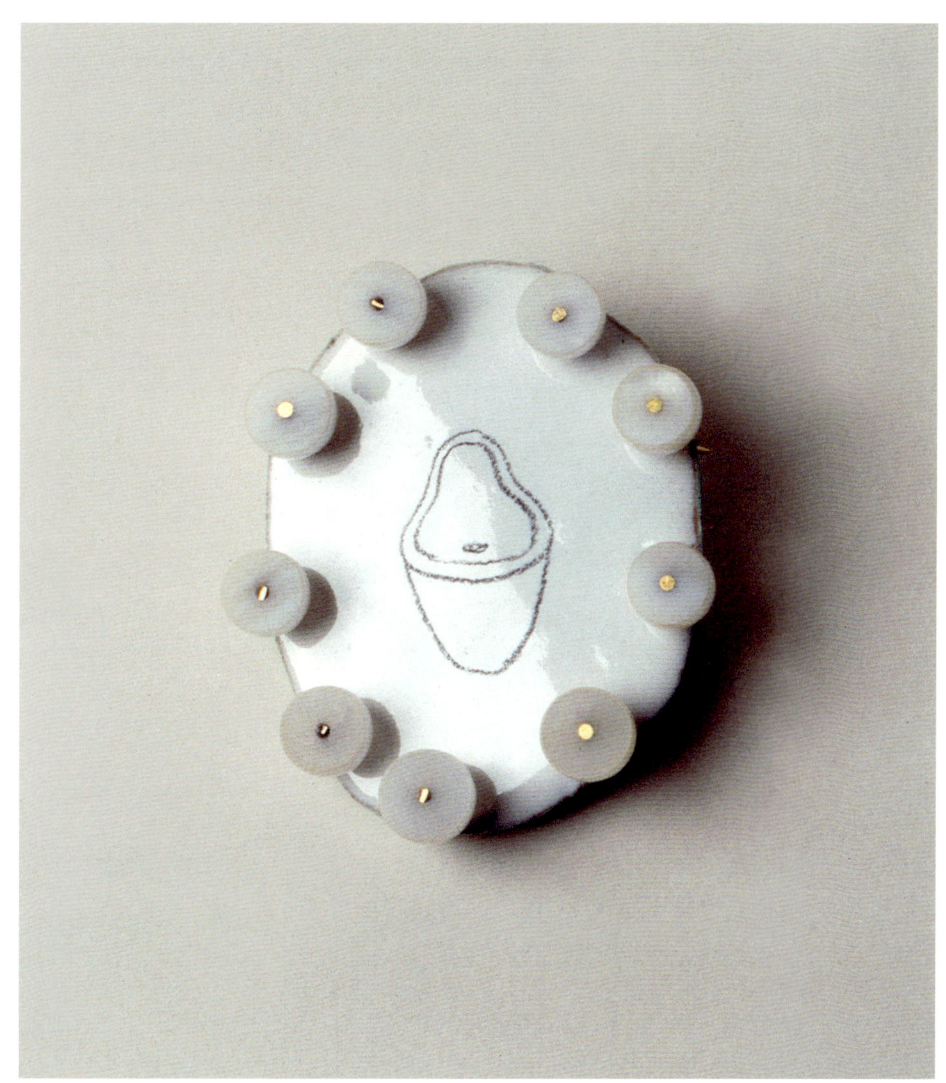

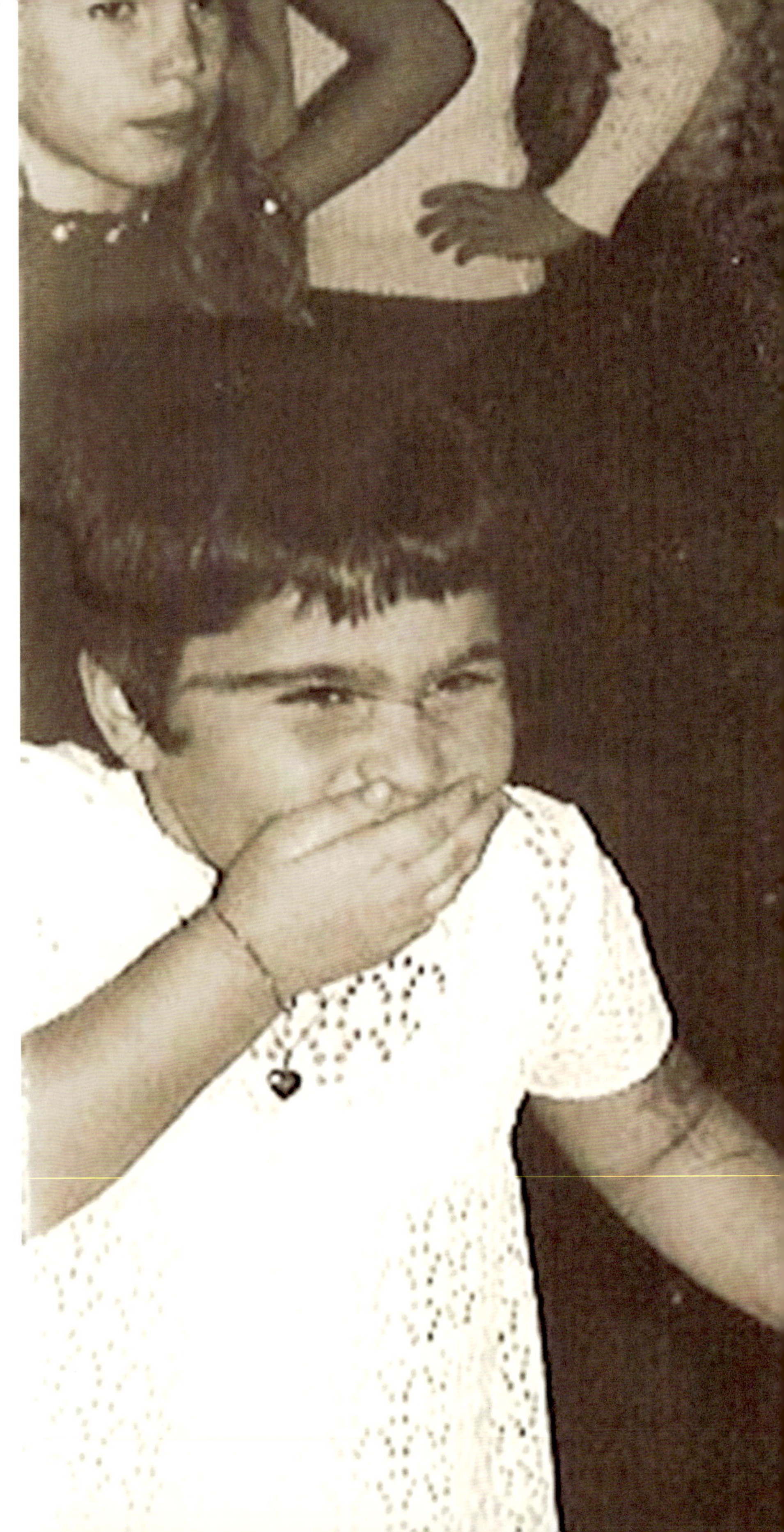

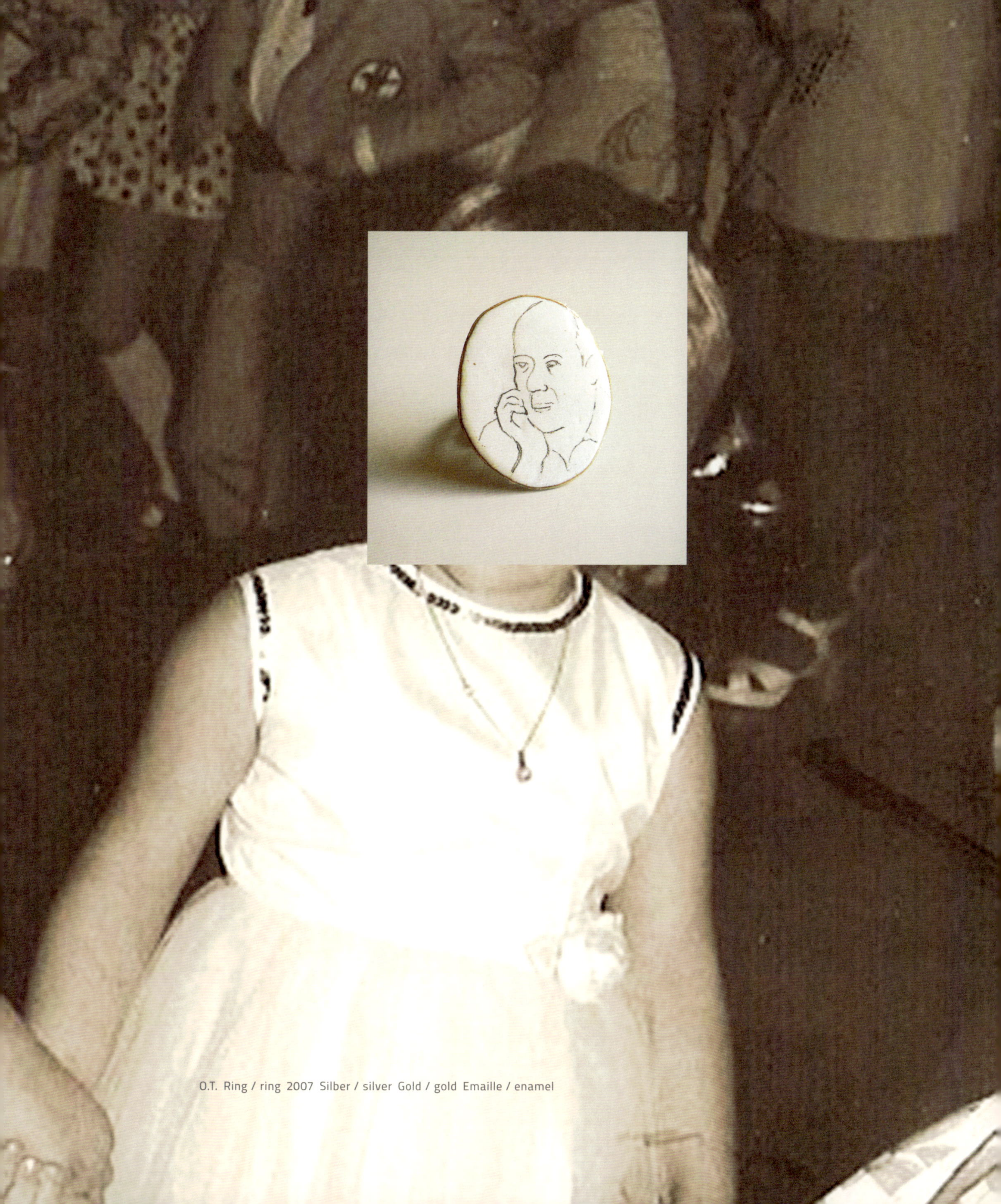

O.T. Ring / ring 2007 Silber / silver Gold / gold Emaille / enamel

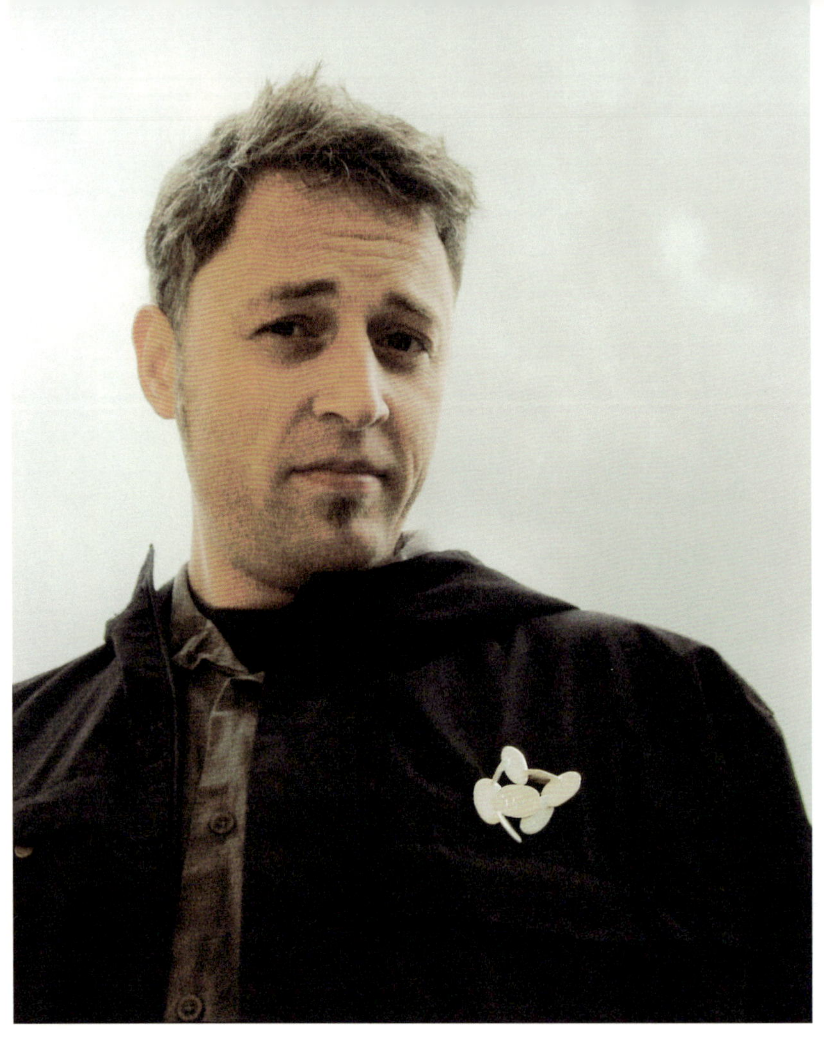

O.T. Brosche / brooch 2003 Silber / silver Gold / gold Emaille / enamel
O.T. Ringe / rings 2004 Silber / silver Emaille / enamel

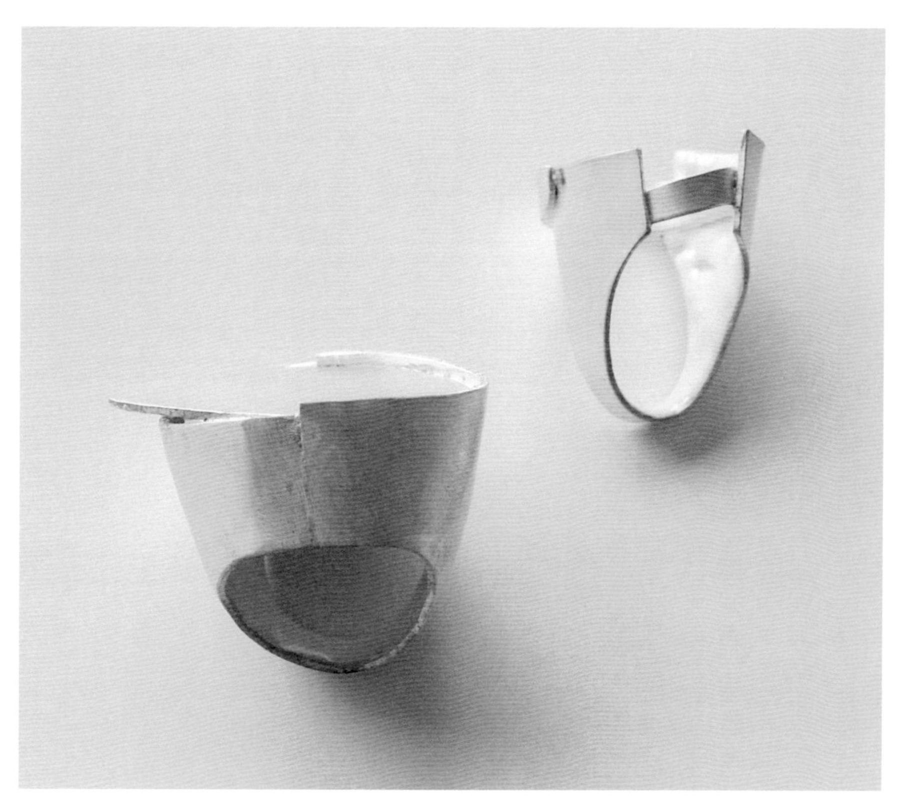

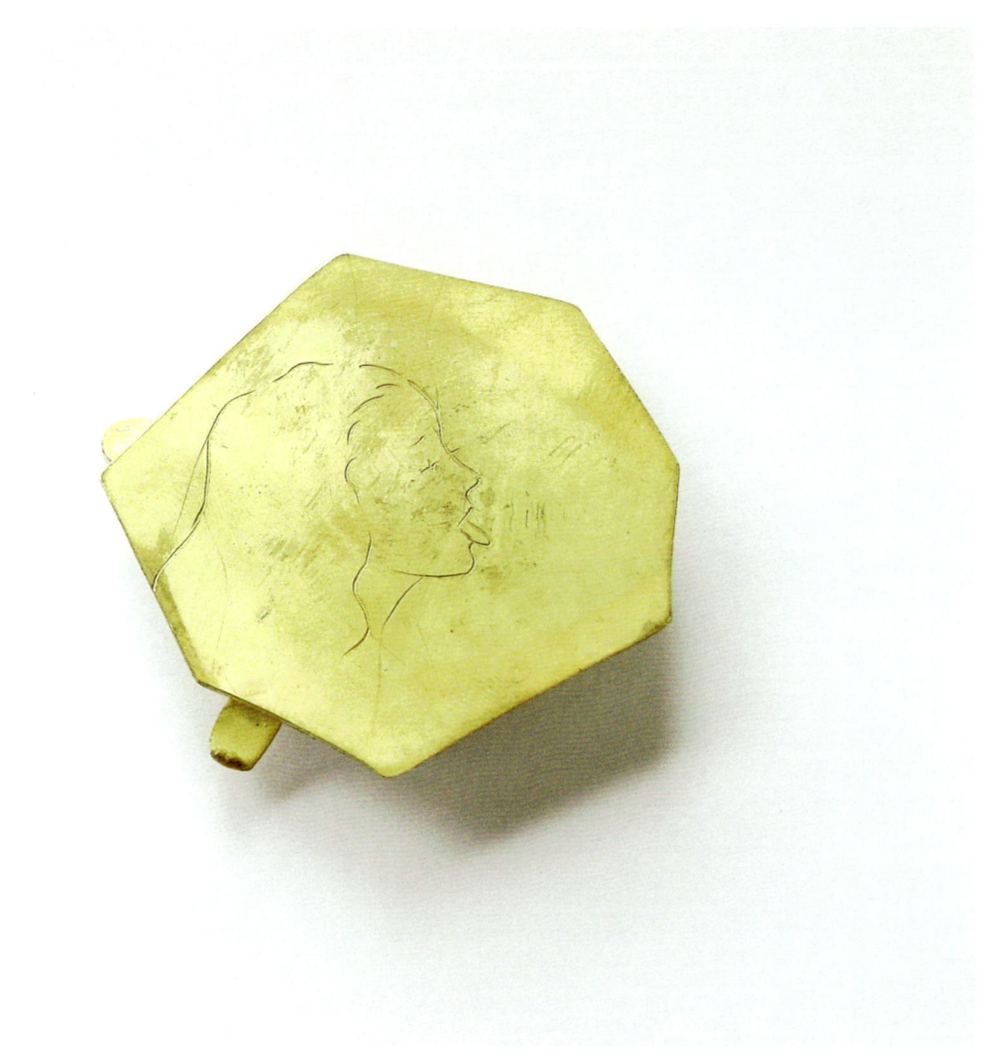

Zeichnungen spielen eine wichtige Rolle in Pontoppidans Frühwerk. Sie graviert störende kleine Zeichnungen auf Silber- oder weiße Emailoberflächen. Störend in dem Sinne, dass diese Zeichnungen unerwartete alltägliche Bilder darstellen, jedoch mit komplizierten Assoziationen. So sehen wir zum Beispiel einen Schuh, eine Lampe oder einen Rettich (Brosche der CODA Sammlung). Viele dieser Objekte sind jedoch nicht mittig, sondern eher ungewöhnlich platziert. Auf den ersten Blick erscheinen die Stücke relativ gängig hinsichtlich Größe und Form, doch die tiefere Bedeutung ist nicht so einfach zu definieren oder zu erschließen. Die Wirkung dieser Widersprüchlichkeit in ihrer Symbolik wird noch verstärkt durch eine bewusst unvollkommene Ausführung (Stichwort »schlampige Verarbeitung«) sowie die Anwendung arbeitsintensiver Techniken wie Niellieren, Emaillieren oder Gravieren. Ihre Zeichnungen haben eine unabhängige Form und Bedeutung, die weit über die einfache Dekoration flacher Oberflächen hinausgeht. Hier versteht es Pontoppidan, ganz bewusst Sand in die gut geölten Räder der sozialen Normen im Fashion- und Schmuckbereich zu streuen, um das aufzumischen, was sie als »die Gewohnheit, bestimmte wiederkehrende Motive der Schmuckindustrie zu feiern« bezeichnet. Indem sie die Linien auf ein Minimum dessen, was nötig ist, um das eigentliche Motiv zu erkennen, reduziert, kommt es zu einer gewissen Einsamkeit oder Verfremdung.[5]
Carin E.M. Reinders

Drawings play an important role in Pontoppidan's early work. She carves disruptive little drawings on silver or white enamel surfaces. Disruptive in the sense that these drawings depict unexpected everyday images with complicated associations. We, for instance, see a shoe, a lamp, a radish (brooch in the CODA collection). Many of these objects are placed out of center or out of perspective. At first glance these pieces look quite normal as far as size and form are concerned but the "meaning" is not so easy to define or to "unlock." The actual effect of the contradiction in her imagery is enforced by the intentional imperfect execution and the labor-intensive techniques such as niello, enameling and carving. Her drawings have an independent form and meaning that go far beyond "just" decorations on a flat surface. Here Pontoppidan deliberately scatters sand into the well-oiled wheels of social codes of fashion and jewelry to disturb what she calls "the habit of celebrating motifs of them found in jewelry." By reducing the lines to a minimum that is needed to recognize the actual motif a certain kind of loneliness or alienation takes place.[5]
Carin E.M. Reinders

O.T. Brosche / brooch 2005 Gold / gold 750/000 Emaille / enamel

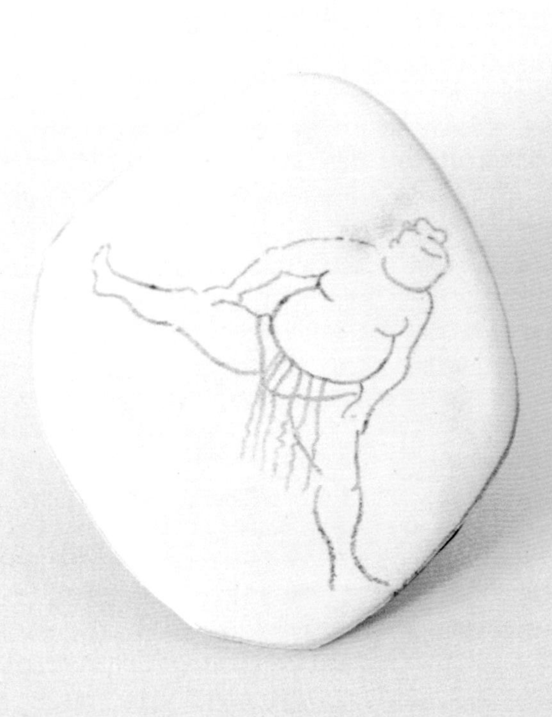

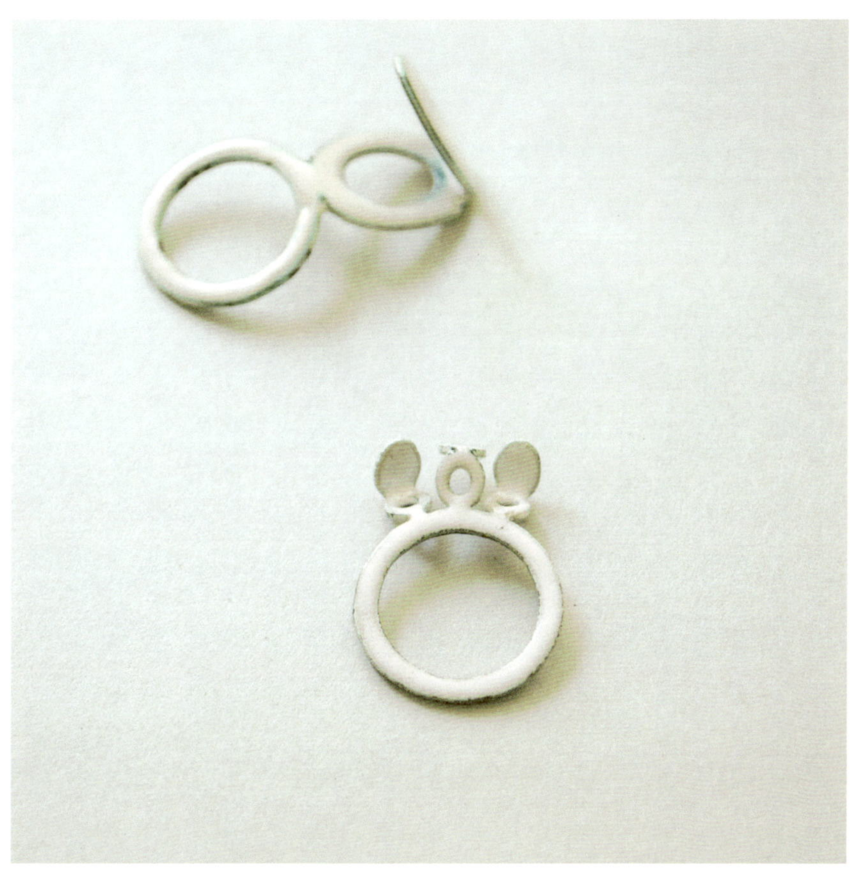

O.T. Brosche / brooch 2005 Silber / silver Gold / gold Emaille / enamel
O.T. Ringe / rings 2001 Silber / silver Emaille / enamel

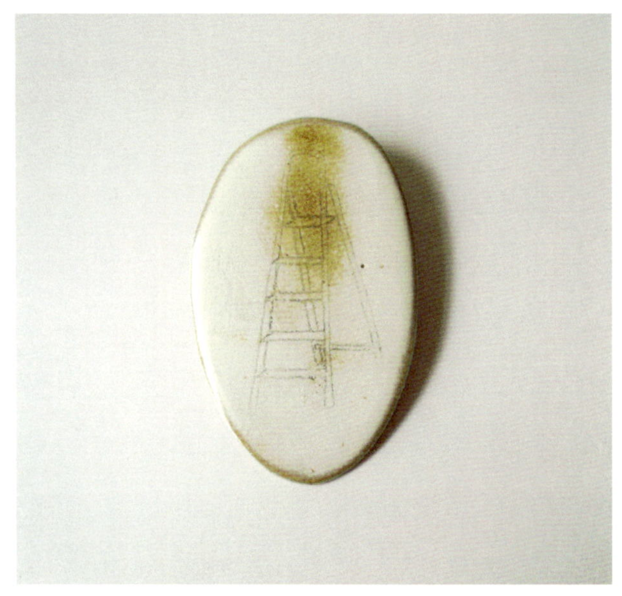

O.T. Brosche / brooch 2007 Silber / silver Gold / gold Emaille / enamel
O.T. (Selbstportrait mit Ziege / Self-Portrait with goat) Brosche / brooch 2002 Silber / silver Gold / gold Emaille / enamel

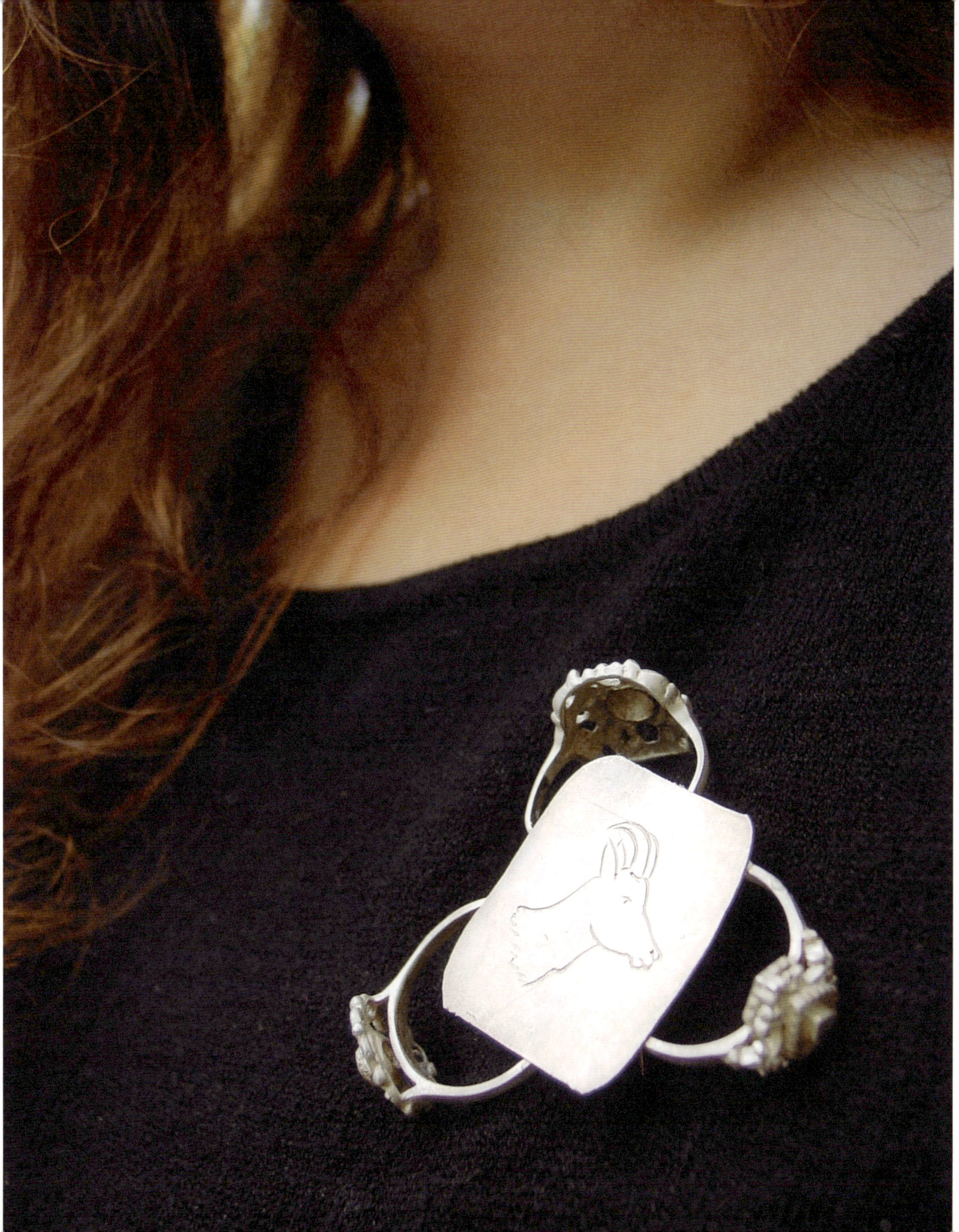

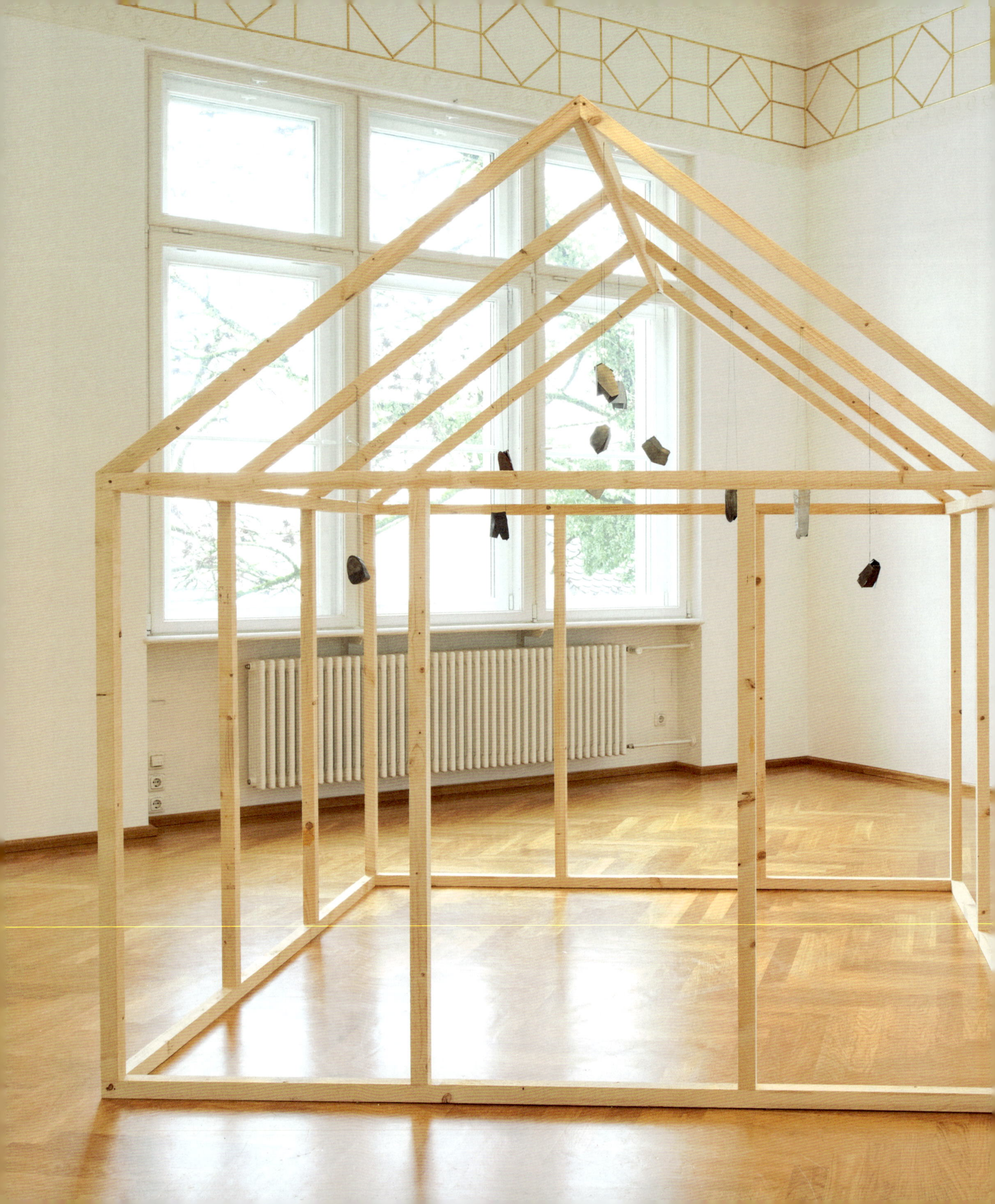

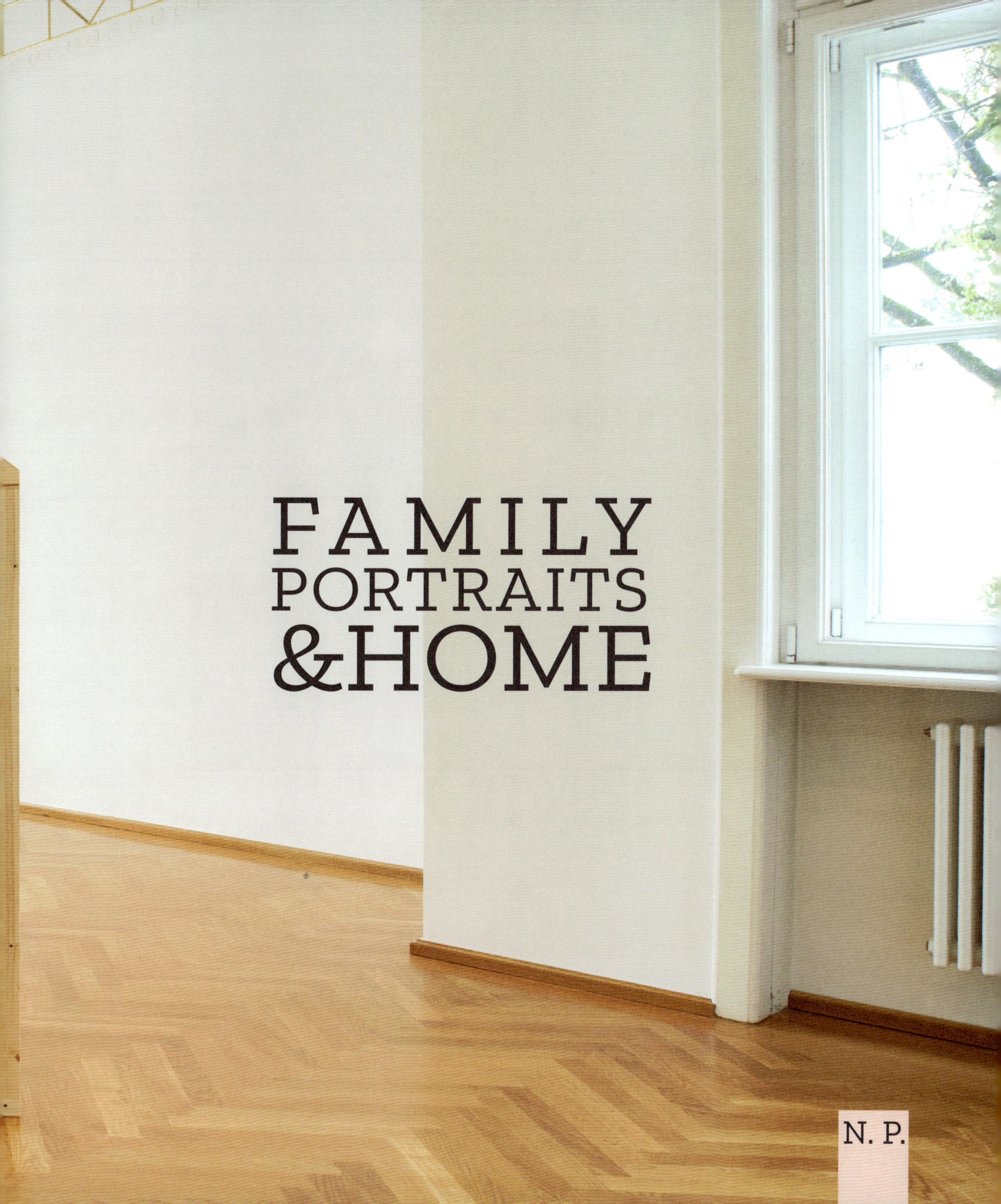
FAMILY
PORTRAITS
&HOME
N. P.

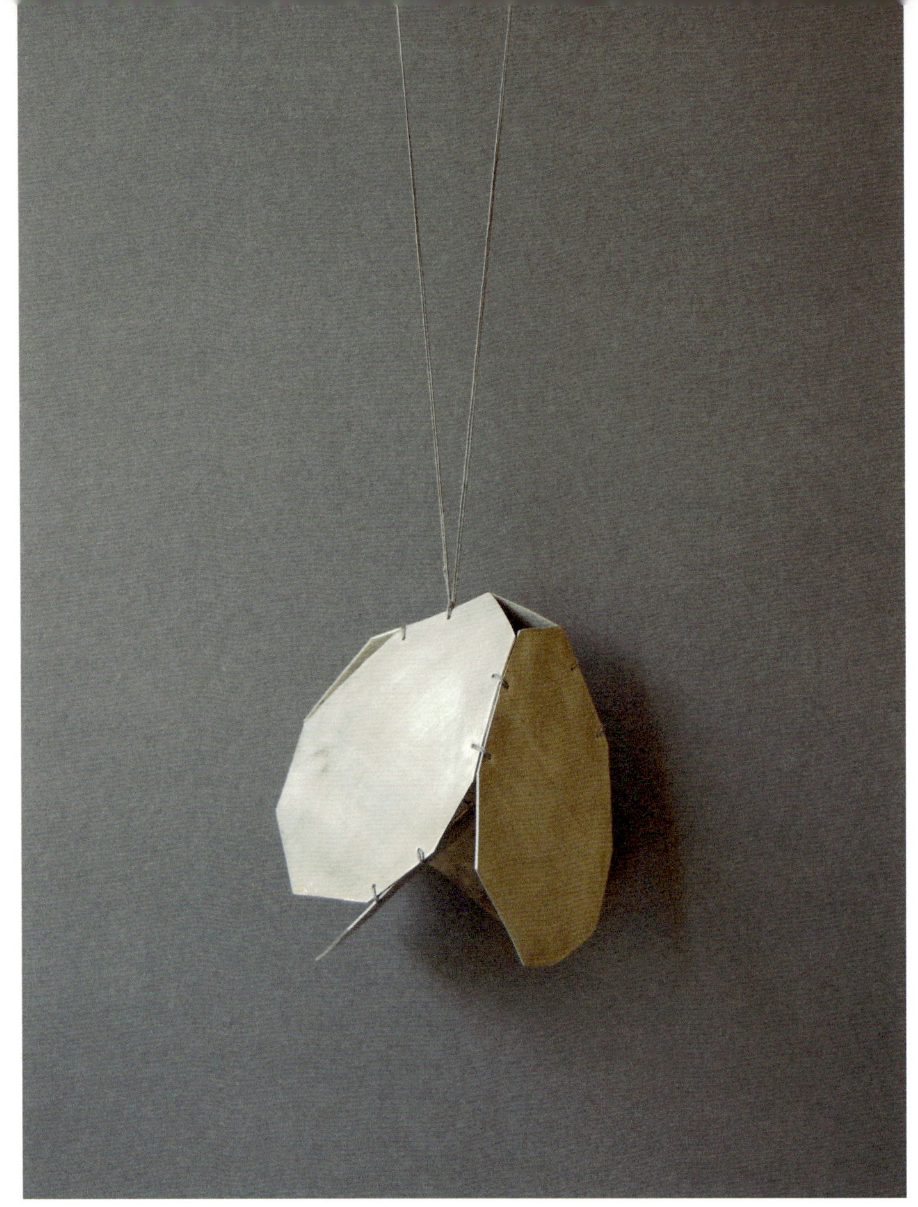

FAMILYPORTRAIT#26 Anhänger / pendant 2010 Zinn / tin Faden / string

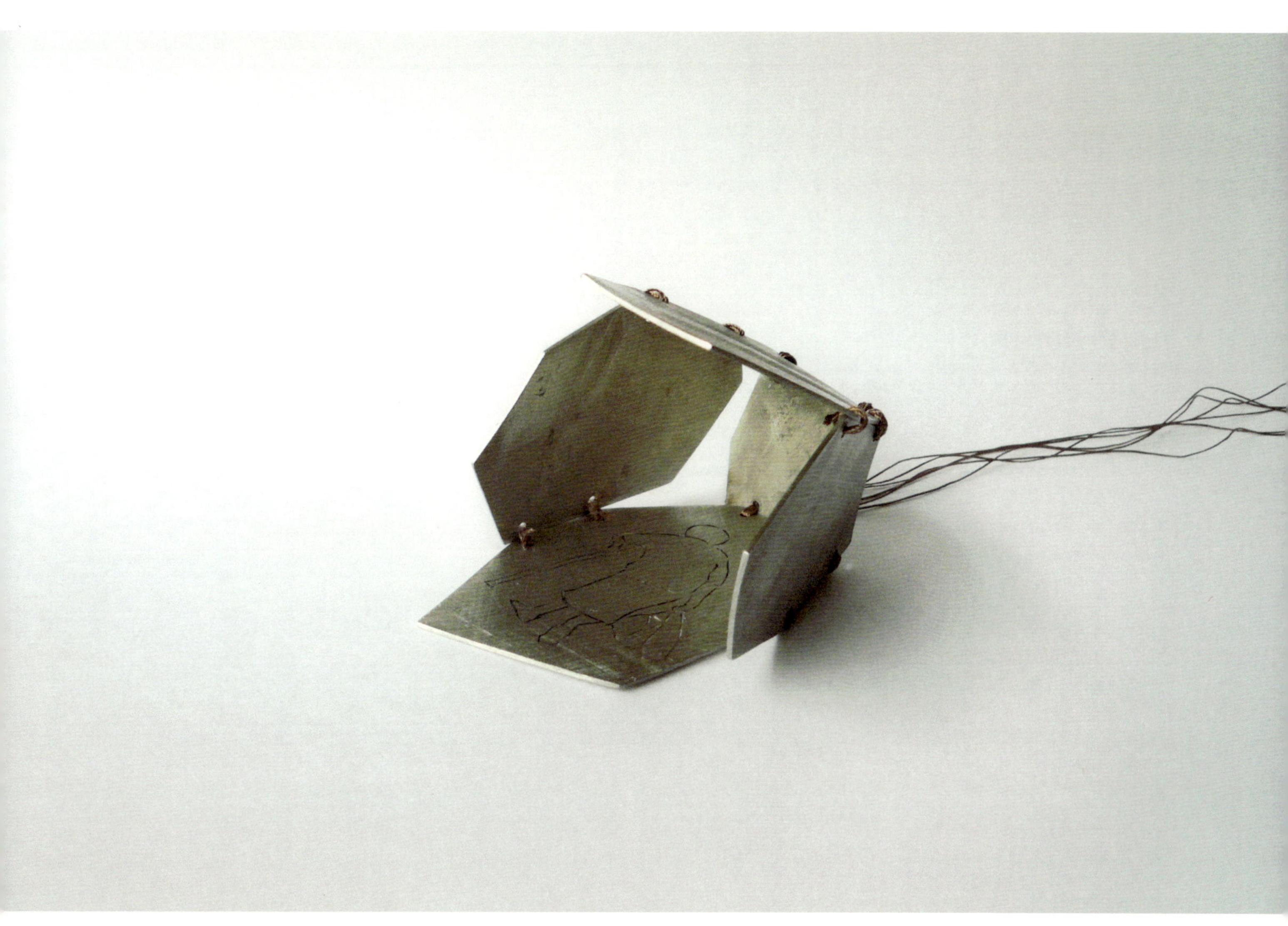

FAMILYPORTRAIT#1 Anhänger / pendant 2007 Zinn / tin Faden / string

Während also Menschen vormoderner Kulturen sich über das Medium Schmuck auf die Höhe Gottes, des Königs, der Ahnen, der Totems beziehen, schmücken sich moderne Menschen mit allem, was mit ihnen selbst auf Augenhöhe steht, das heißt, sie schmücken sich mit sich selbst. So erforscht Karen Pontoppidans künstlerische Reflexion die Möglichkeiten, dass man mithilfe des Schmucks mit bestimmten Ebenen des eigenen Daseins in Beziehung tritt: mit dem biologischen Körper, dem Animalischen in einem selbst oder dem archaischen Familienkollektiv.[6]
Pravu Mazumdar

Whereas man in pre-modern cultures alludes to the elevated level of god, of the king, of ancestors, of totems via the medium of jewelry, modern man adorns itself with everything on a par with themselves—that is, they adorn themselves with themselves. Karen Pontoppidan's artistic reflection explores the possibilities that, with the aid of jewelry, people can enter into a relationship with certain levels of their own being: with the biological body, the animalistic in one's self, or the archaic family collective.[6]
Pravu Mazumdar

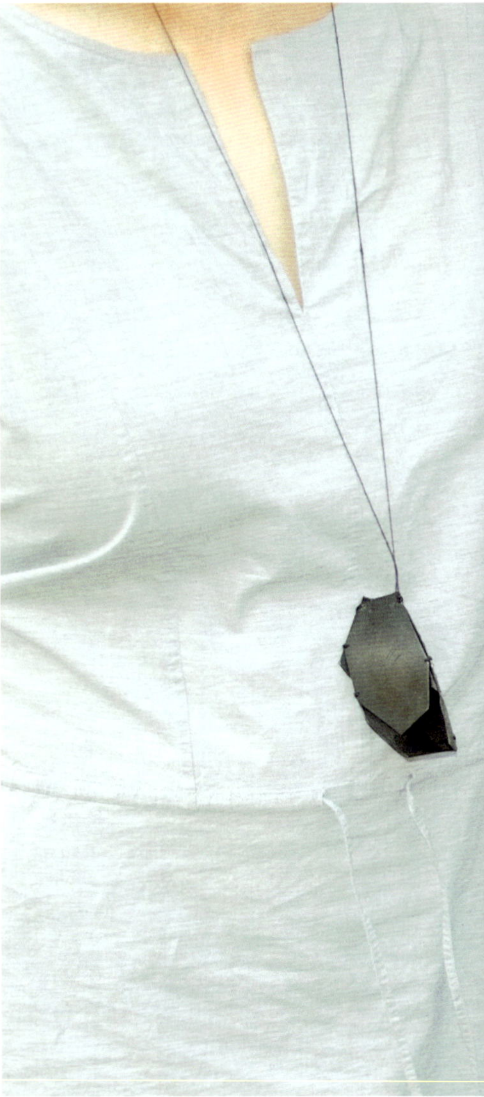

FAMILYPORTRAIT#2 + #20 + #1 Anhänger / pendants 2007–2009
Zinn / tin Faden / string Farbe / paint

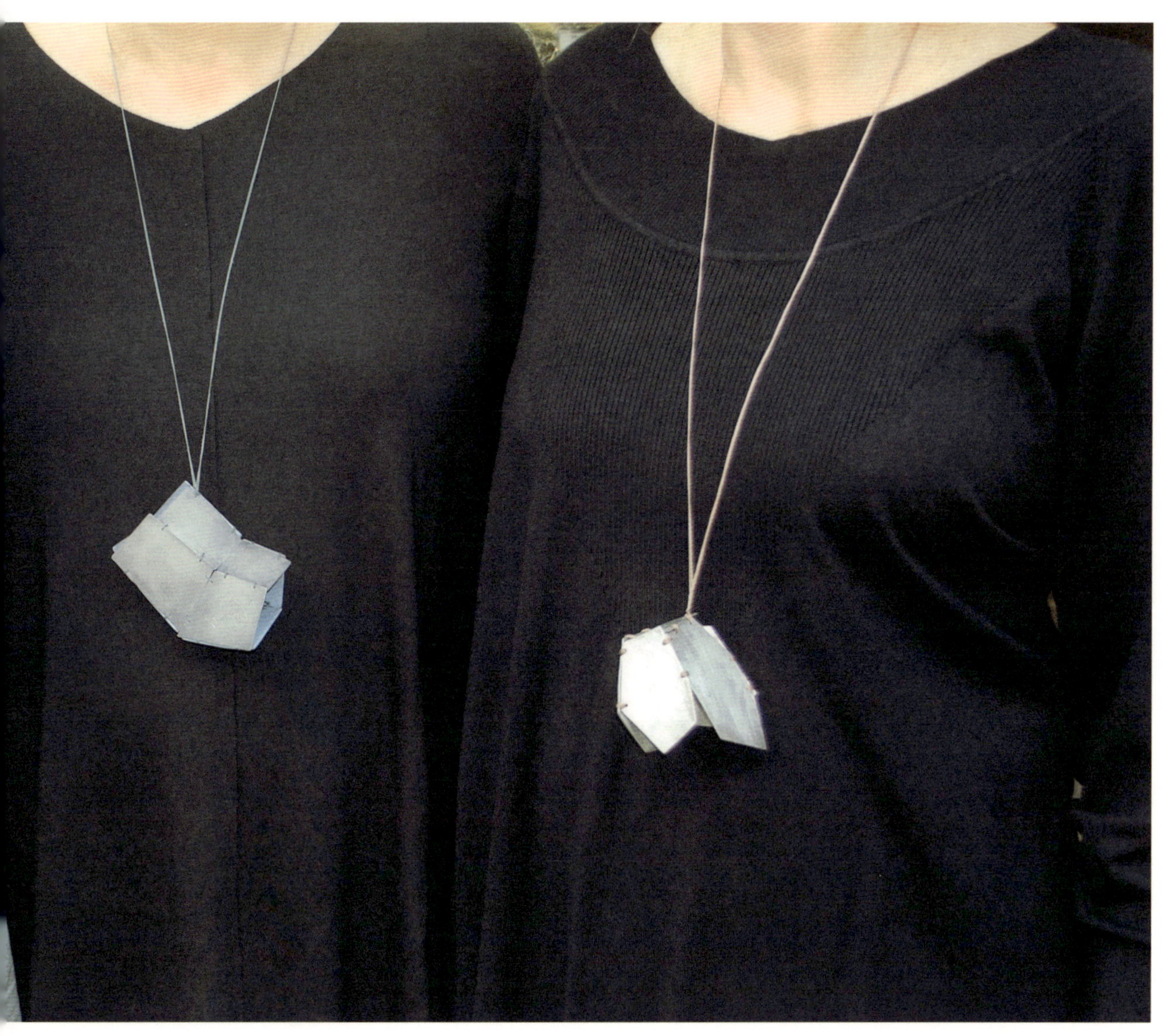

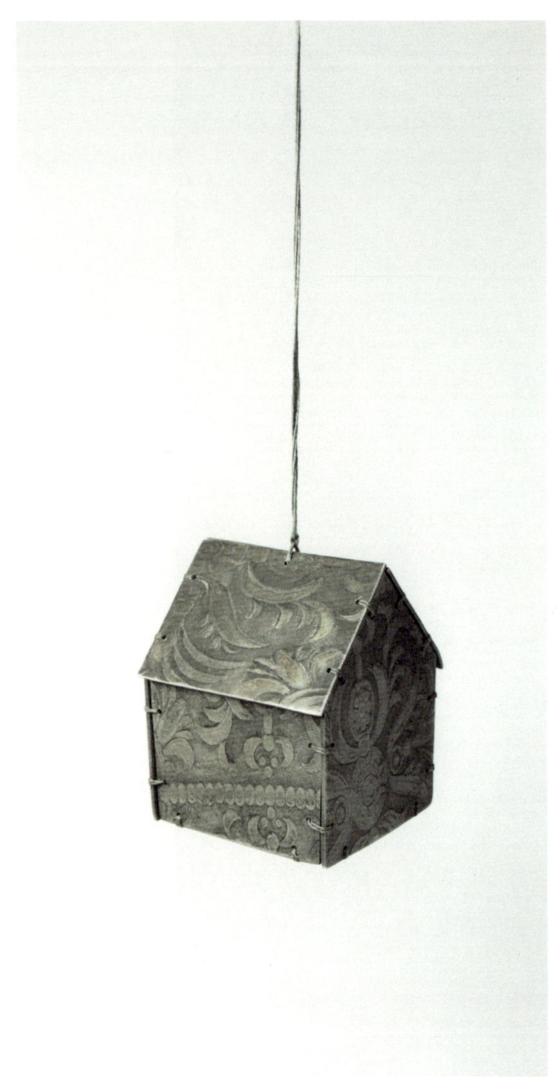

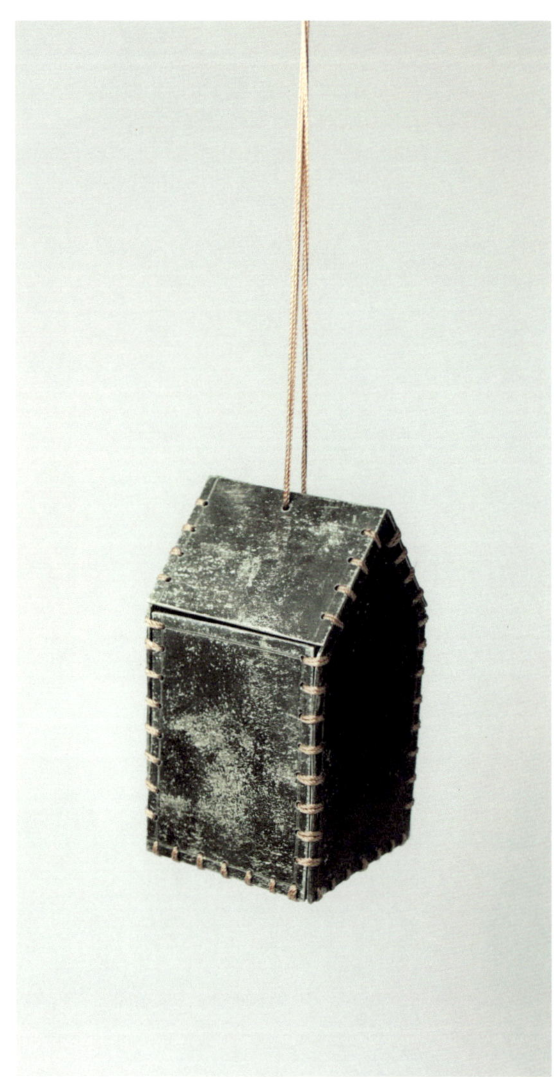

HOME#16 Anhänger / pendant 2009 Zinn / tin Faden / string
HOME#3 Anhänger / pendant 2007 Zinn / tin Faden / string
HOME#14 + #15 Anhänger / pendants 2009–2010 Zinn / tin Faden / string

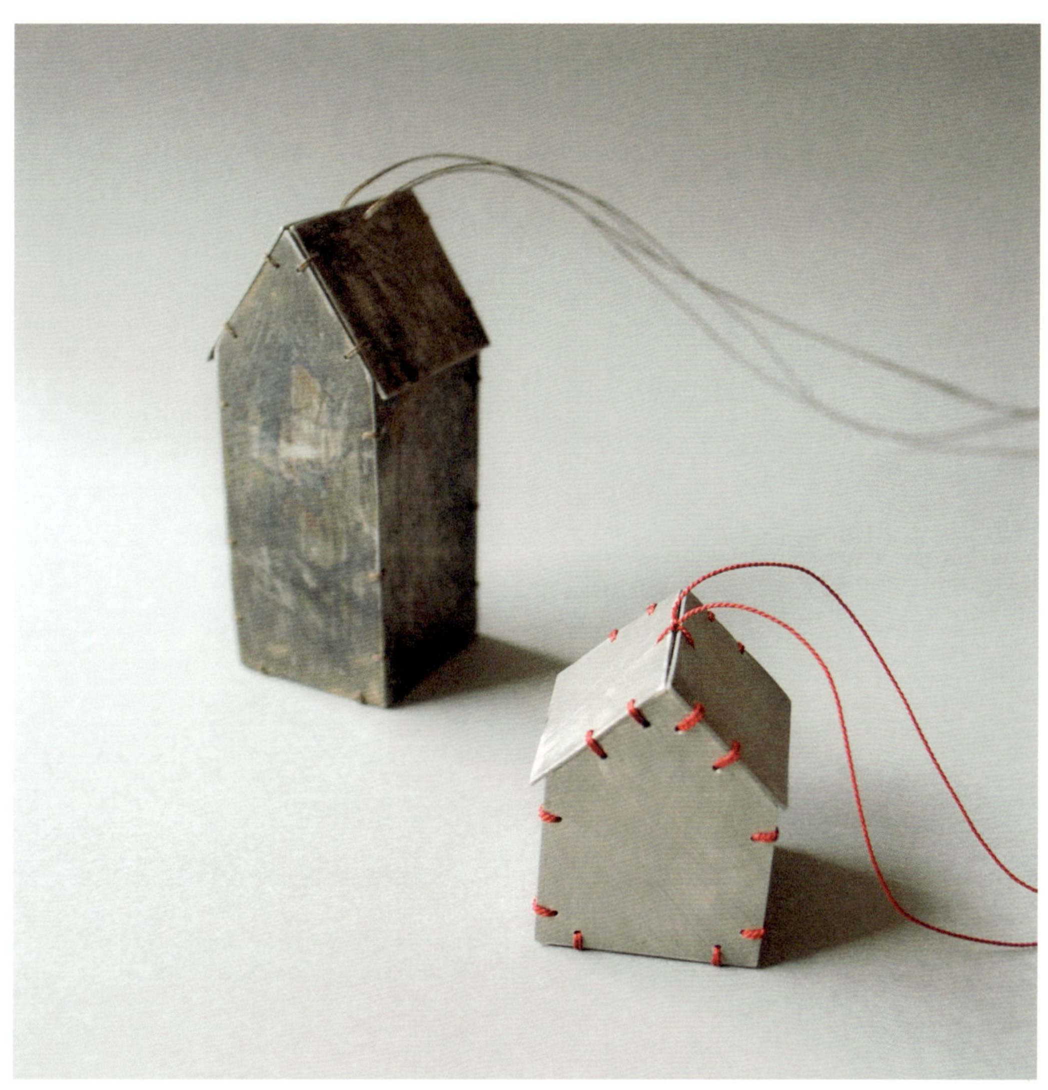

N. P.

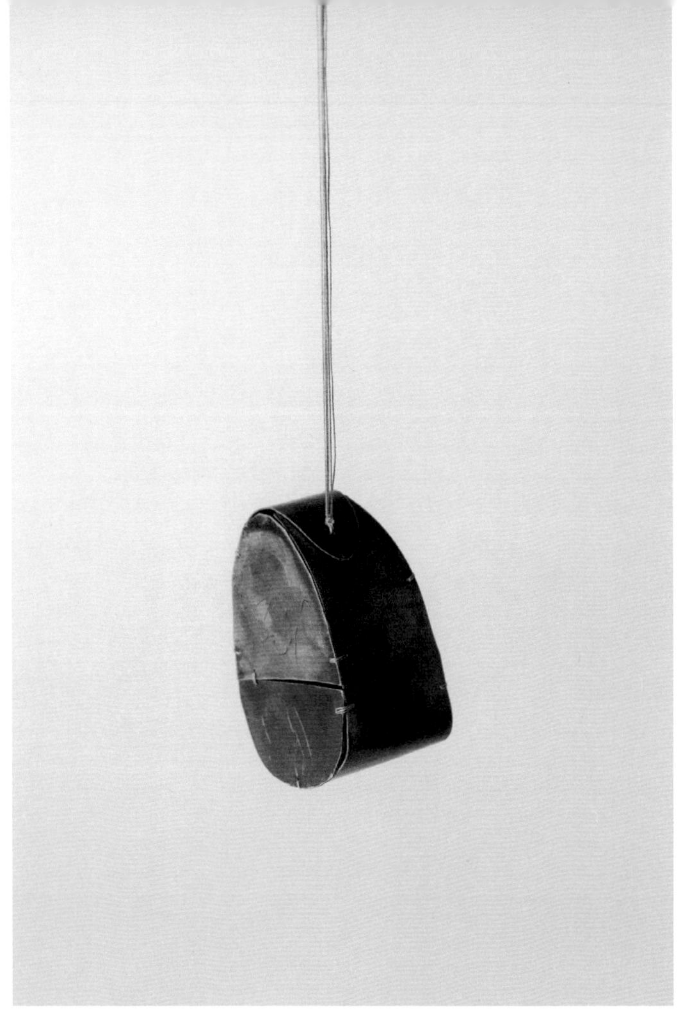

Familie – das sind Menschen, die durch unsichtbare Bande und über viele Generationen miteinander verbunden sind. Wie diese Beziehungen, so ist auch diese Arbeit Pontoppidans schwer zu greifen: eine ganz eigene, reizvolle Mischung an Verschlossenheit und Aufsässigkeit. [...] In jeder Familie bestimmen einige Familienmitglieder die Gefühle und Empfindungen, die in dieser Familie dominieren; und in jeder Familie verschwinden die Individuen unweigerlich im Schmelztiegel der Zeit. FAMILYPORTRAITS ist eine Hommage an die Sicherheit, aber auch an die Flüchtigkeit des Lebens.[7] Ward Schrijver

Family stands for people connected to one another by invisible bonds, for long lines through history. Like these relationships, the work Pontoppidan makes is elusive: a strange, enticing mixture of reticence and recalcitrance. . . . Certain people are always the foundation of the sentiments within a family. And in every family, all of the beloved individuals inevitably disappear in the melting point of time. FAMILY PORTRAITS is a tribute to the security of life as well as its elusiveness.[7] Ward Schrijver

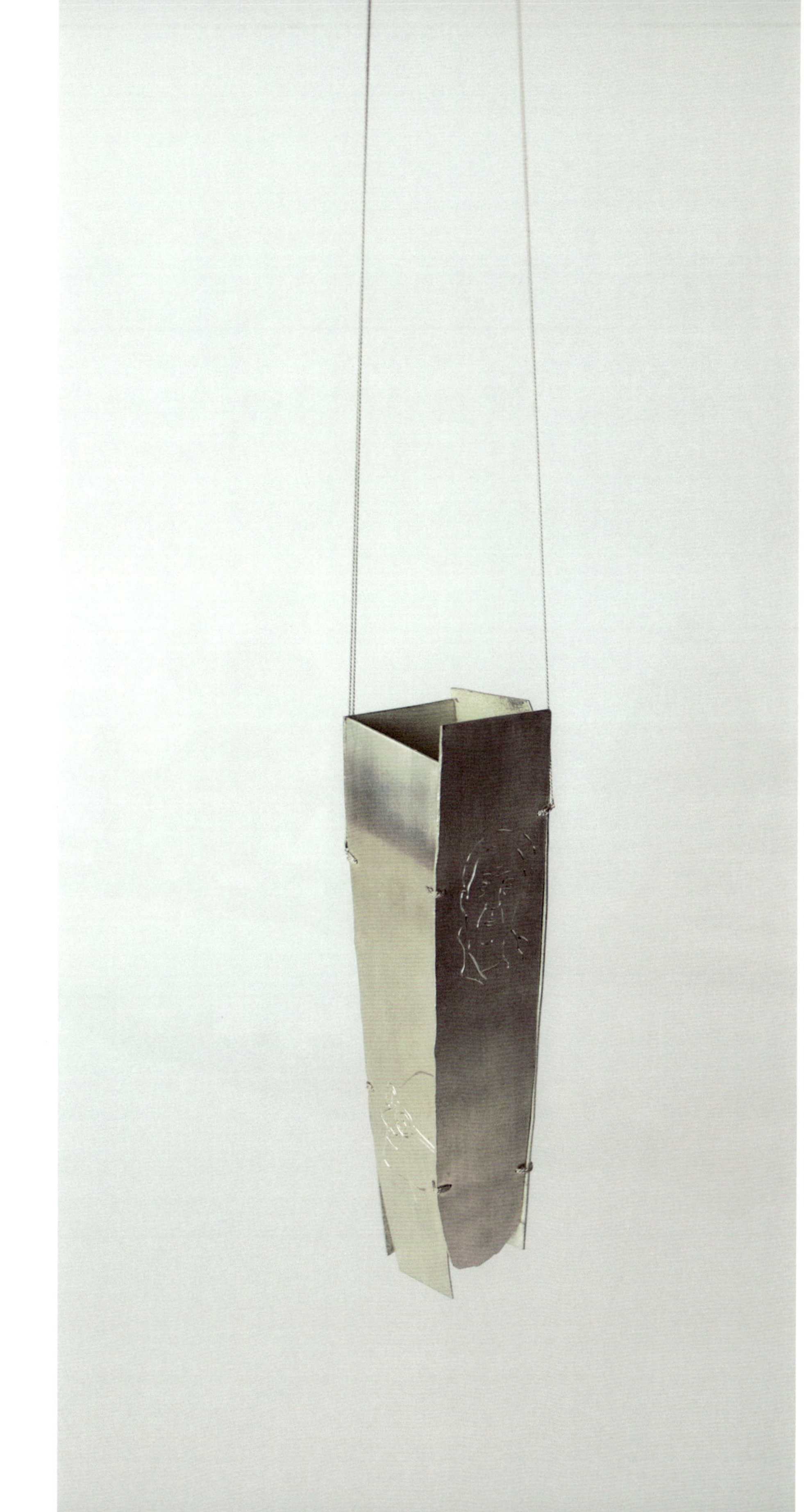

FAMILYPORTRAIT#11 Anhänger / pendant
2008 Zinn / tin Faden / string

FAMILYPORTRAIT#4 Anhänger / pendant 2007
Zinn / tin Faden / string Farbe / paint

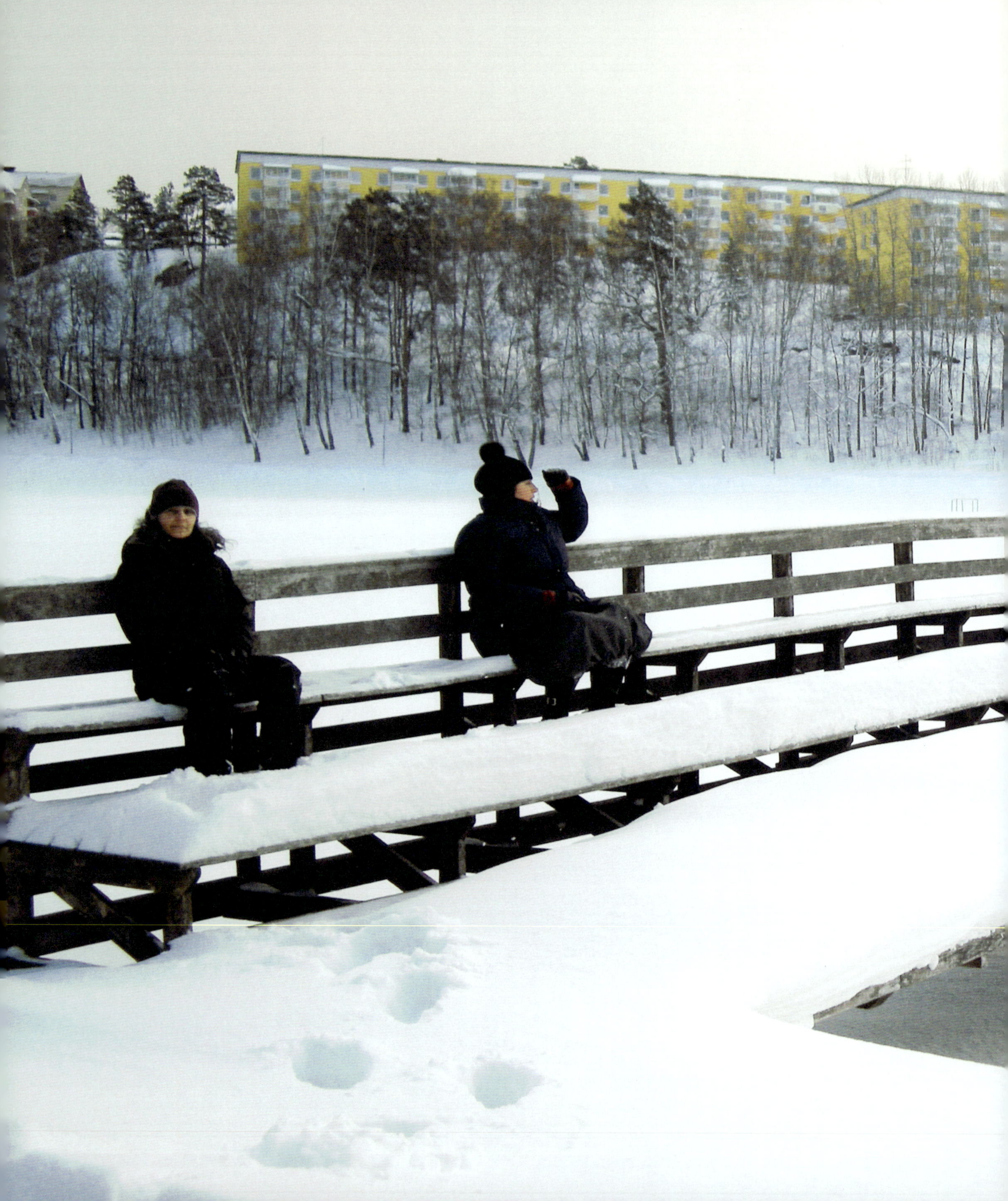

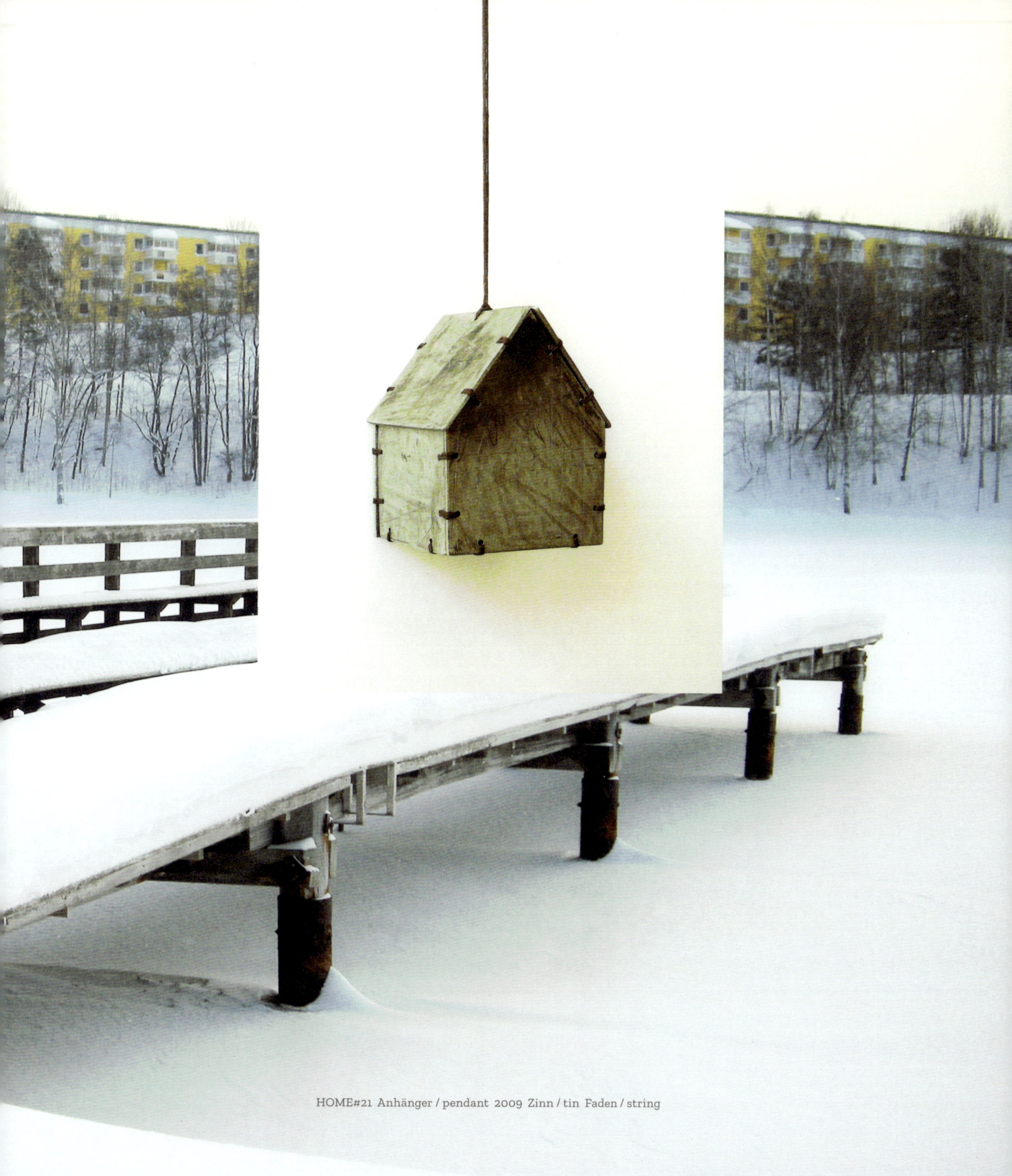

HOME#21 Anhänger / pendant 2009 Zinn / tin Faden / string

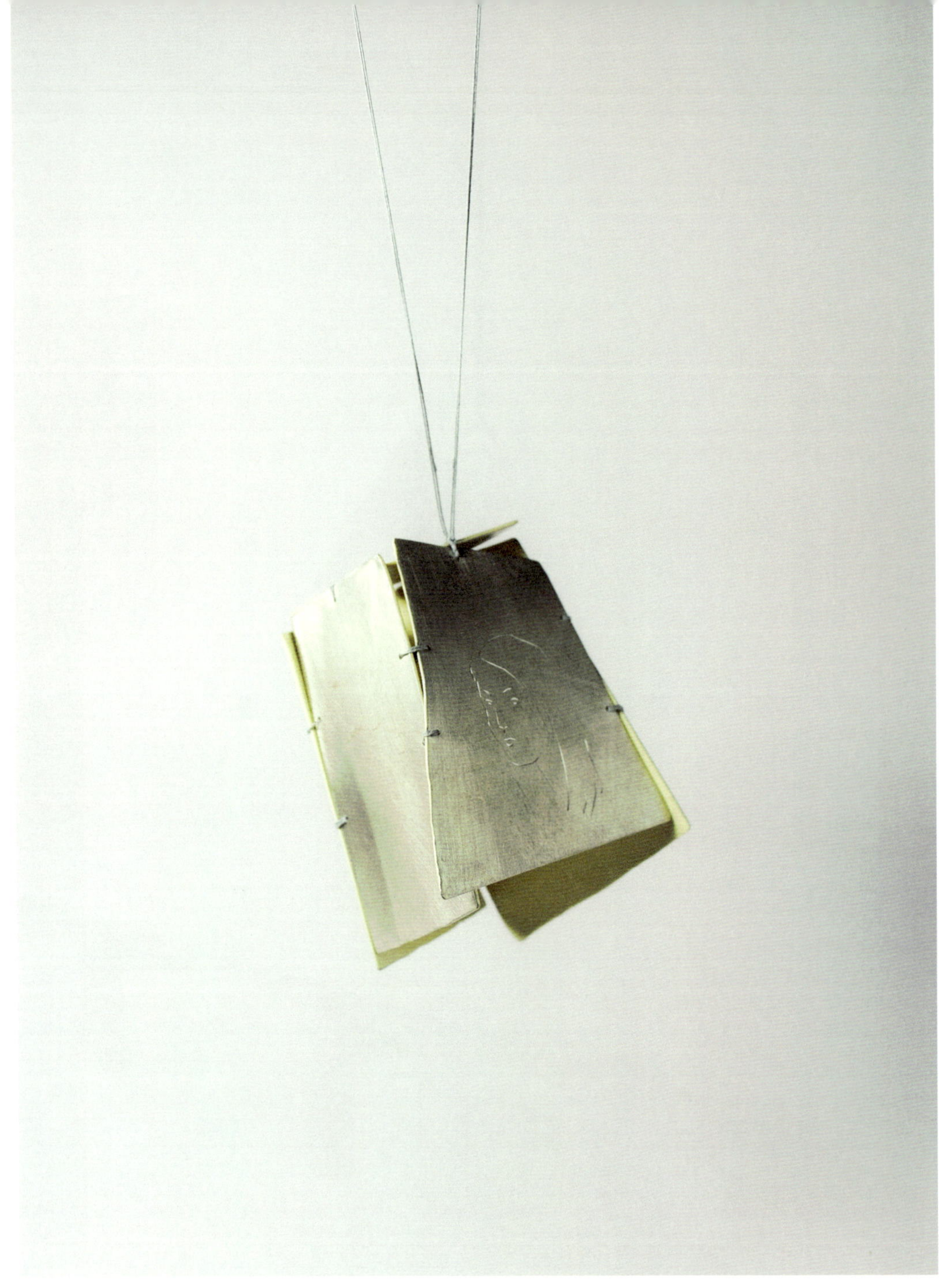

FAMILYPORTRAIT#24 Anhänger / pendant 2009 Zinn / tin Faden / string Farbe / paint
HOME#33 Anhänger / pendant 2010 Zinn / tin Faden / string Farbe / paint

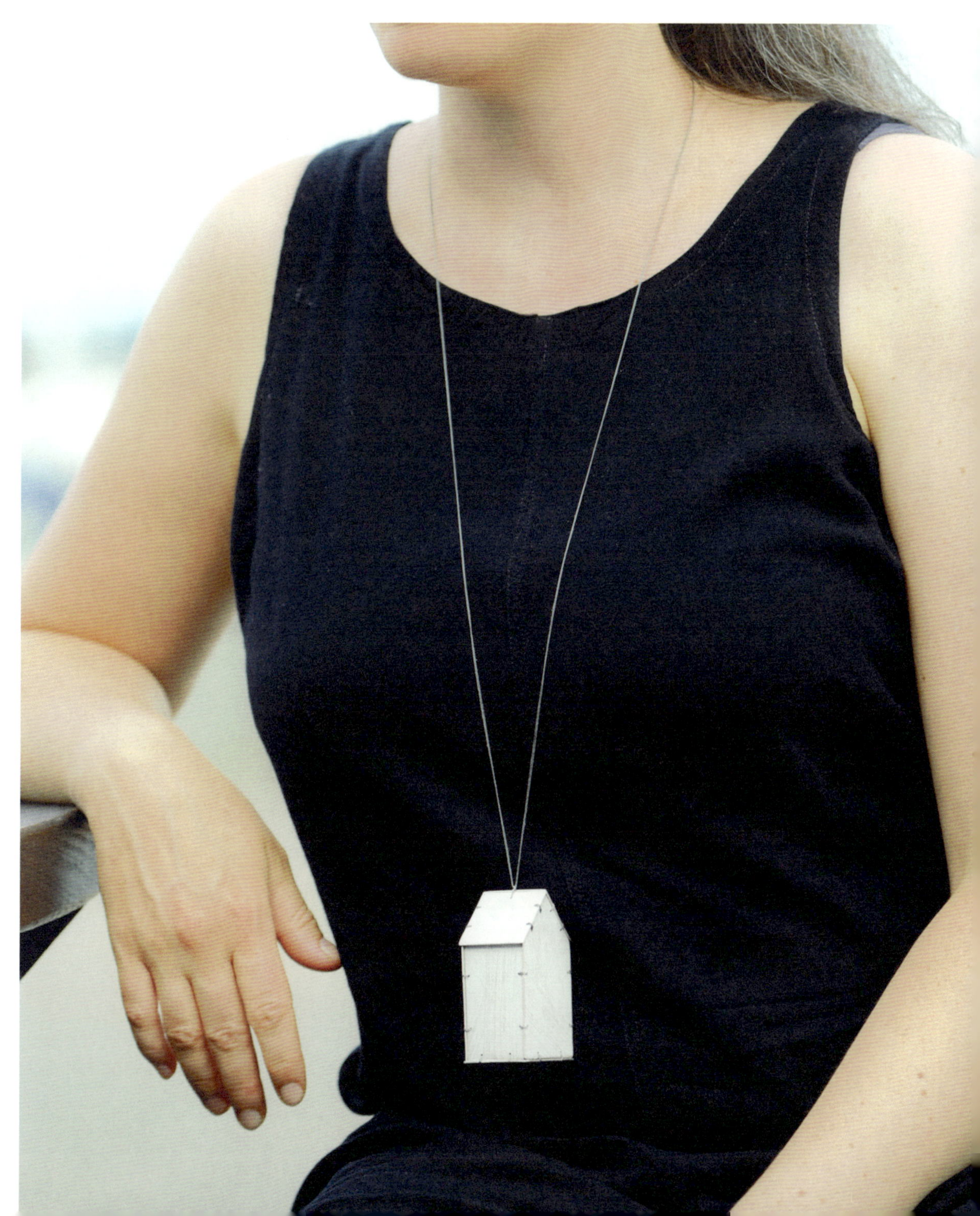

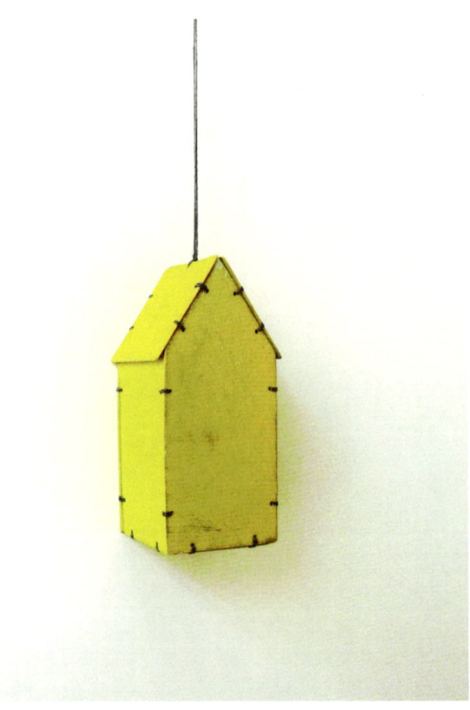

HOME#18 Anhänger / pendant 2009 Zinn / tin Faden / string Farbe / paint

Materialien haben ihre eigene Sprache, sie können mit Autorität etwas ausdrücken. Deswegen ist Material in meinen Arbeiten als sinngebend zu verstehen.[8]
N.P.

Materials have their own language; they can express something with authority. That is why material can be seen as bestowing meaning in my works.[8]
N.P.

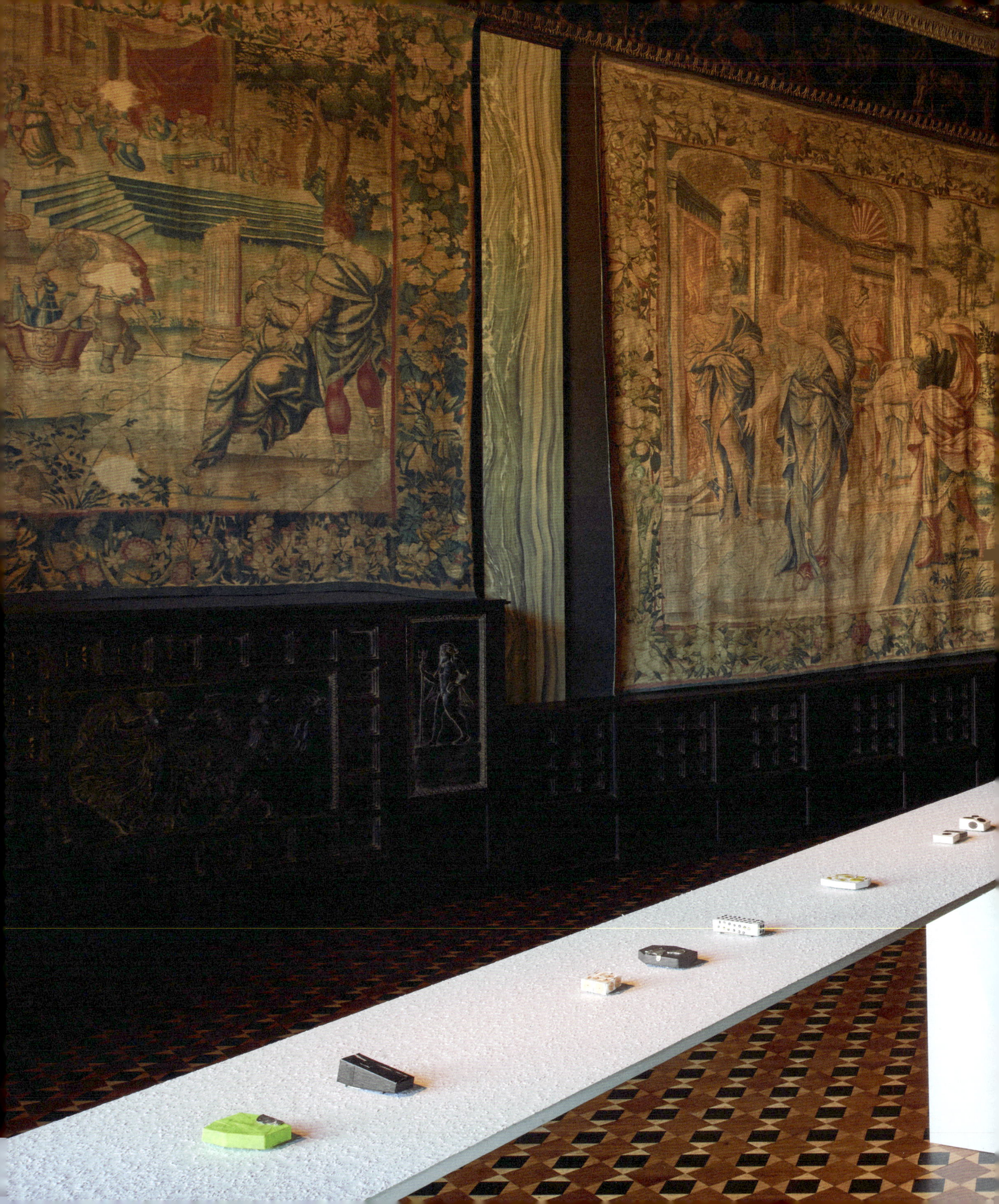

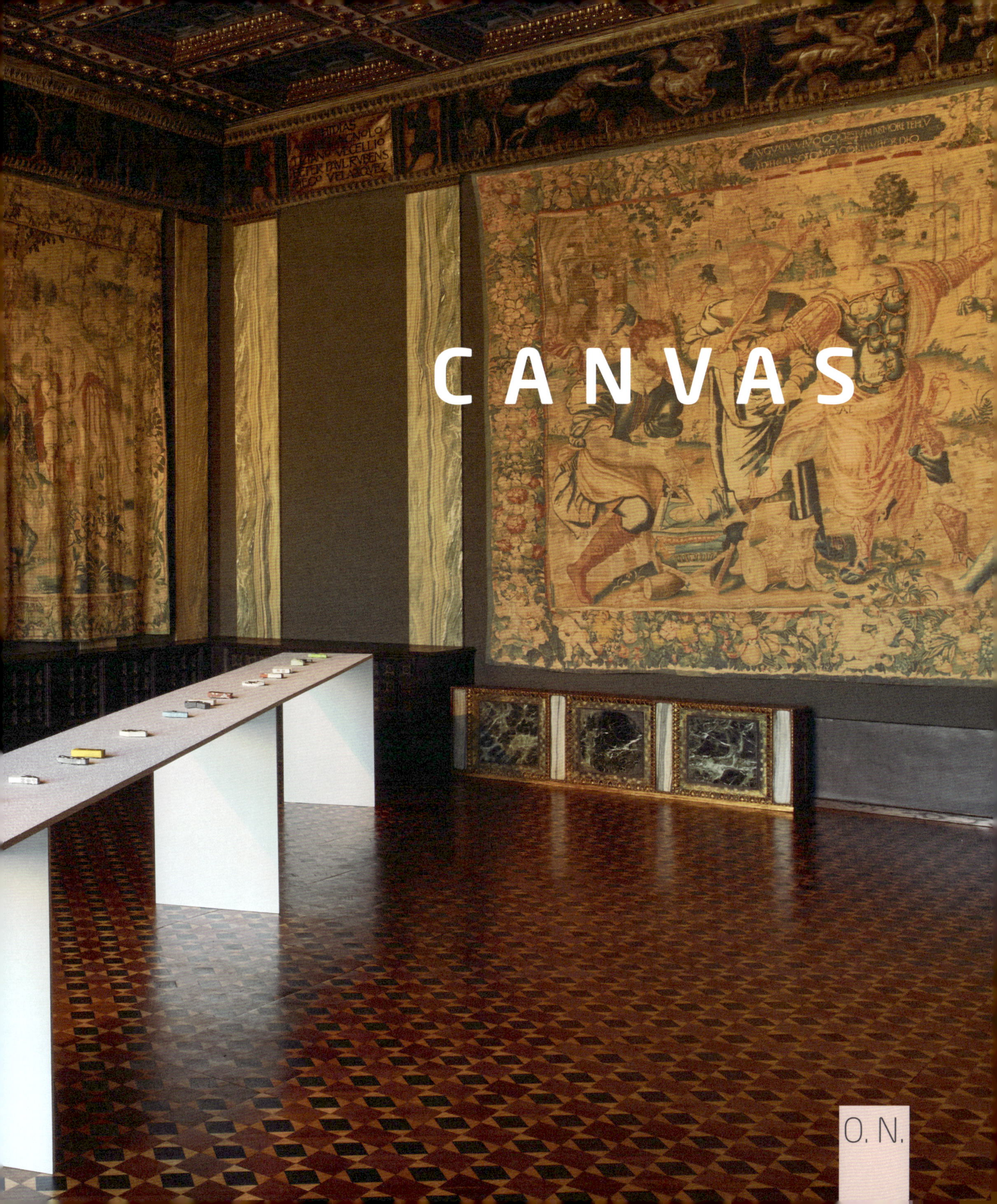
CANVAS
O. N.

Pontoppidan befindet sich im Kampf mit den verschiedenen Medien der Kunst: Während sie einst die herausragendsten Porträts und Tierbilder in Silber gravierte, so malt sie nun auf Leinwand; jenem Medium der großen Gesten, bei ihr reduziert auf intime Größe. Auf den Leinwänden tauchen Spuren von Geschichten, Fragmente von Erinnerungen auf. Diese stellt sie nicht nur in Farbe dar; sie fügt auch Elemente aus assoziationsreichen Materialien, etwa Zinn, Blei oder Edelmetalle, hinzu. Ihr zufolge ist die Frage, ob es dabei um »die Kunst des Handwerks oder das Handwerk der Kunst« gehe. Natürlich gibt es darauf keine eindeutige Antwort. Was zählt, ist die Qualität – und die ist in ihrem Fall garantiert.[9]
Ward Schrijver

Pontoppidan has engaged in battle with codes: whereas once she drew the most superb portraits and animals on silver, now she has resolved to paint on canvas. The medium of the grand gesture, reduced on an intimate scale. On the canvas appear vestiges of stories, fragmented recollections. She does not only express these using paint, but also by adding elements of materials rich in associations like tin, lead and precious metal. As Pontoppidan phrases it, are we involved now with "the art of making craft or the craft of making art"? There is of course no unequivocal answer, only the quality counts, and that is guaranteed in her case.[9]
Ward Schrijver

CANVAS#58 Brosche / brooch 2011 Leinwand / canvas Holz / wood Silber / silver Eisen / iron Zinn / tin

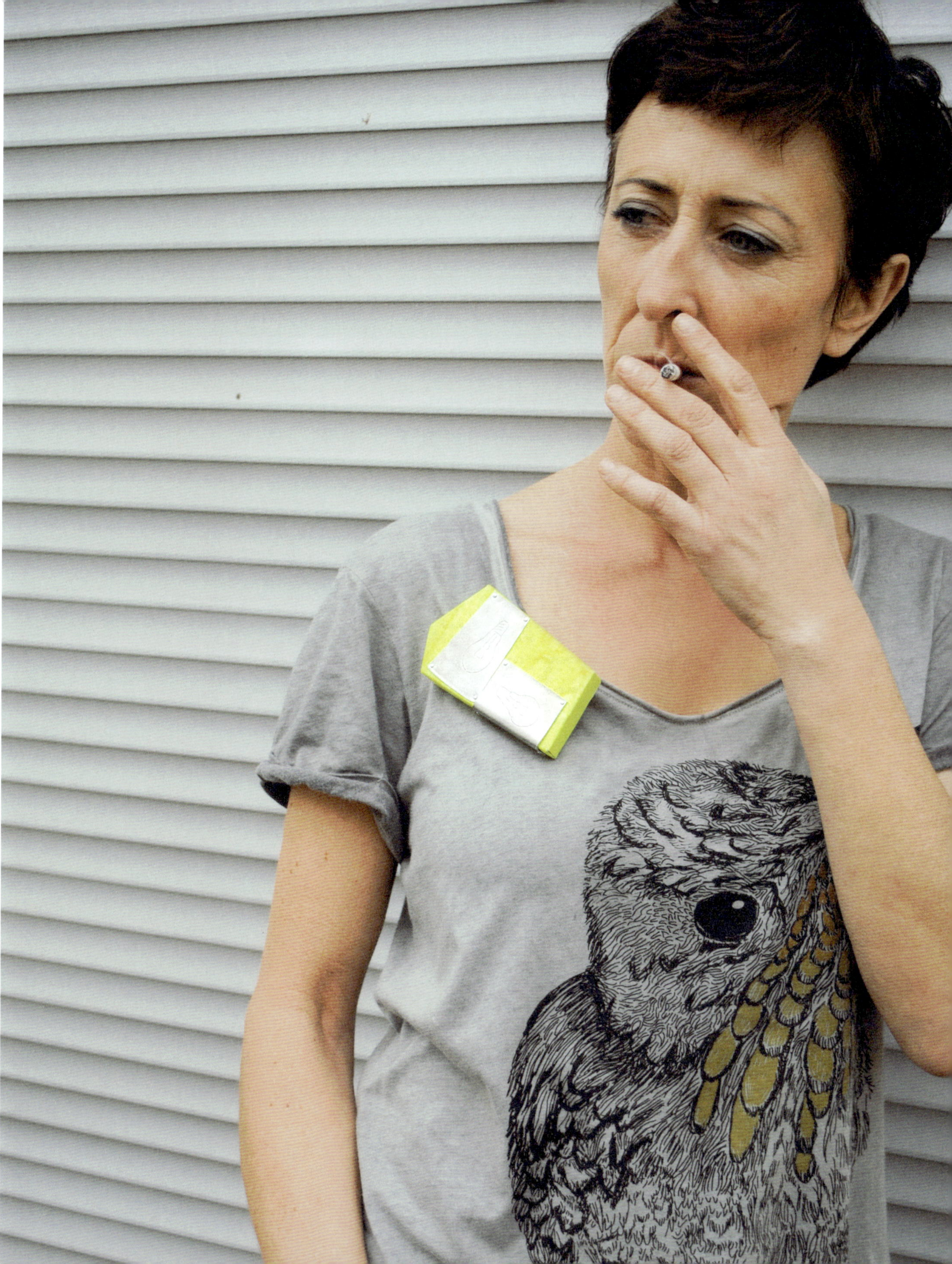

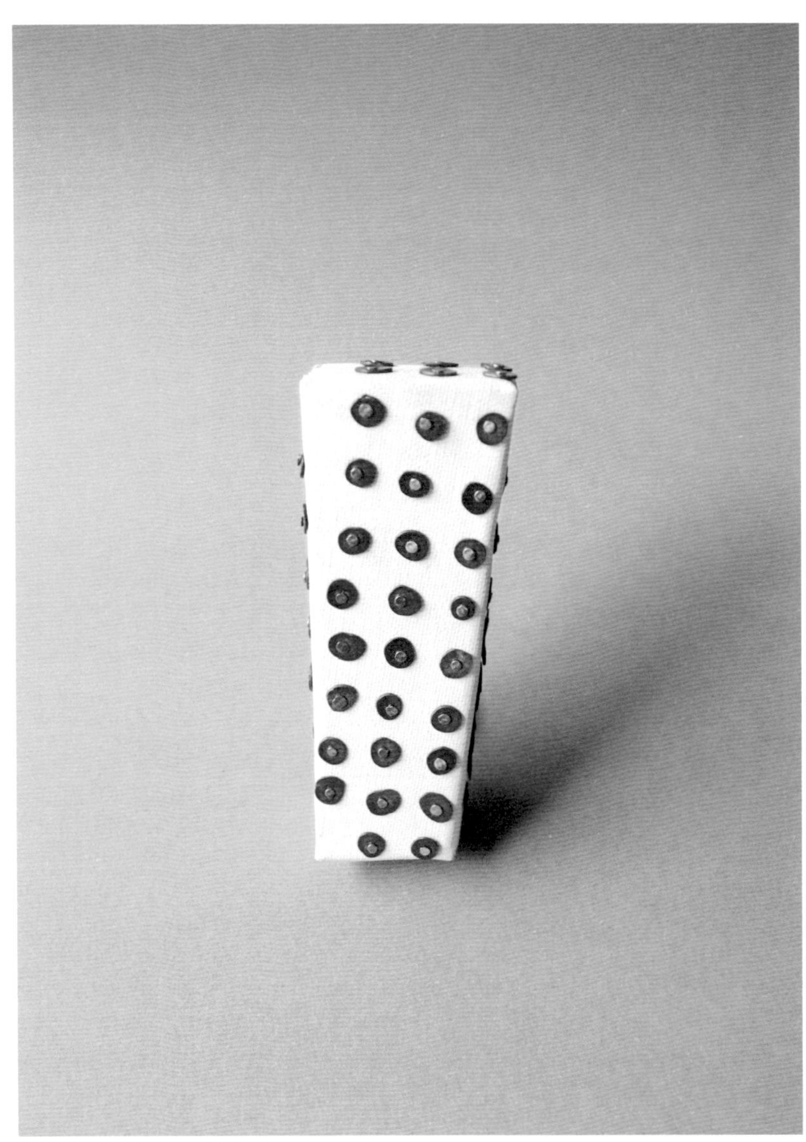

CANVAS#2 Brosche / brooch 2010 Leinwand / canvas Holz / wood Silber / silver Eisen / iron Schrot / shot

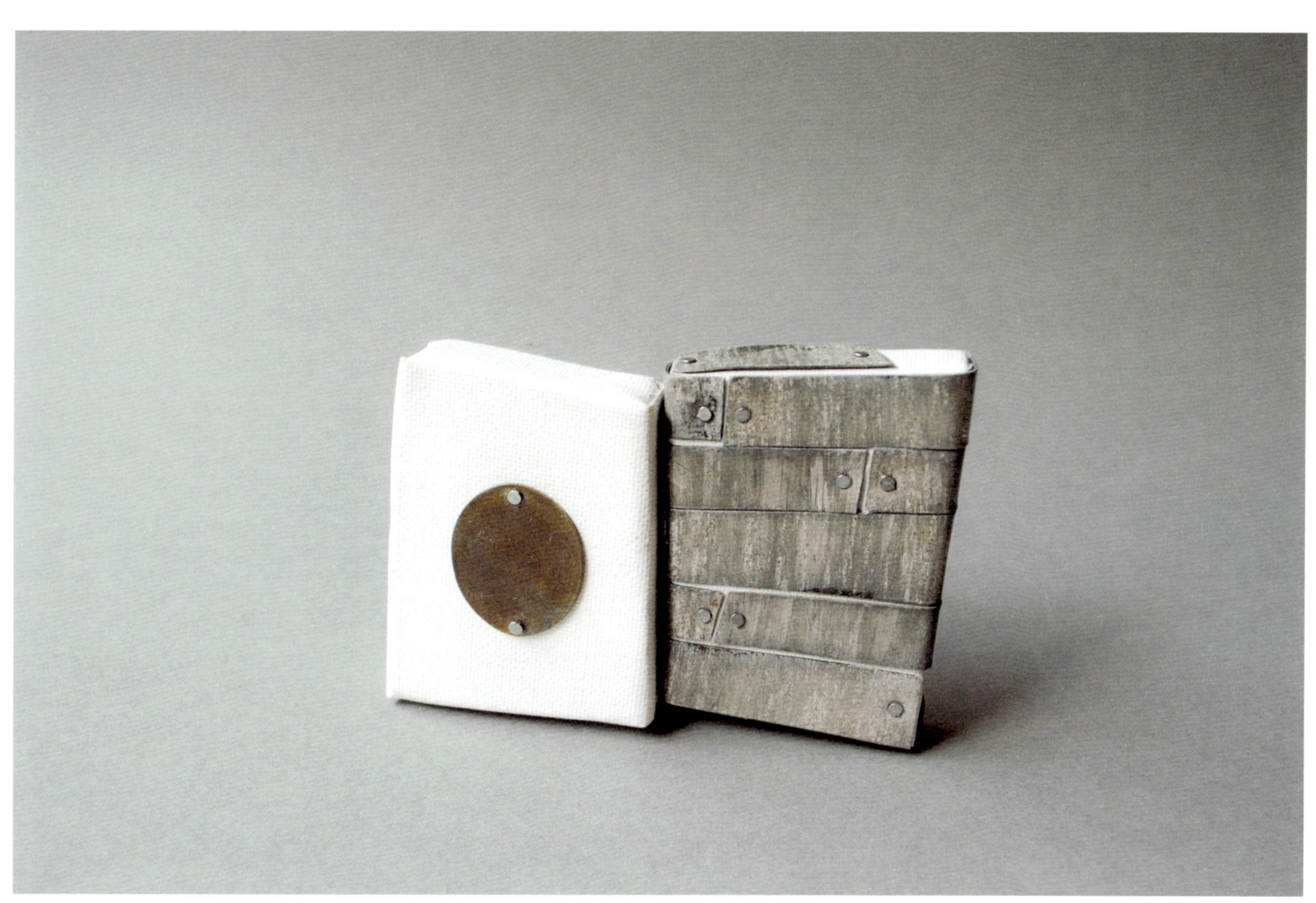

CANVAS#8 Brosche / brooch 2010 Leinwand / canvas Holz / wood Silber / silver Eisen / iron Zinn / tin Münzen / coins

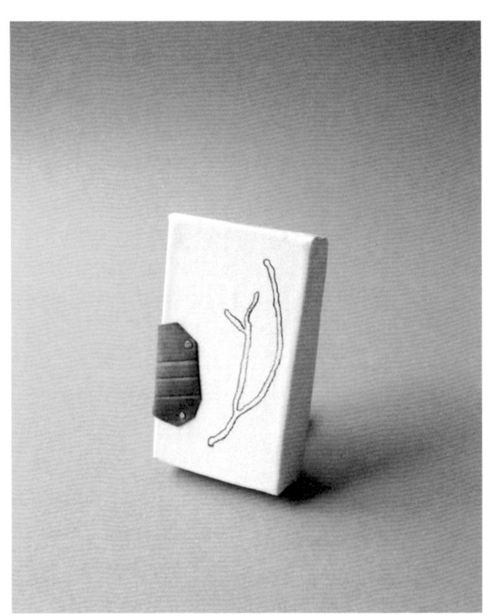

Die eigentliche Frage ist nicht, ob ein Schmuckstück angenehm zu tragen ist; sondern vielmehr, ob die Botschaft des Schmuckstücks für den potenziellen Träger*in so viel Bedeutung hat, dass dieser gewillt ist, dieses Stück – ungeachtet jeglicher Konsequenzen – am eigenen Körper zu tragen.[10]
O.N.

The question is not if a piece of jewelry is comfortable to wear, the question is if the expression of the piece is so meaningful to the potential wearer that she or he is willing to add the piece to their body—no matter the consequences.[10]
O.N.

CANVAS#1318 Brosche / brooch 2011 Leinwand / canvas Holz / wood Silber / silver Eisen / iron Zinn / tin Gold / gold
CANVAS#3 Brosche / brooch 2010 Leinwand / canvas Holz / wood Silber / silver Eisen / iron Zinn / tin

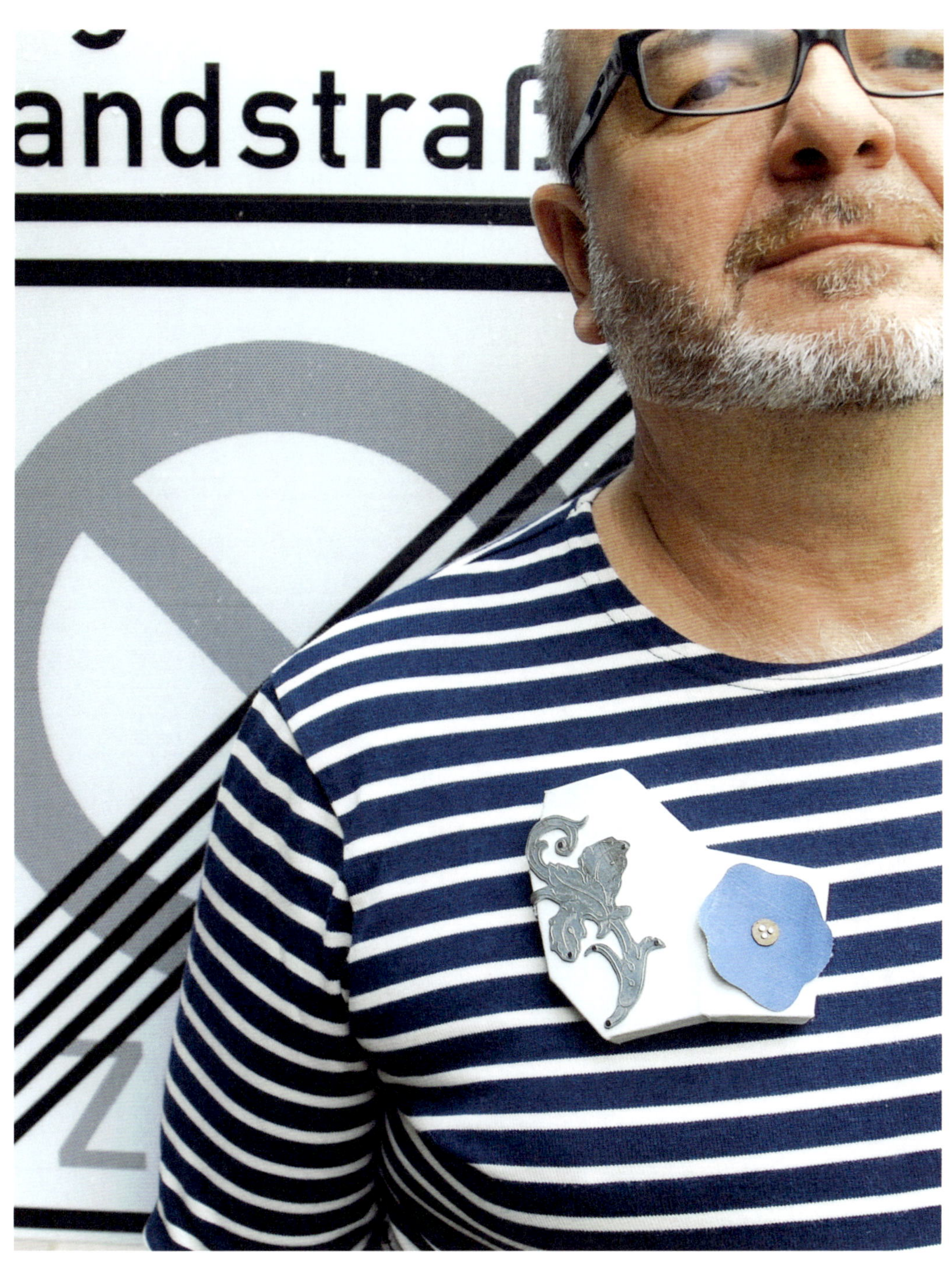
andstraß

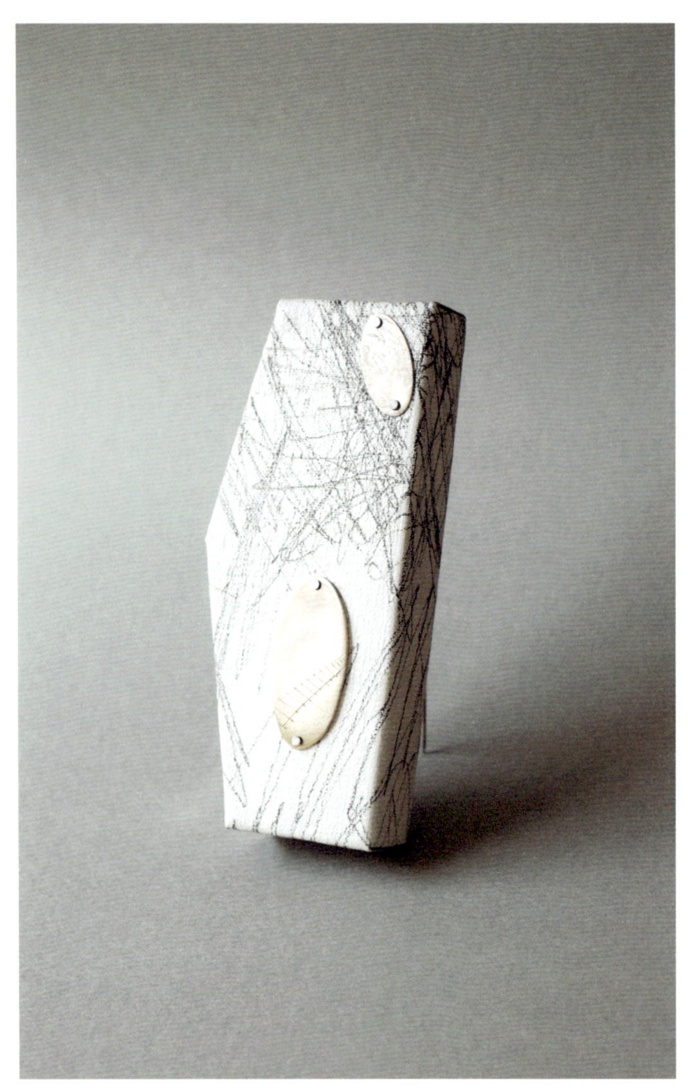

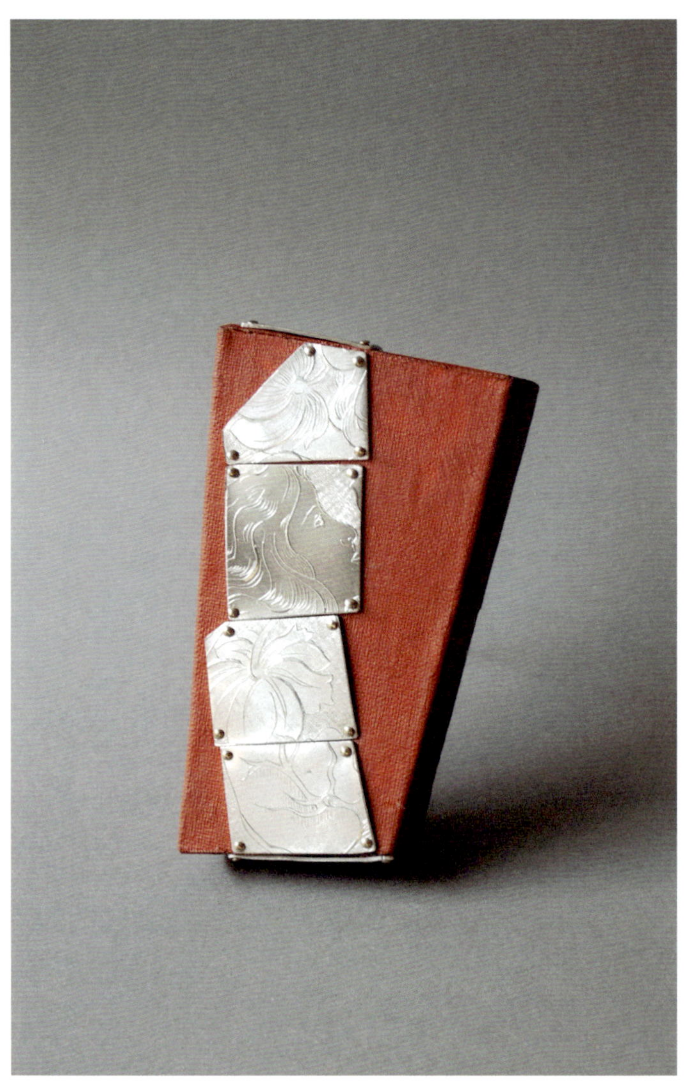

CANVAS#26 + #17 + #6 + #30 Broschen / brooches 2011 Leinwand / canvas Holz / wood Silber / silver Eisen / iron Zinn / tin Schrot / shot

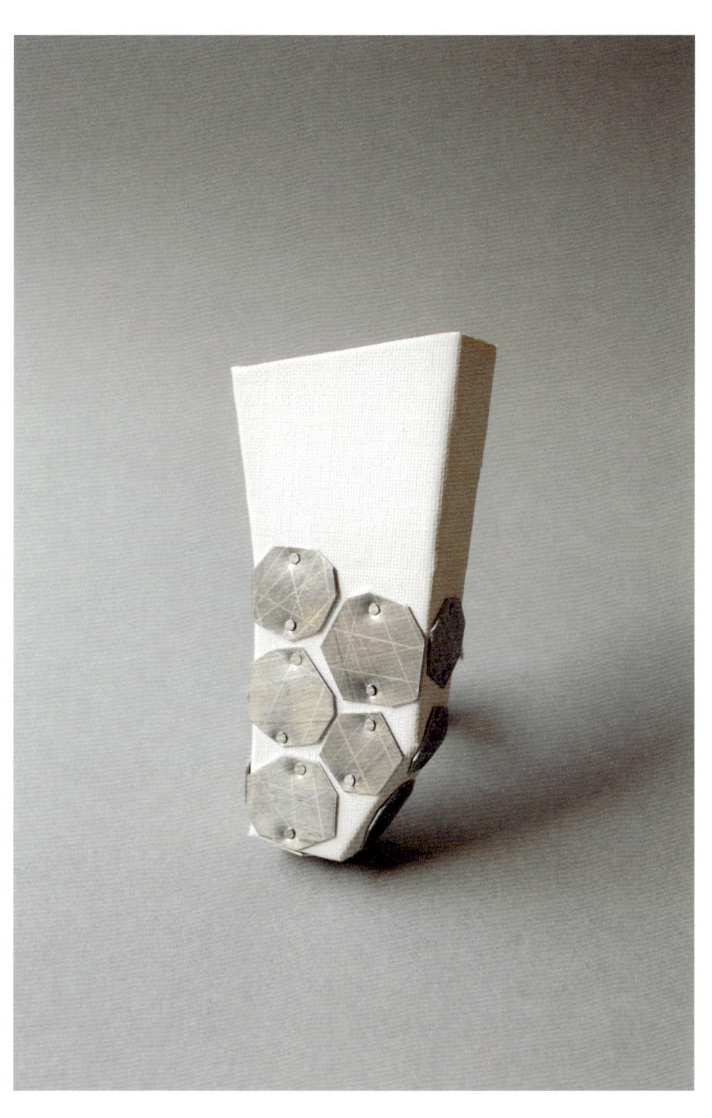

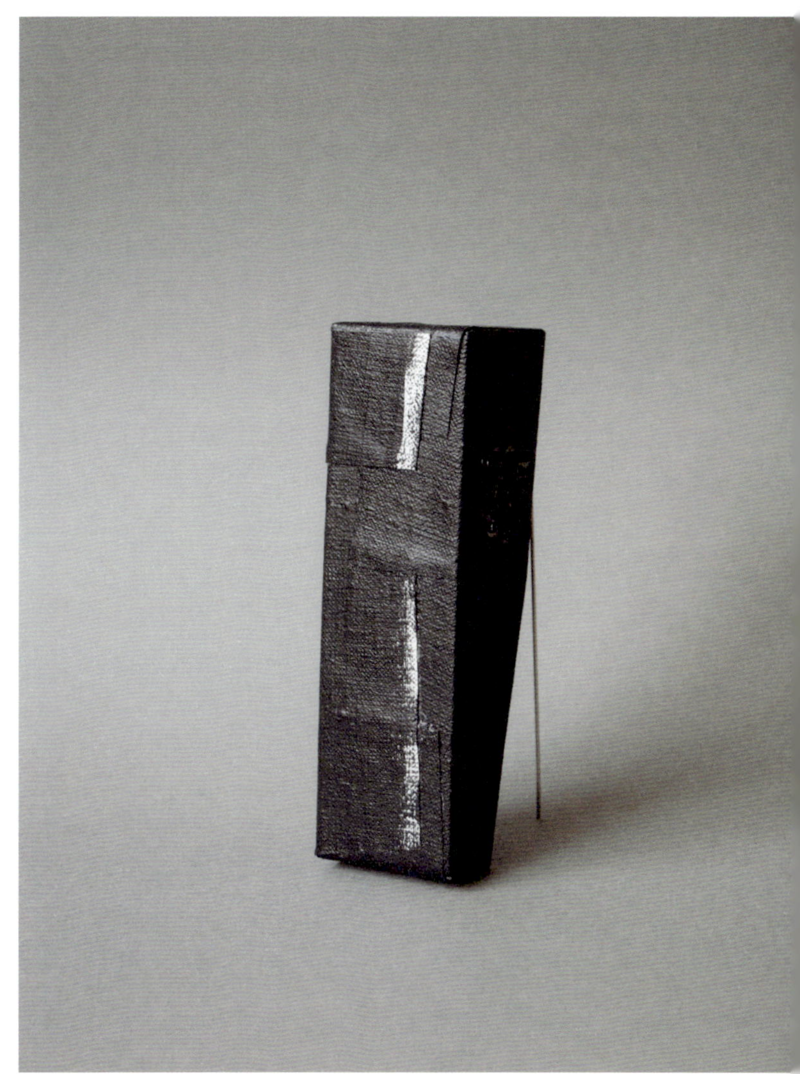

O. N.

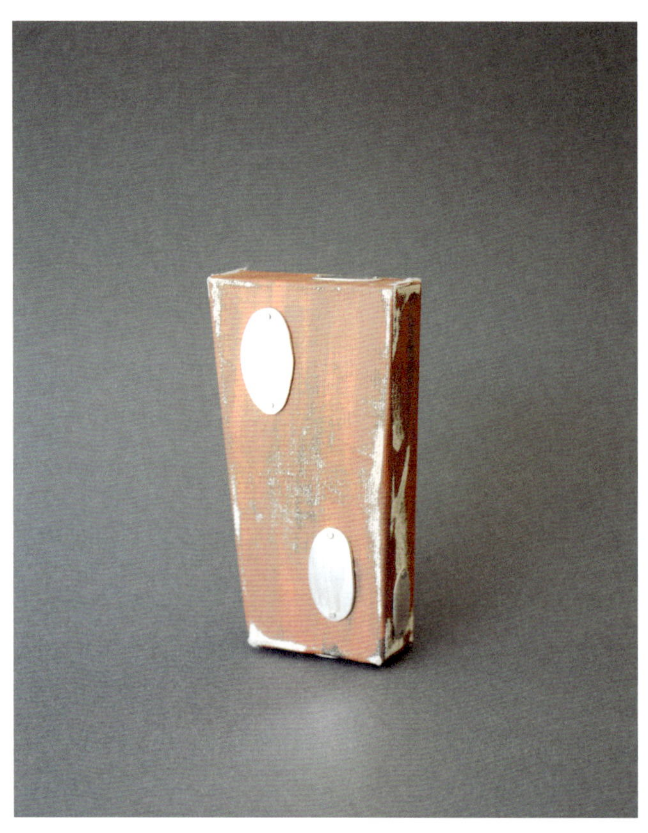

CANVAS#11 Brosche / brooch 2011 Leinwand / canvas Holz / wood Silber / silver Eisen / iron
CANVAS#56 Brosche / brooch 2011 Leinwand / canvas Holz / wood Silber / silver Eisen / iron Zinn / tin

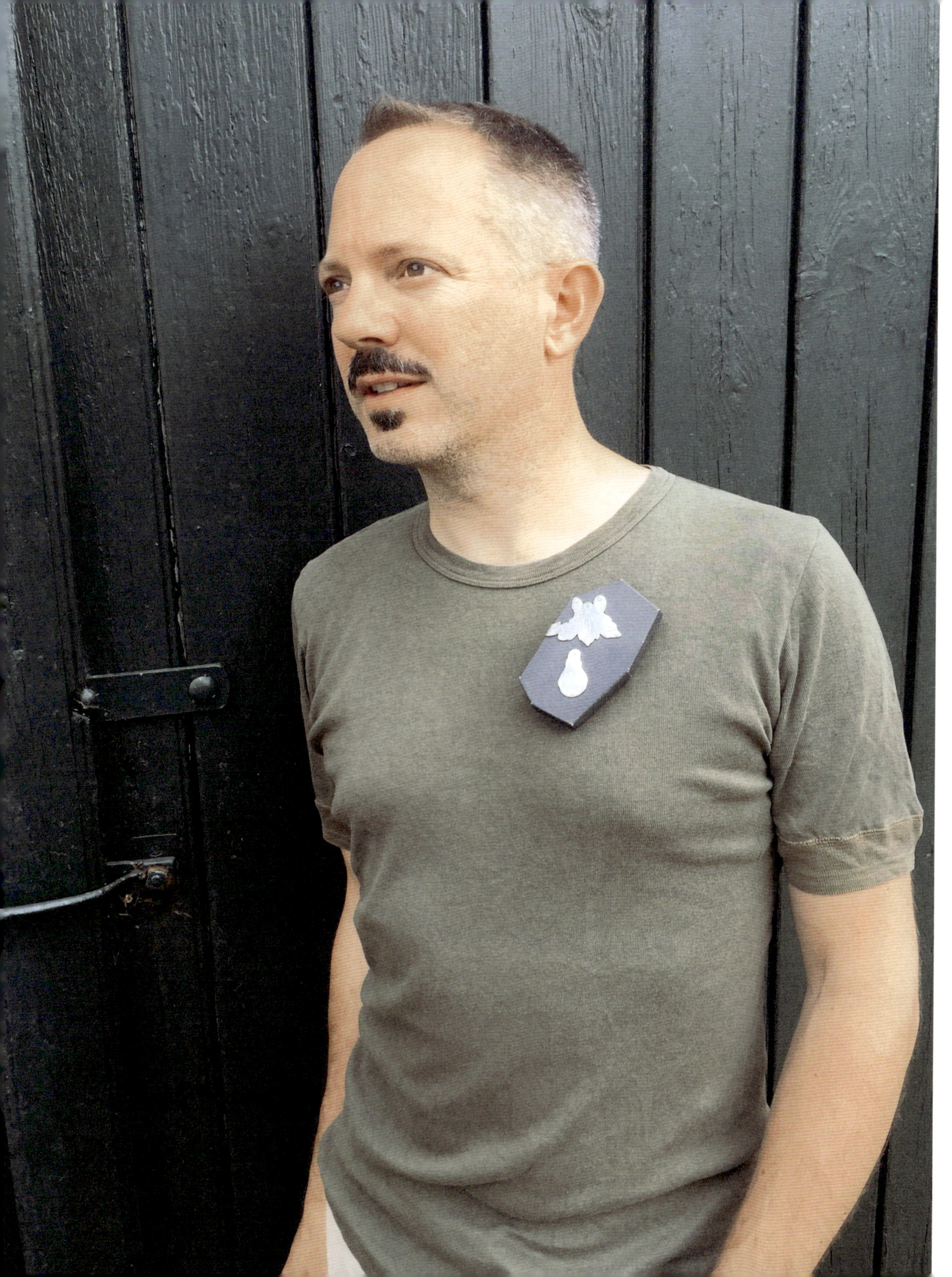

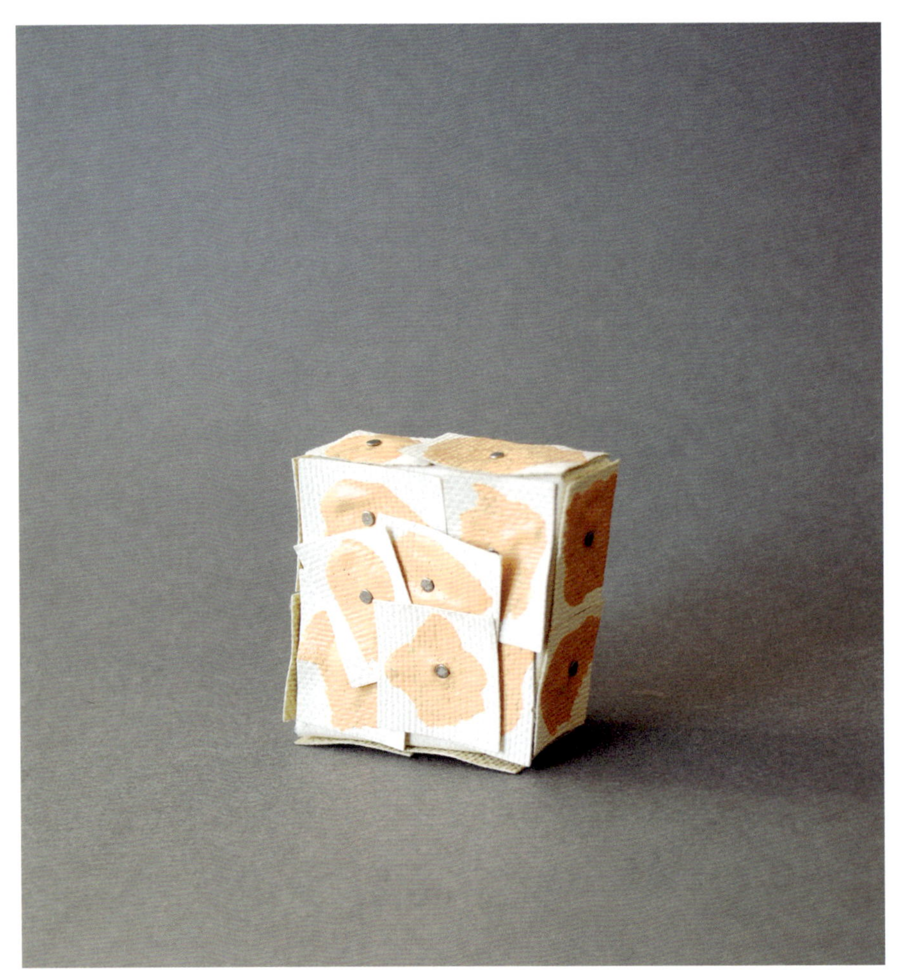

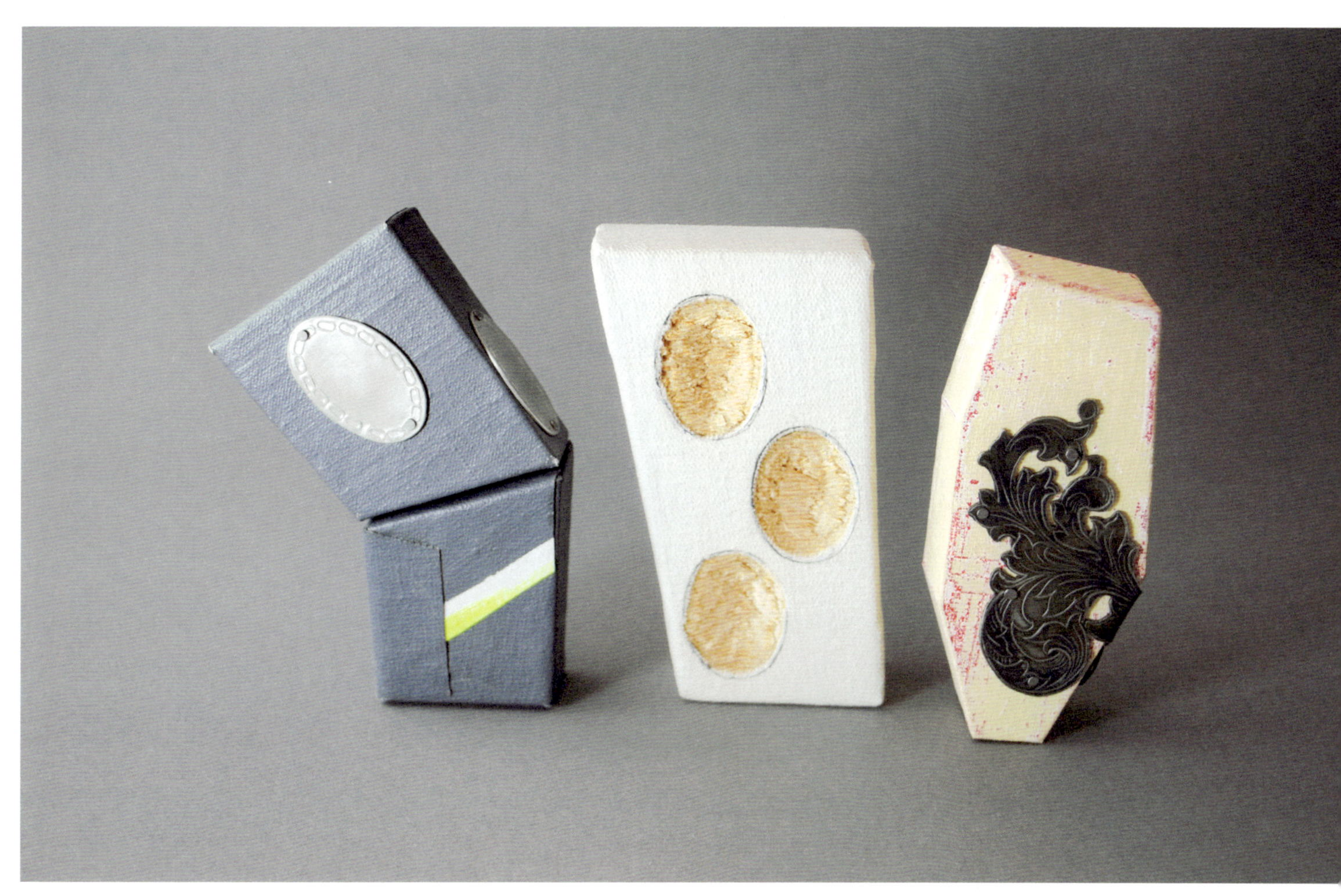

CANVAS#61 Brosche / brooch 2011 Leinwand / canvas Holz / wood Silber / silver Eisen / iron
CANVAS#51 + #27 + #54 Broschen / brooches 2011 Leinwand / canvas Holz / wood Silber / silver Eisen / iron Zinn / tin

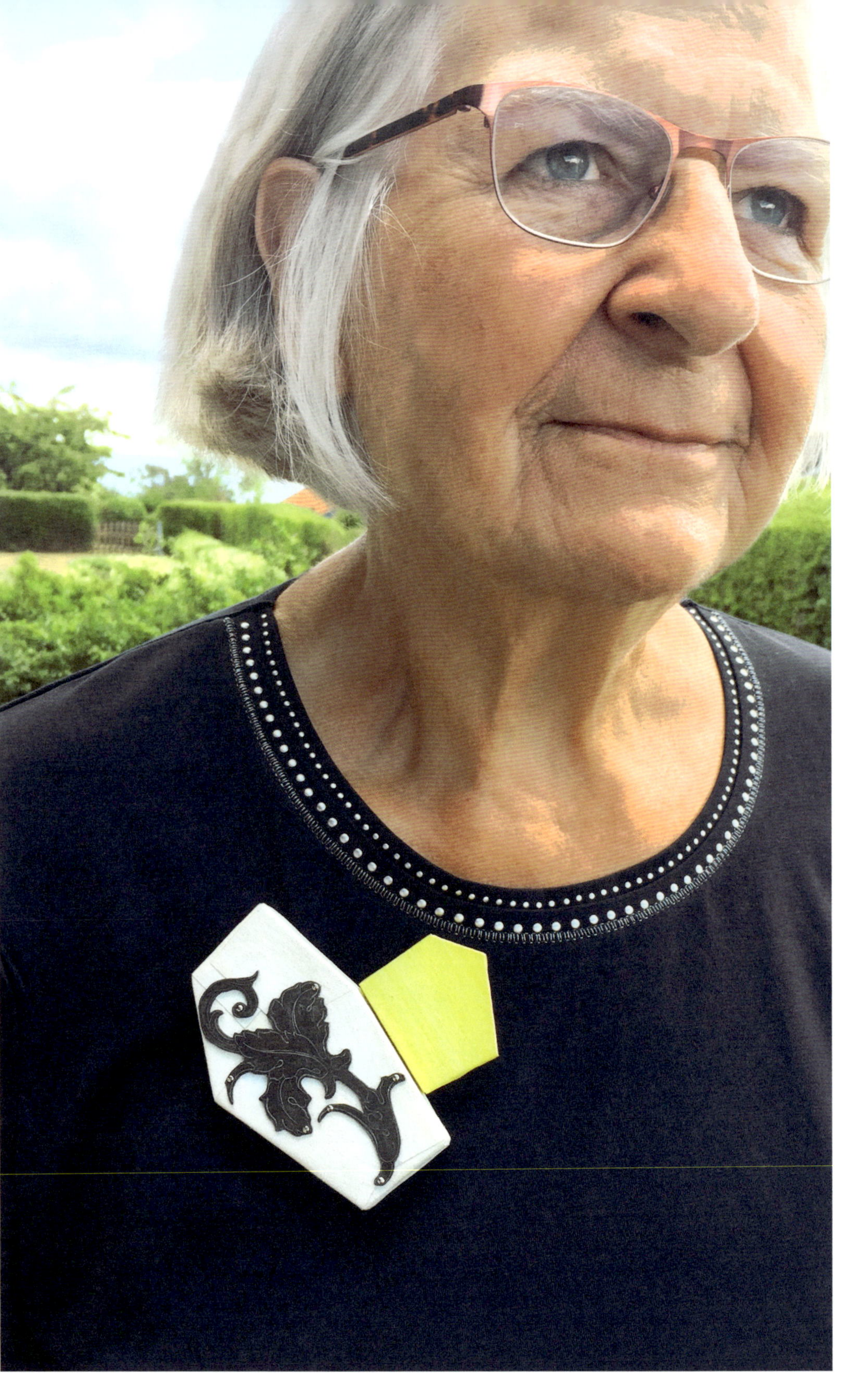

Meiner Meinung nach erfüllt Schmuck in einer Kultur einen ganz konkreten Zweck. Er ist nicht nur dekoratives Beiwerk modischer Auftritte; Schmuck ist vielmehr ein essenzieller Gegenstand, wenn es darum geht, Identitäten innerhalb Gesellschaften zu bilden und (wieder-)herzustellen.[11]
O.N.

For me jewelry has a purpose within a civilization. It is not only a decorative addition to attain a stylish appearance; it is an essential object for creating and re-creating systems of identity within societies.[11]
O.N.

CANVAS#38 Brosche / brooch 2011 Leinwand / canvas Holz / wood Silber / silver Eisen / iron Zinn / tin

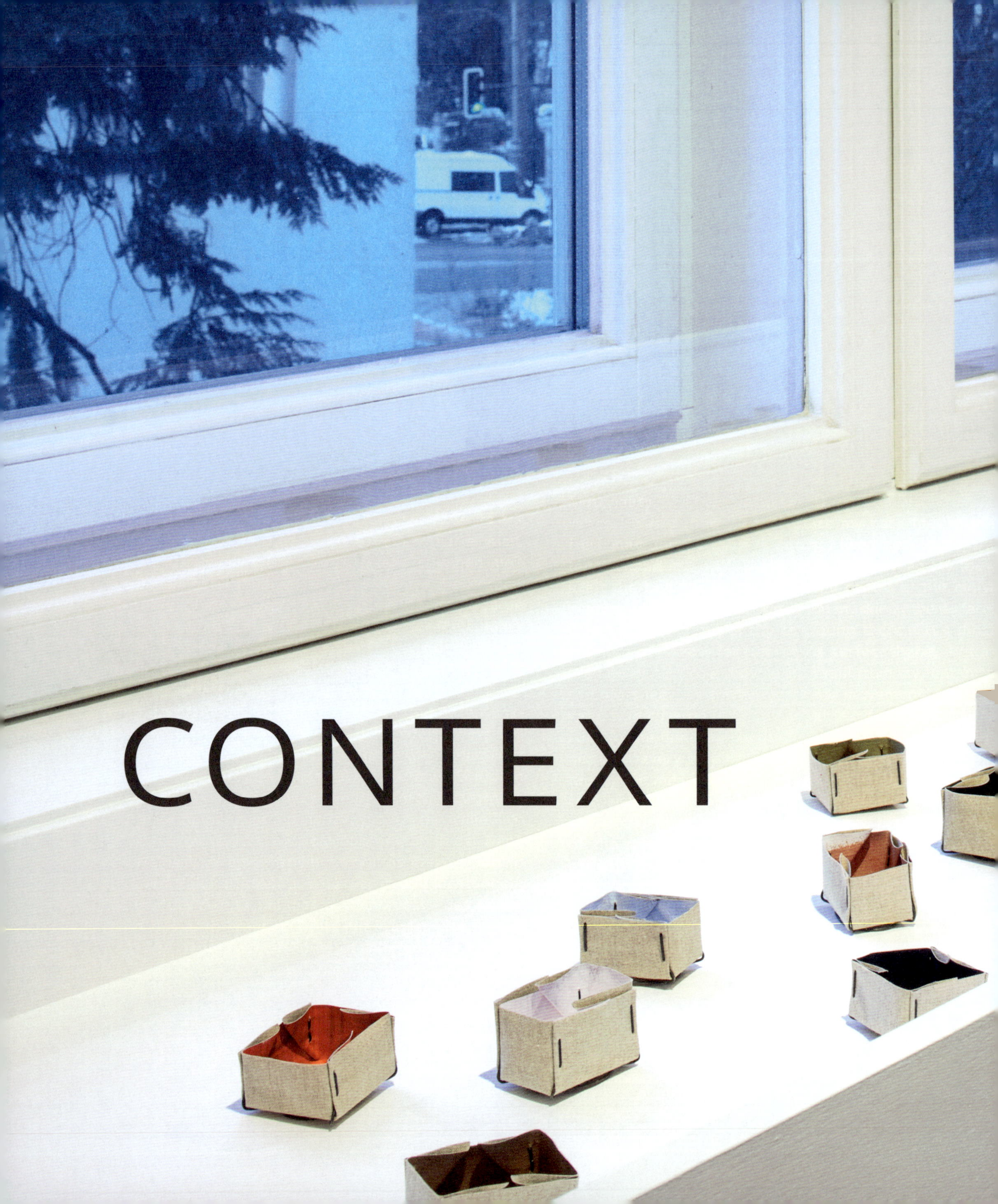

CONTEXT

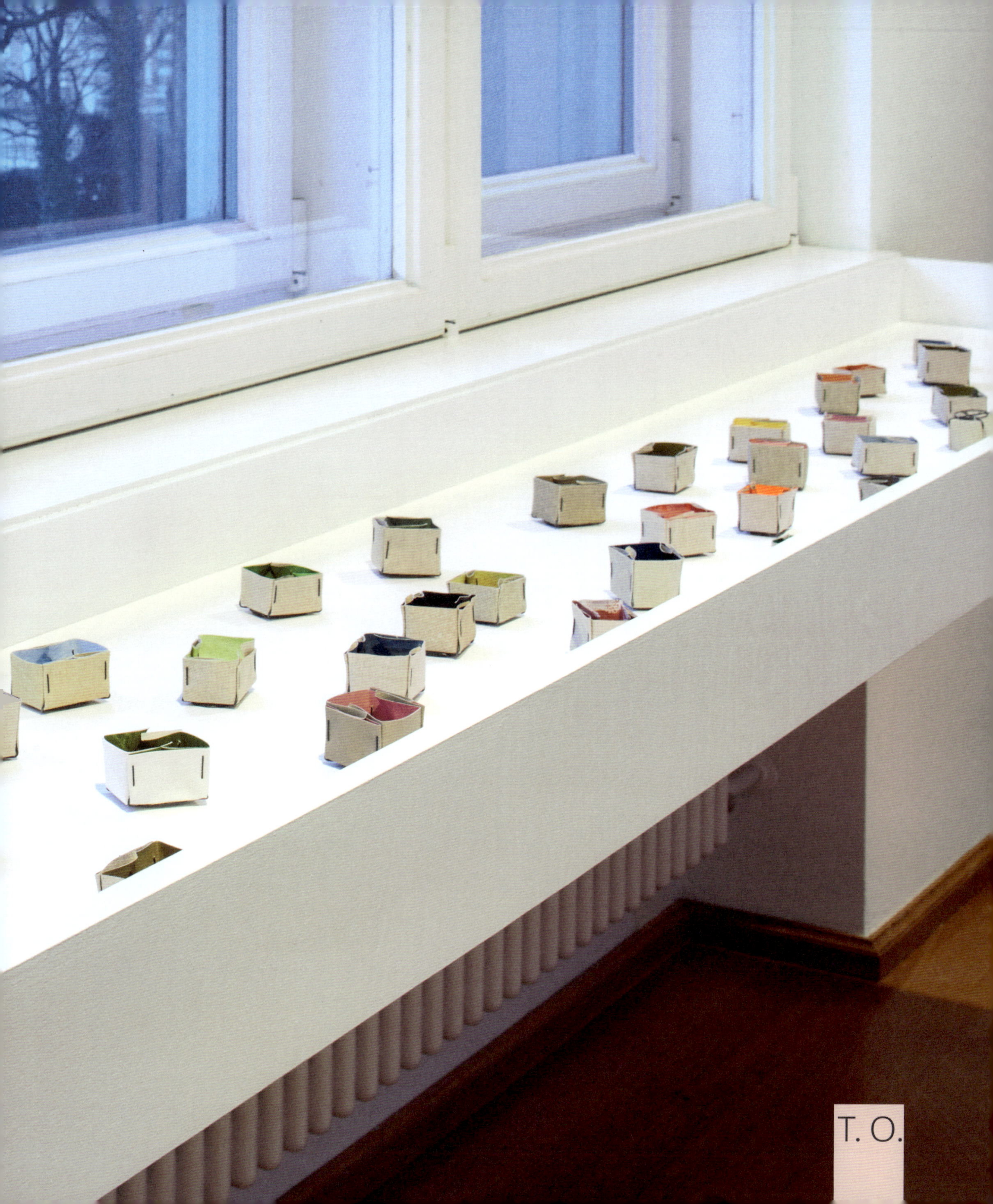

T. O.

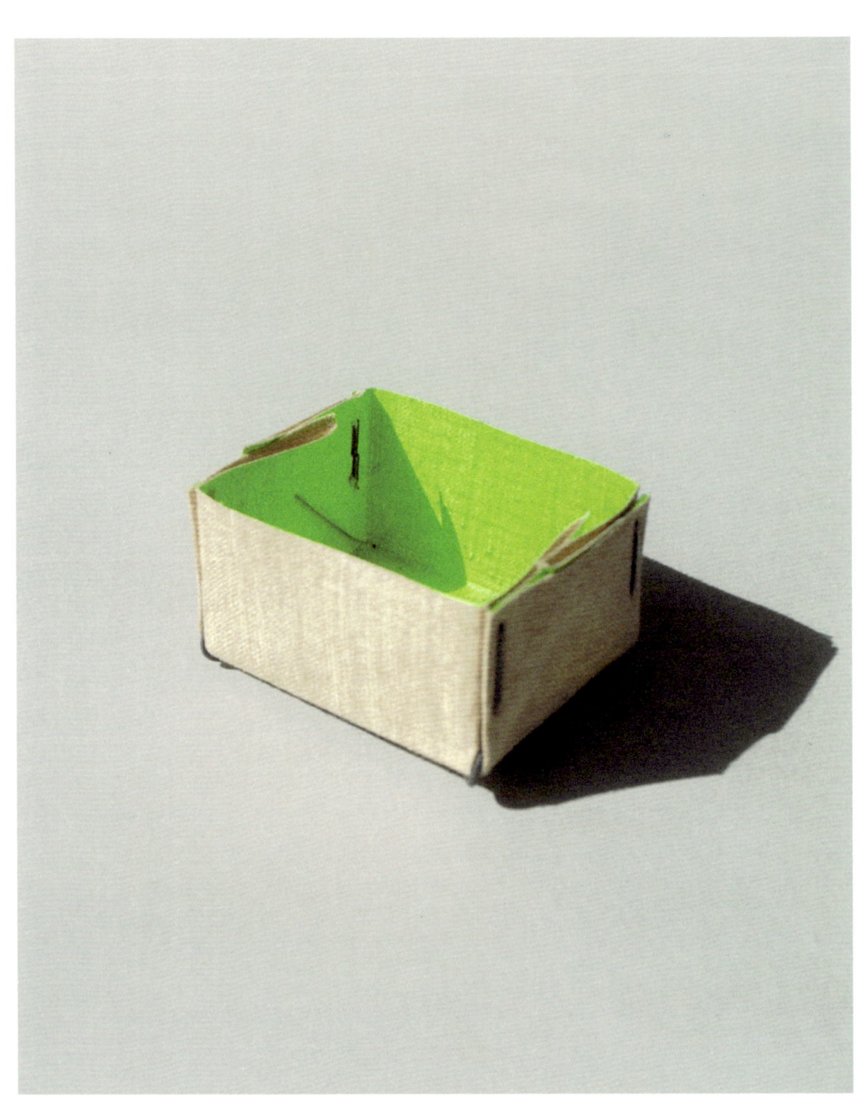

CONTEXT Broschen / brooches 2013 Leinwand / canvas Silber / silver Farbe / paint

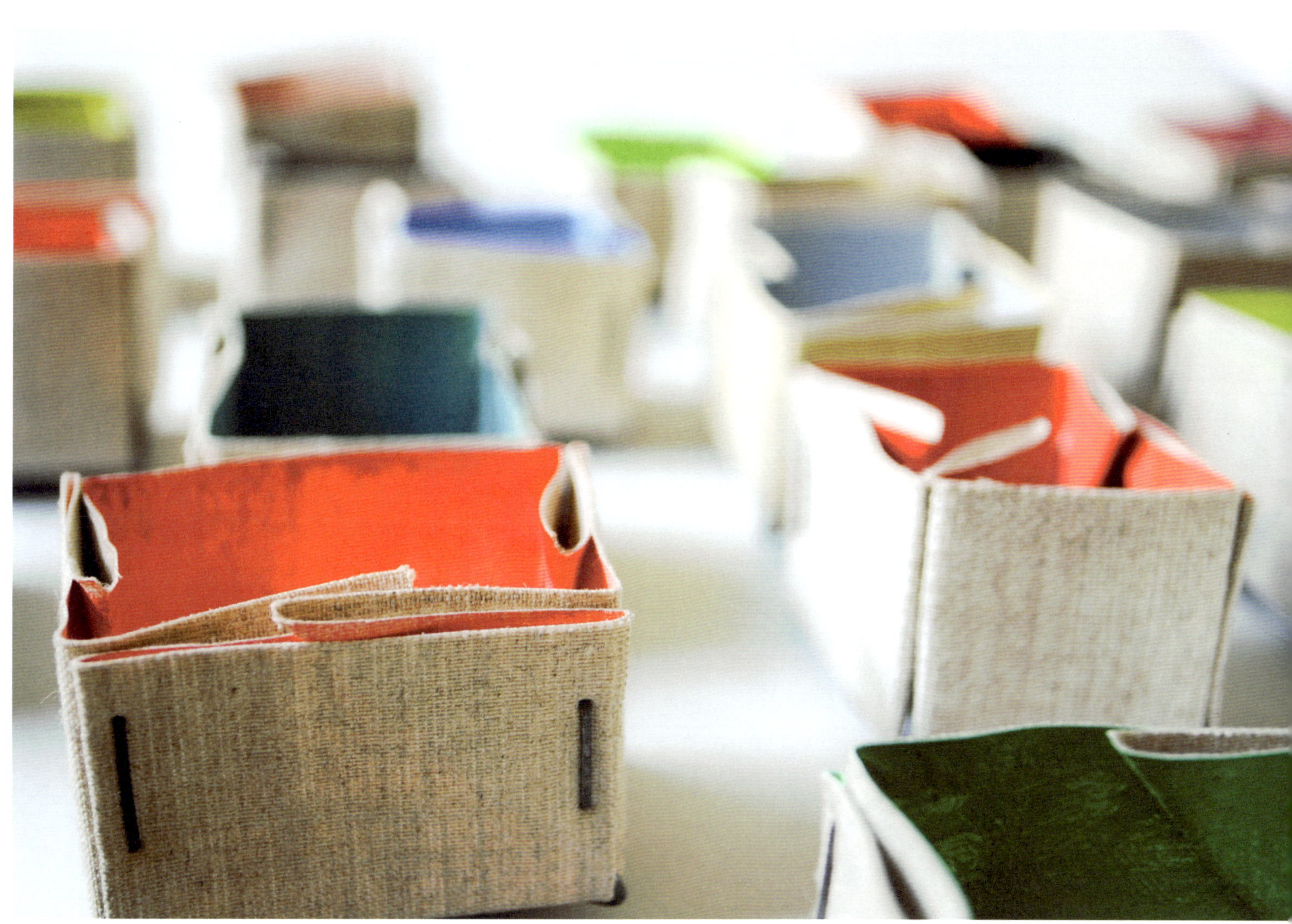

T. O.

Bei dieser Arbeit ist Pontoppidan nicht nur am Endprodukt interessiert. Vielmehr ist der gesamte Schaffensprozess Teil des Konzepts. Juweliere fertigen ihre Arbeiten zumeist in der Abgeschiedenheit ihrer Studios. Fine-Art- und Industriedesign-Künstler hingegen sind zunehmend darauf angewiesen, dass andere bestimmte Tätigkeiten für sie übernehmen. Pontoppidans einfache Schlussfolgerung: Sie holte sich fachmännische Hilfe für ihre neue Arbeit.[12]
Ward Schrijver

Instead of just focusing on the end product, this time she also incorporated the making of the work into the concept. Whereas the jeweler makes his or her work mostly in the solitude of the studio, fine art and industrial design artists rely more and more on execution by others. It led Pontoppidan to a simple conclusion. She enlisted specialized assistance to produce her new work.[12]
Ward Schrijver

CONTEXT Brosche / brooch 2013 Leinwand / canvas Silber / silver Farbe / paint

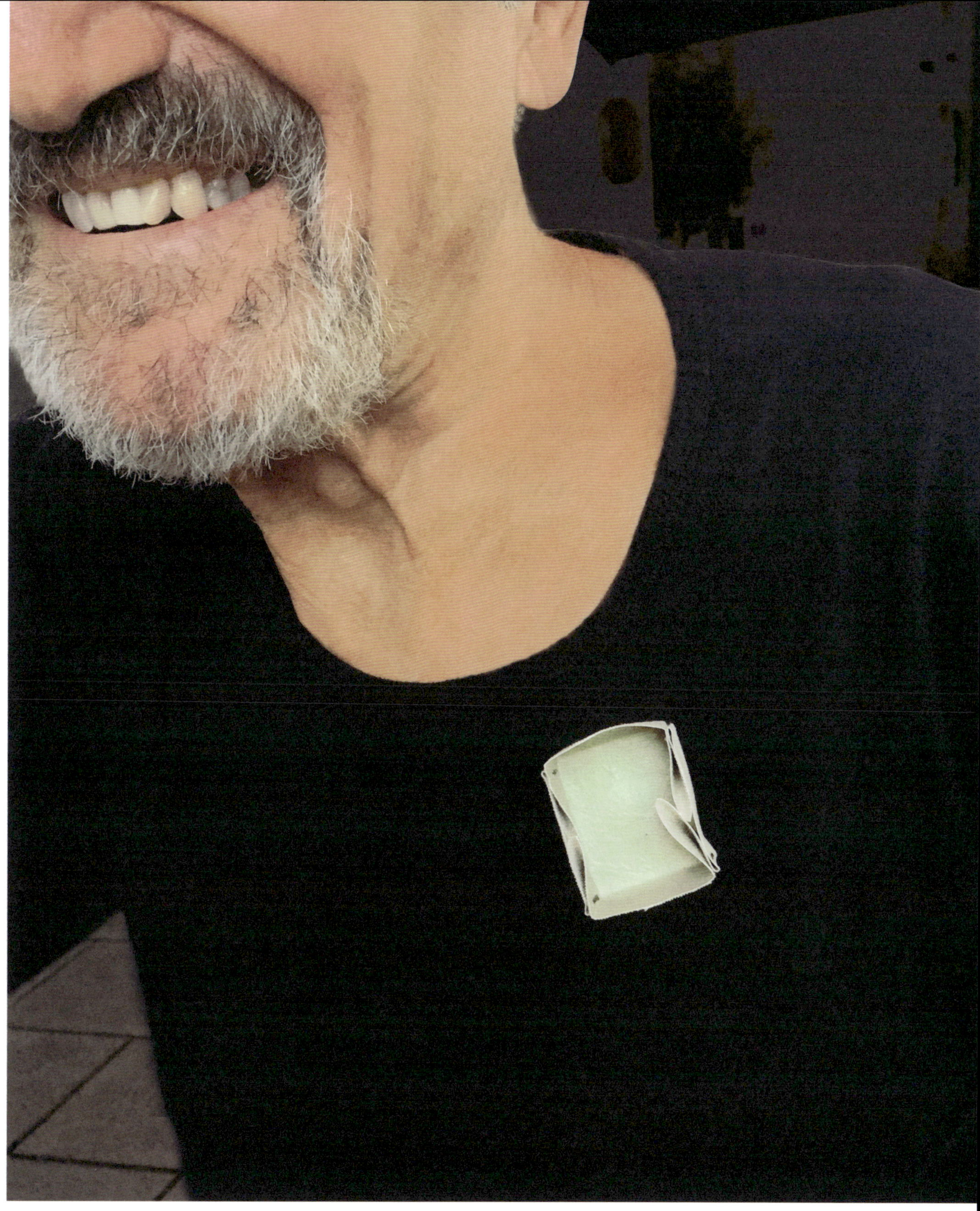

T. O.

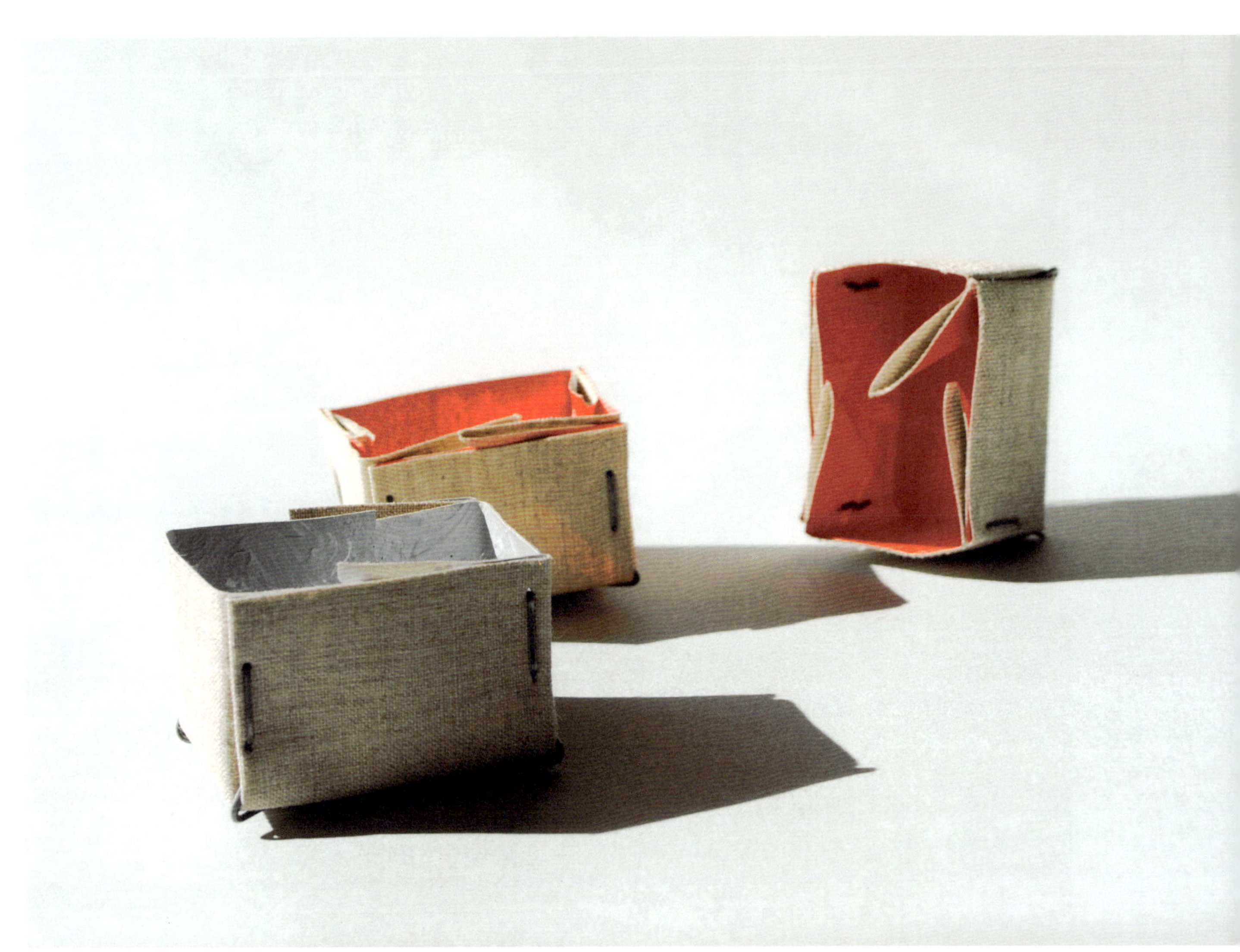

CONTEXT Broschen / brooches 2013 Leinwand / canvas Silber / silver Farbe / paint

T. O.

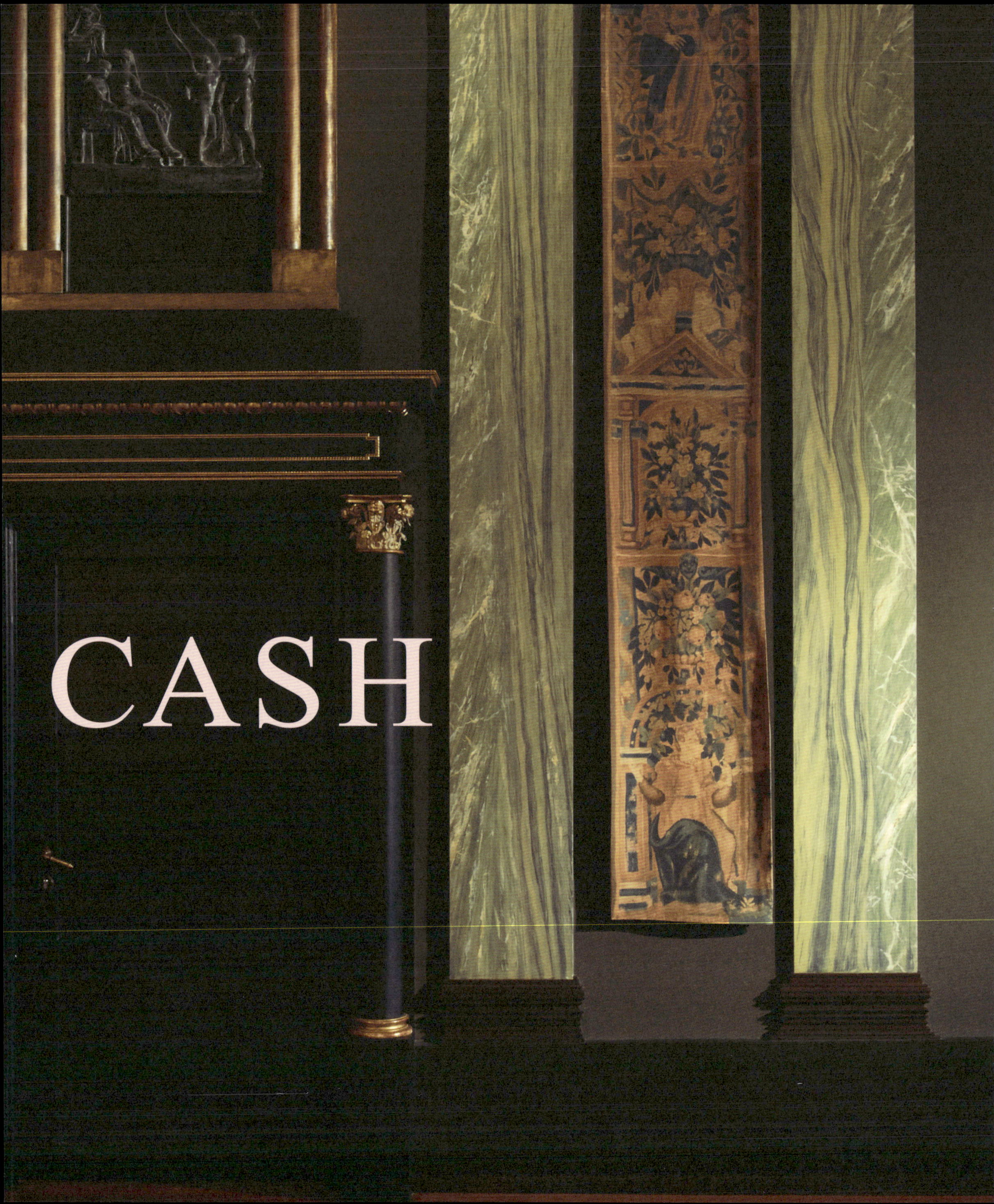

CASH

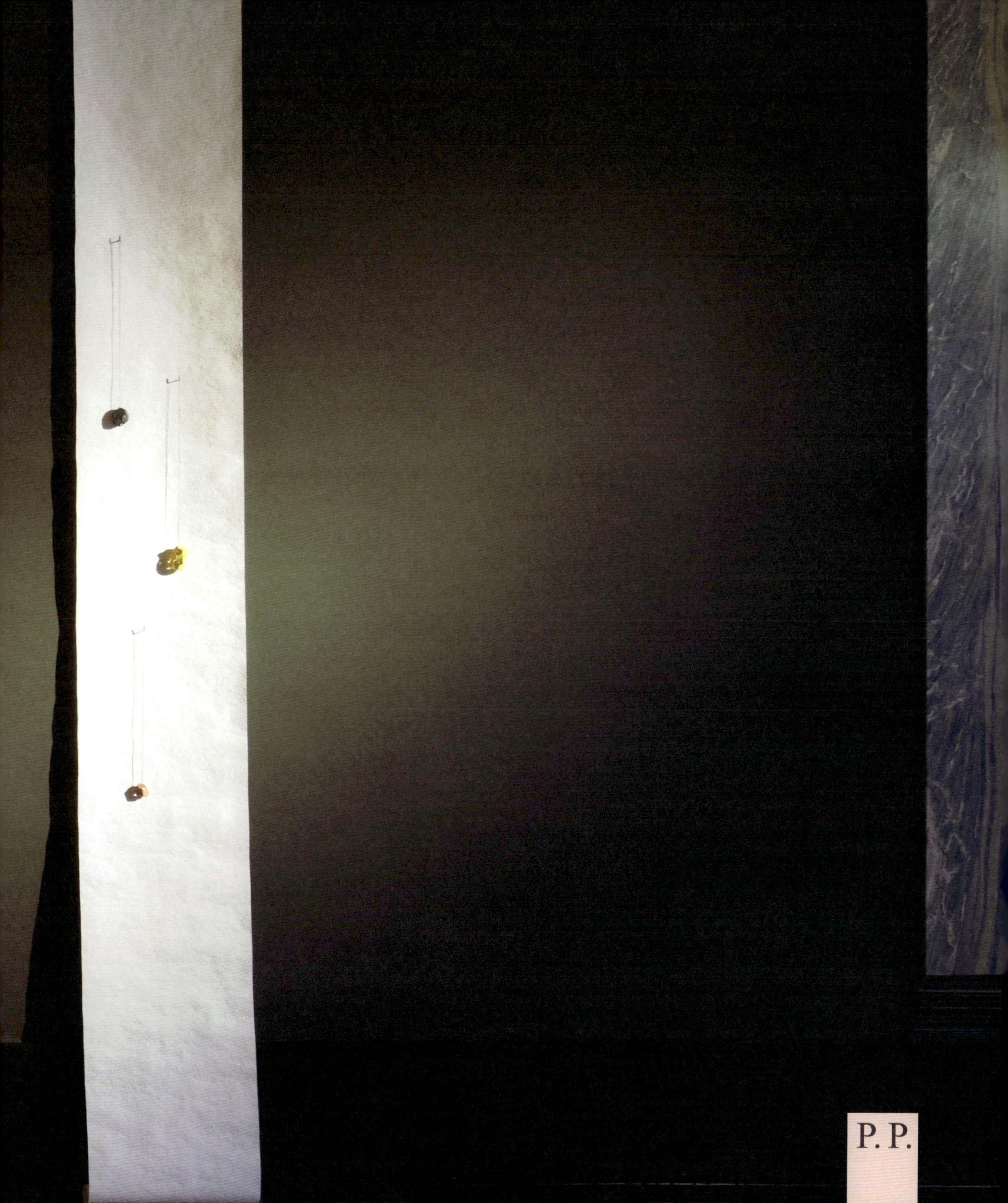
P. P.

Obwohl sie alle traditionalistischen Versuchungen, welche die Schmuckkunst zuweilen heimsuchen, gnadenlos im Keim erstickt, obwohl ihre Arbeiten starke Tendenzen zu Absurdität, Verfremdung und Spielereien aufweisen, so weiß sie dennoch ihre Wurzeln in der Schmuckherstellung und im Goldschmiedehandwerk zu schätzen, auch wenn dies nicht immer sofort sichtbar ist. Denn wäre dies nicht der Fall, wäre ihr »fieser« Ansatz bei Weitem nicht so effektiv. In ihrem Schaffensprozess unterliegen die Schmuckstücke einem mysteriösen Wandel – einerseits konzeptionelle Auseinandersetzung und kritische Reflexion, andererseits ästhetische und dekorative Rekapitulation; all dies verschmolzen in kompakter und handlicher Form.[13]
CURRENT OBSESSION

Although she mercilessly eradicates all traditionalistic temptations besetting jewelry art, although her work displays a strong proclivity toward things like absurdity, defamiliarization and play, she values her background in jewelry and the goldsmith's craft, even though this is not always immediately visible. Were that not the case, her "nasty" approach could never be quite so effective. For the process involved in her work, jewelry is subjected to a mysterious transformation, with conceptual action and critical reflection on the one hand and aesthetic and ornamental recapitulation on the other melting into a compact and handy form.[13]
CURRENT OBSESSION

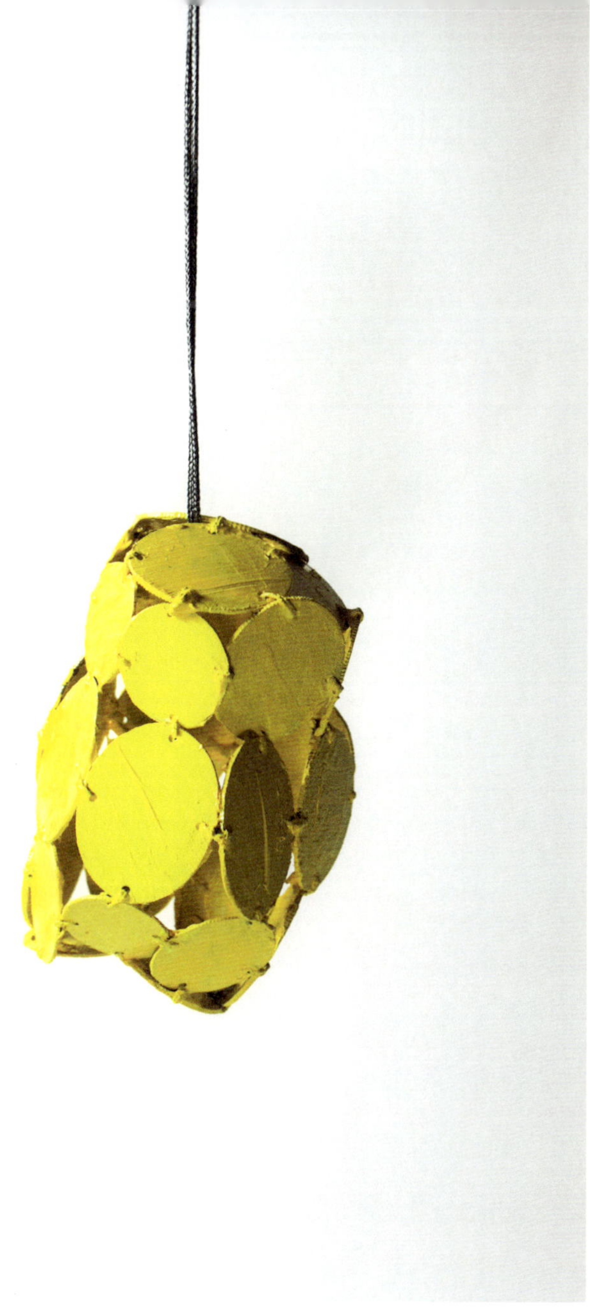

CASH#2 Anhänger / pendant 2013 Silbermünzen / silver coins Faden / string Farbe / paint

Das Suchen und Erkennen von Ähnlichkeiten zwischen den verschiedenen Serien Pontoppidans ist keine leichte Aufgabe. Pontoppidan selbst sagt: »Ich habe keinen bestimmten Stil, aber es scheint eine innere Logik zwischen allen Schaffensperioden zu geben.«[14]
Carin E.M. Reinders

Looking and trying to recognize the similarities between the series by Pontoppidan is perhaps no easy task. Pontoppidan says: "I do not have a style, but there seems an inner logic between all periods."[14]
Carin E.M. Reinders

CASH#11 Anhänger / pendant 2015 Silbermünzen / silver coins Faden / string Farbe / paint

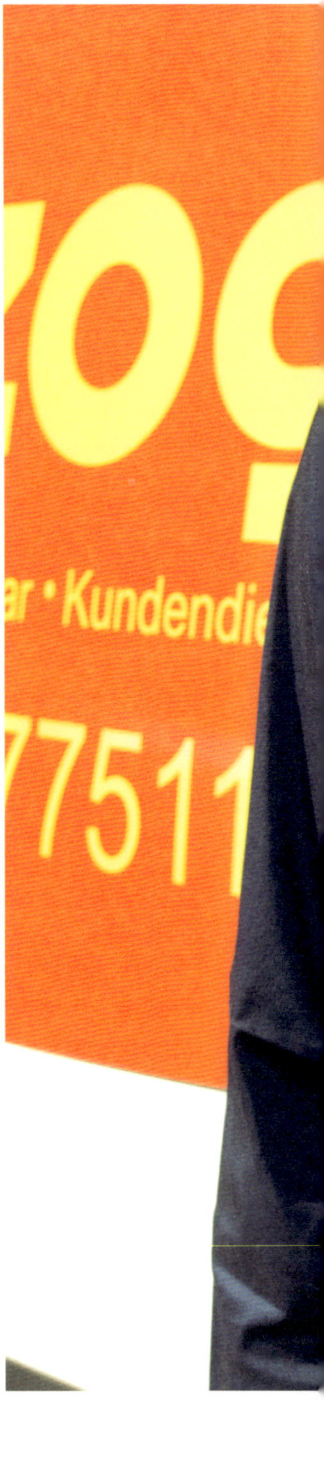

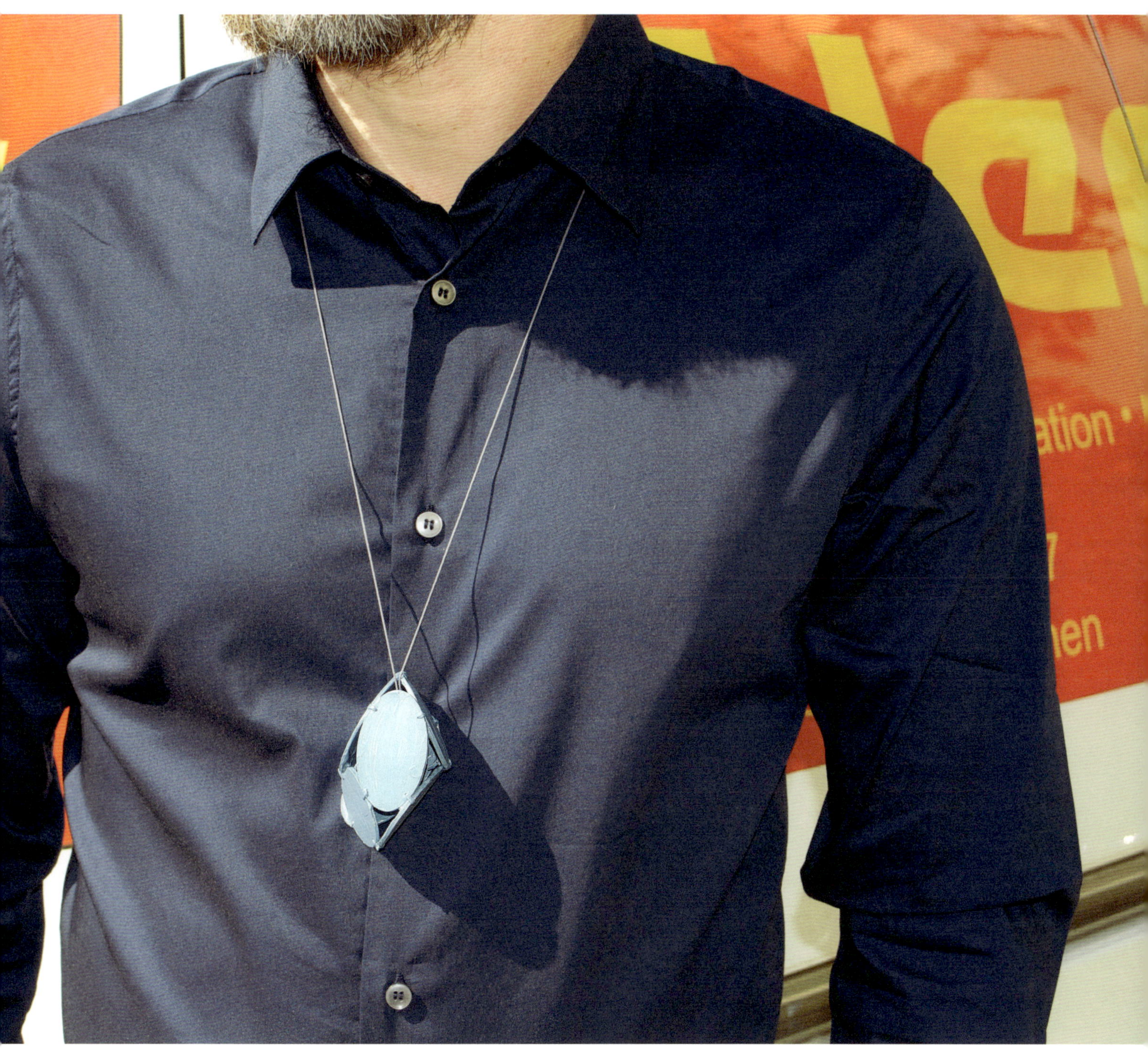

P. P.

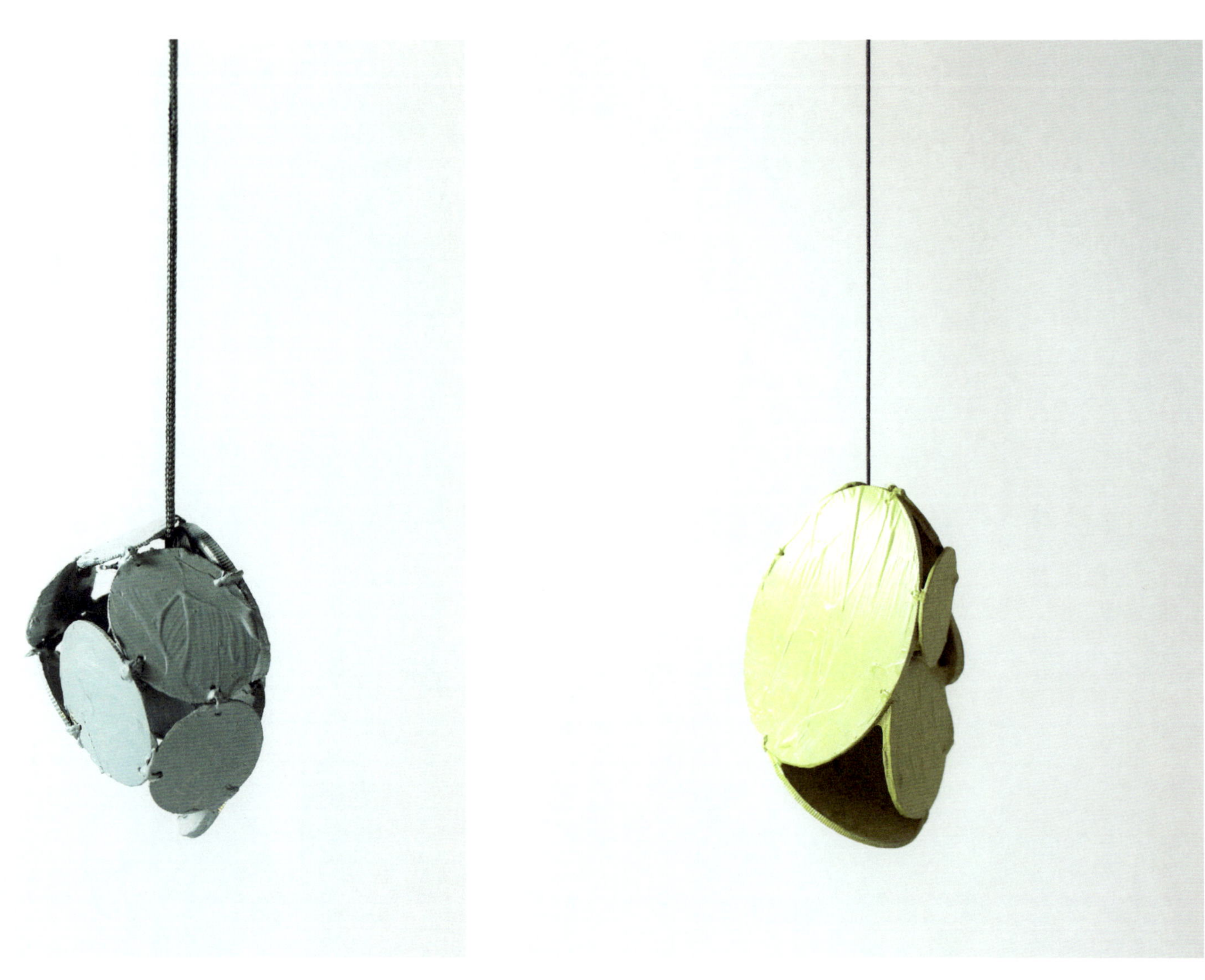

CASH#4 + #8 + #13 + #3 Anhänger / pendants 2013–2015 Silbermünzen / silver coins Faden / string Farbe / paint

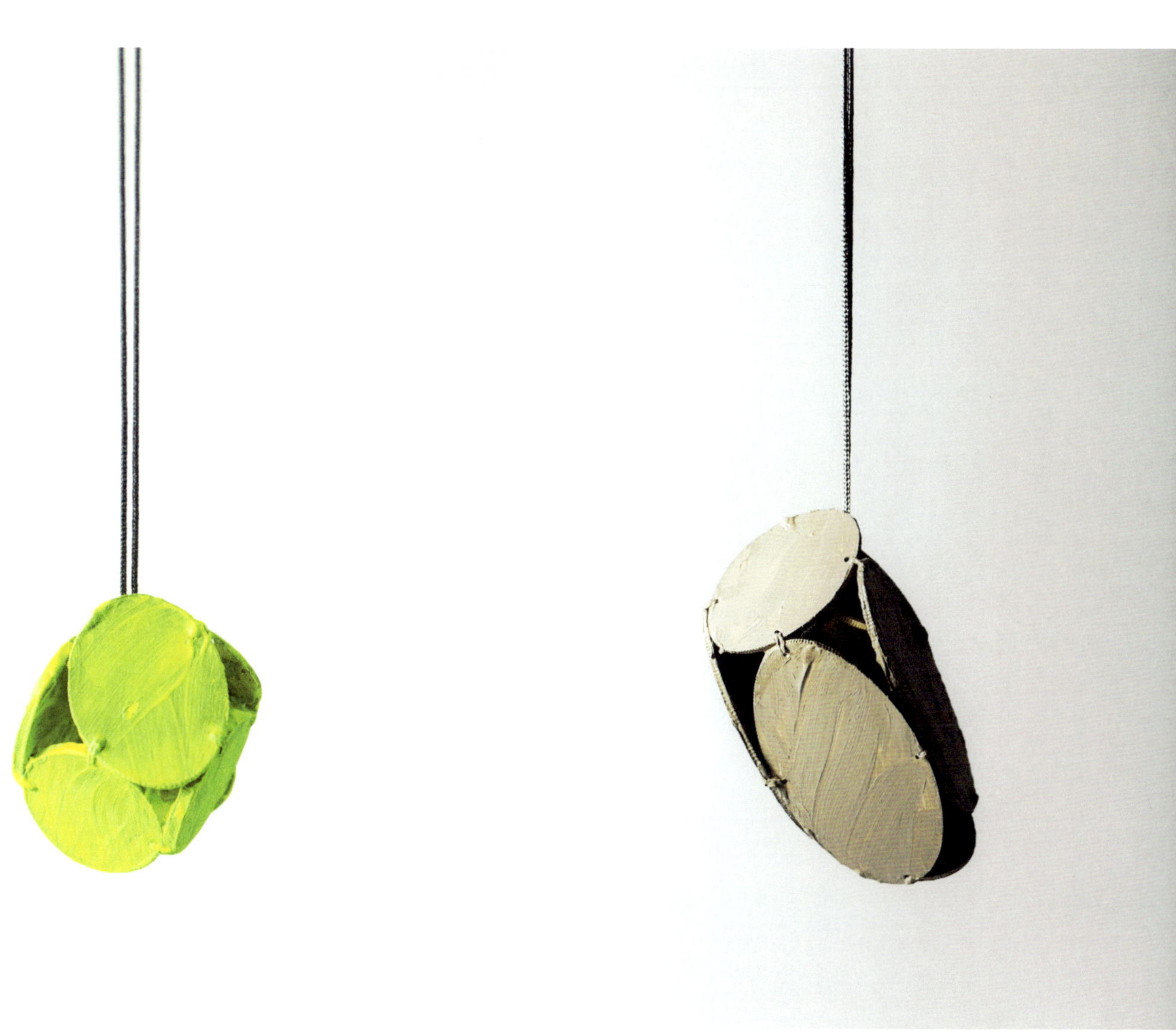

Im Werk Pontoppidans finden wir keine Statements zur Monarchie oder deren öffentlichen Wahrnehmung. Sie befasst sich mit der Welt der Kunst; damit, wie Geld Kreativität kontrolliert. Sie hat sich bereits in anderen Werken mit diesem Thema auseinandergesetzt: In der Serie CANVAS ging sie der Frage nach, ob Schmuck, der aus bemalten Leinwänden gefertigt wird, automatisch als Kunst zu verstehen ist; in ihrer Arbeit CONTEXT prüft sie, welchen Stellenwert die persönliche Mitarbeit des Künstlers hat. Und nun fertigt Pontoppidan CASH: Schmuckanhänger, die aus Sammlermünzen aus Feinsilber bestehen. Sie walzte diese, um ihre Form und ihren politischen Wert zu verändern, und versah sie dann mit einer dicken Farbschicht. Das verwendete Material ist typisch für die Schmuckherstellung, das Finish das universelle Medium der Kunst. Das Schöne an diesen Werken ist, dass sie – im Unterschied zu an der Wand hängenden Gemälden – am Körper getragen werden können und sich die Farbe nach und nach ablöst, worin sich wiederum die Doppeldeutigkeit dieser Arbeit offenbart.[15]
Ward Schrijver

With Pontoppidan, we find no statements about monarchy or public stature, her stance concerns the art world, how money controls creativity. She has dealt with the subject before; in her CANVAS series, she considered whether jewelry made from painted canvas automatically distinguishes it as art—and with CONTEXT she investigated the importance of an artist's personal participation. This time Pontoppidan made CASH: pendants composed of collectors coins, made of fine silver. She rolled them down to alter the shape and political value and covered them in a thick layer of paint. The material is characteristic for jewelry, the finish the universal code for art. The nice thing about them is that, in contrast to a painting hanging on the wall, they can be worn and in due course the paint will gradually wear of revealing the double meaning of the work.[15]
Ward Schrijver

CASH#7 + #6 + #4 Anhänger / pendants 2014 Silbermünzen / silver coins Faden / string Farbe / paint

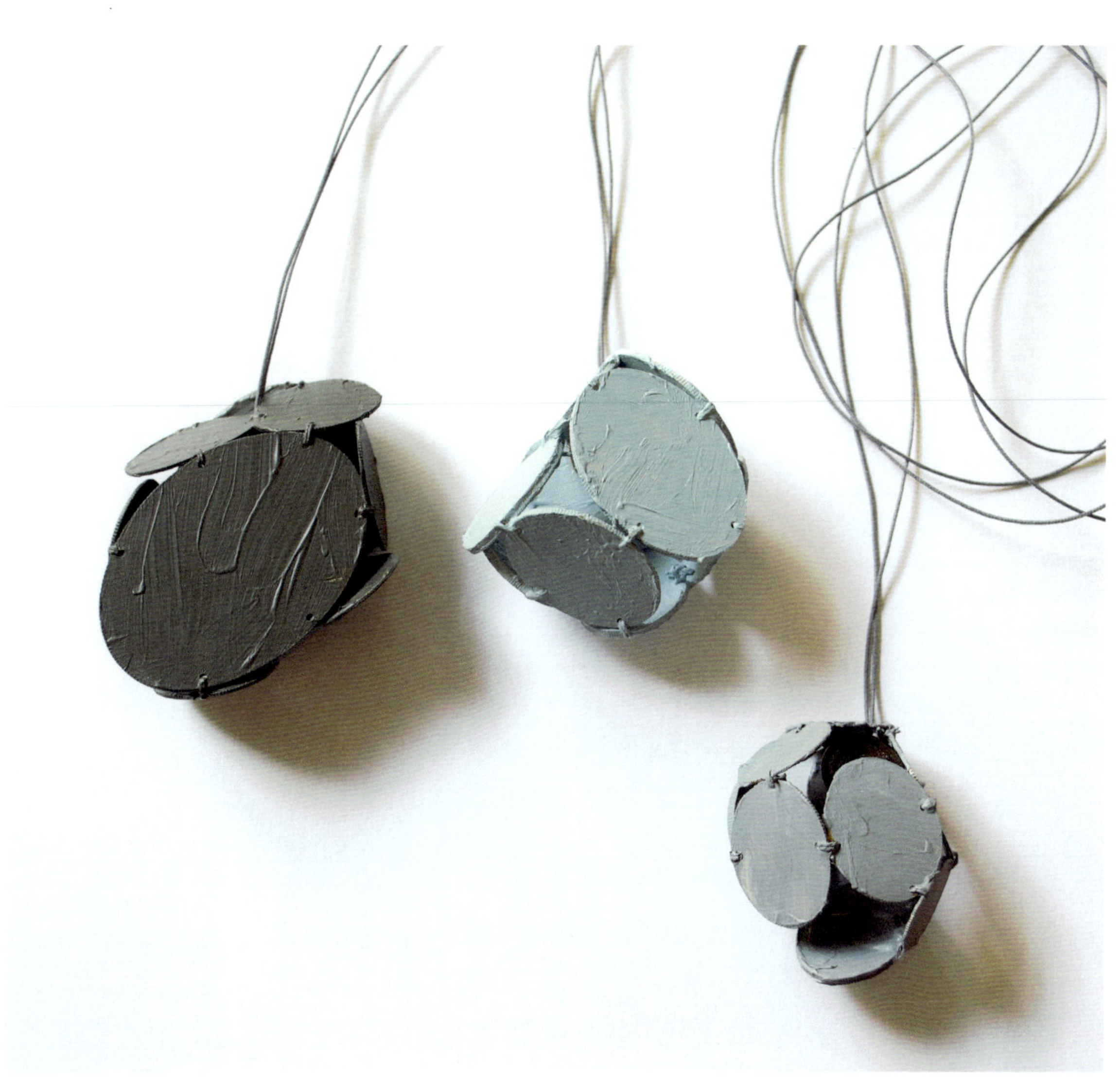

P. P.

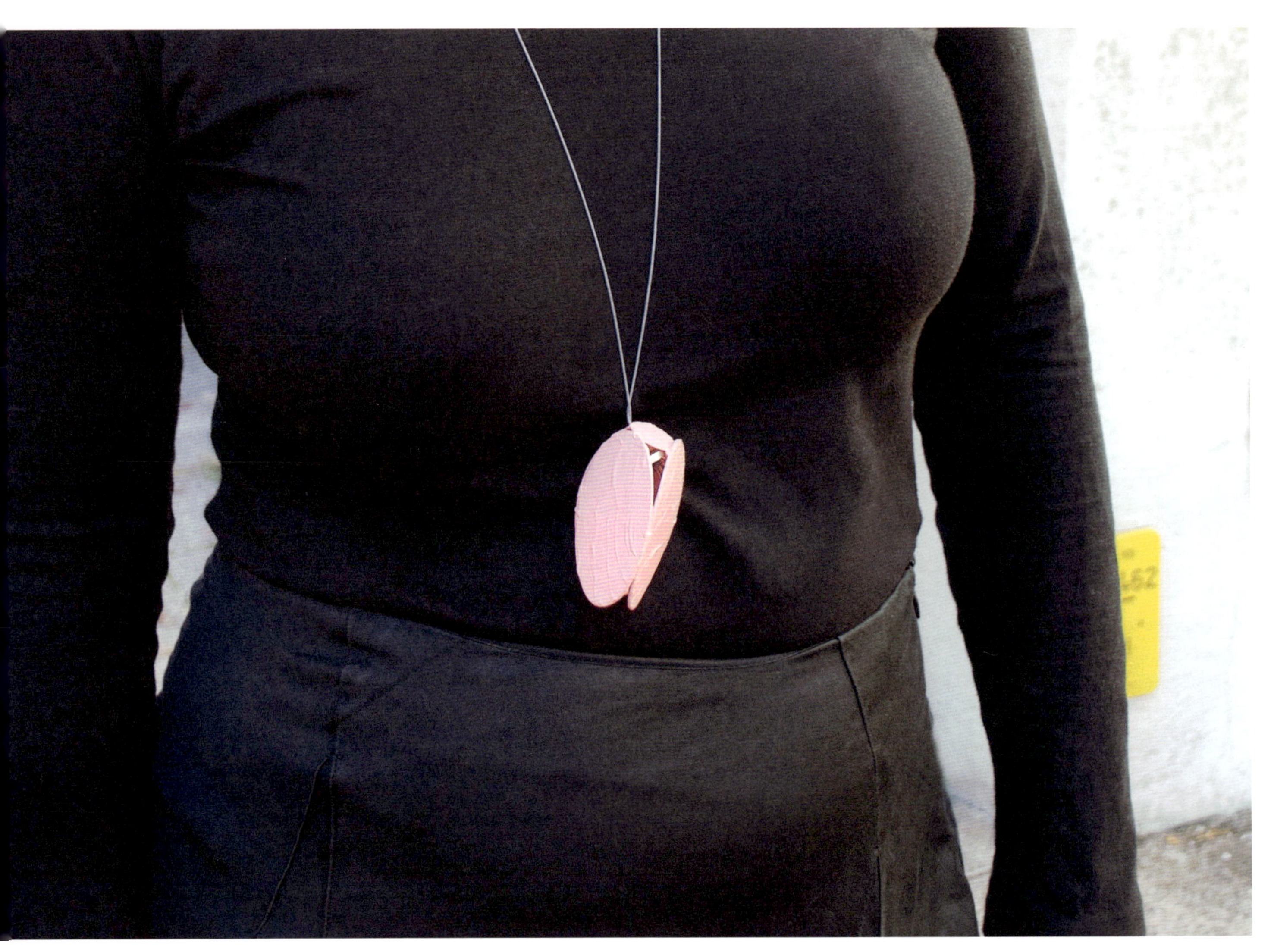

CASH#9 Anhänger / pendant 2014 Silbermünzen / silver coins Faden / string Farbe / paint

CASH ist so etwas wie eine abschließende Bemerkung zu dem mit ästhetischem Verhalten verbundenen ökonomischen System. Kunst offenbart sich immer mehr als einfache Definition, abhängig von Sachen wie Kontext, Erfolg und Ambiente, in der die einzelnen Objekte verankert sind.[16]
CURRENT OBSESSION

CASH constitutes something like a concluding remark on the economic system associated with aesthetic behaviour. Art reveals itself more and more as a simple definition, dependant on things like context, success and ambience, in which the individual objects are anchored.[16]
CURRENT OBSESSION

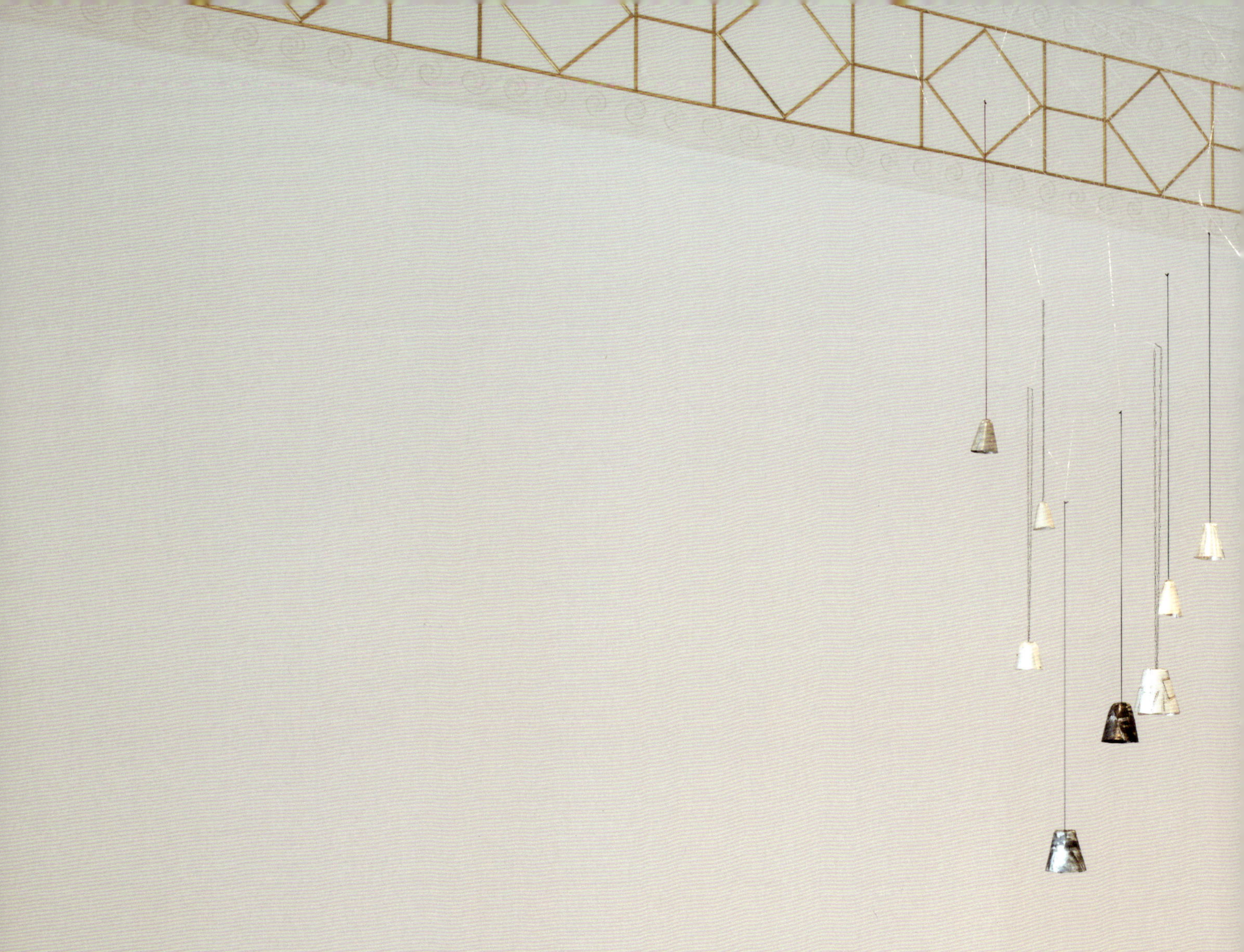

KNELL – The Gender Bell

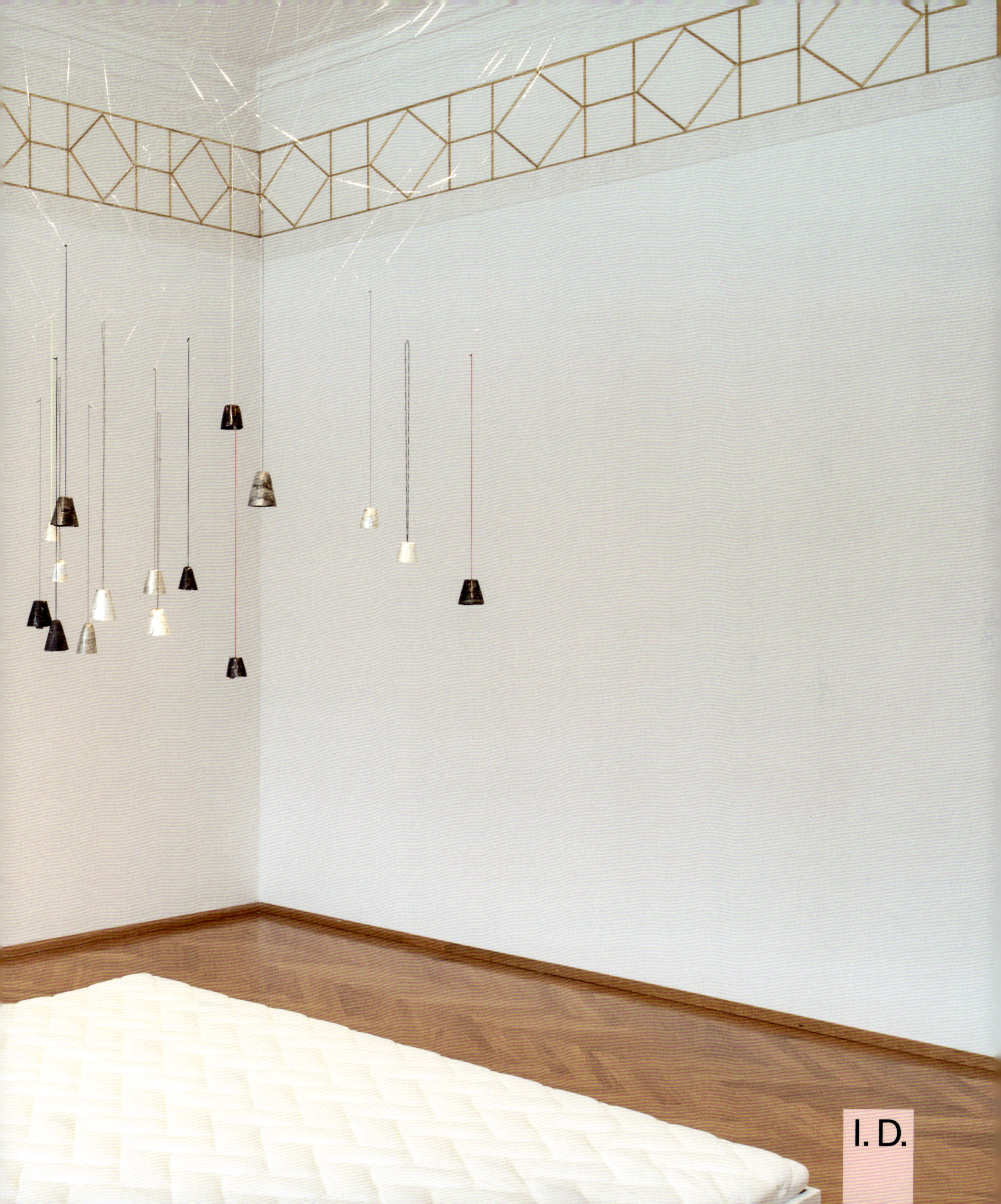

I. D.

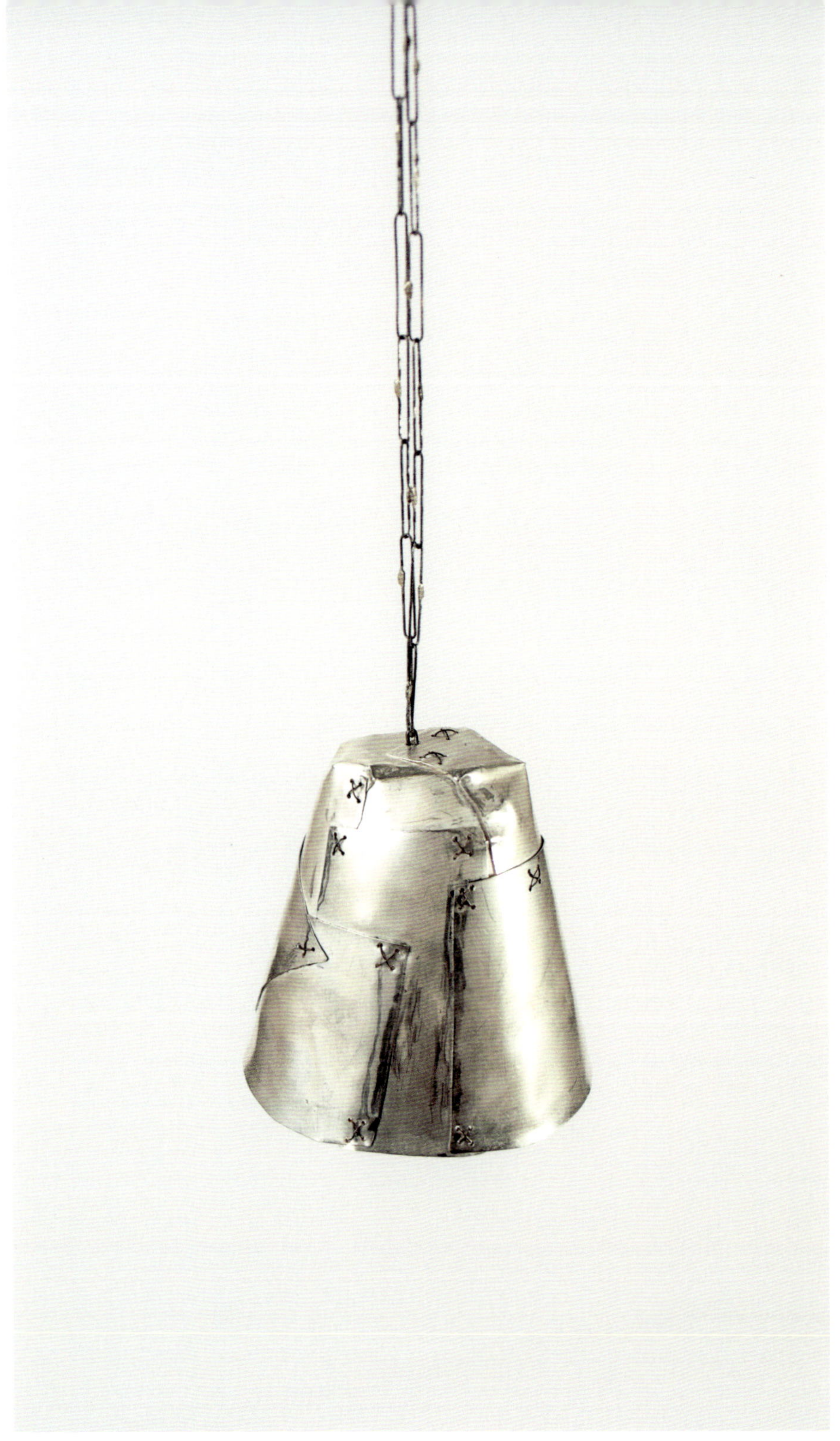

Diese Glockenketten sind trotzig, anrührend, selbstbewusst, zart. Sie erscheinen als passendes Bild einer Totenglocke, aber – wie auch im Titel benannt – spiegeln sie Fragen von Gender. Die Glocke weist ihren weiblichen oder männlichen Träger aus in seinem Bewusstsein von jemand anderem bzw. anderer, aber auch von sich selbst. Die Glocke macht ihren Träger präsent. In ihrer Funktion eines Klangkörpers bedeutet die Glocke Mahnung, aber auch Warnung. Die Glocke schafft Erinnerung und sie erreicht Aufmerksamkeit. Damit erfüllt der Schmuck einen gesellschaftlichen Auftrag und wird zu einer politischen Aussage.[17]
Angelika Nollert

These bell necklaces are defiant, touching, self-confident, delicate. They appear as an apposite image of a death knell yet reflect issues of gender—as mentioned in the title. The bell identifies its female or male wearer in its awareness of another, or others, but also of itself. The bell makes its wearer present. As a body of sound, the bell means monition but also admonition. The bell creates memories and it attracts attention. In doing so, the jewelry fulfills a social duty and becomes a political statement.[17]
Angelika Nollert

KNELL#3 Anhänger / pendant 2016 Silber / silver Eisen / iron Zinn / tin

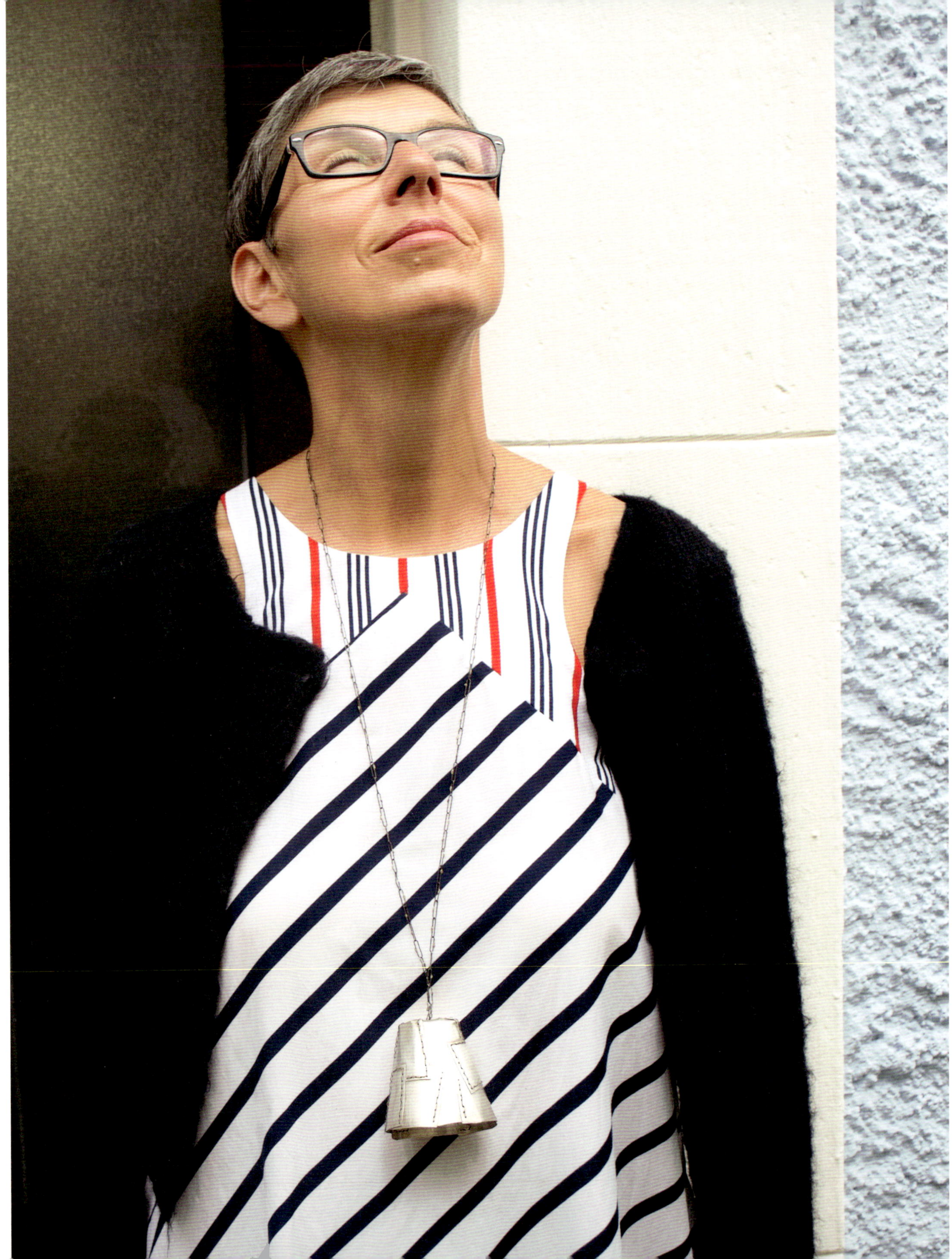

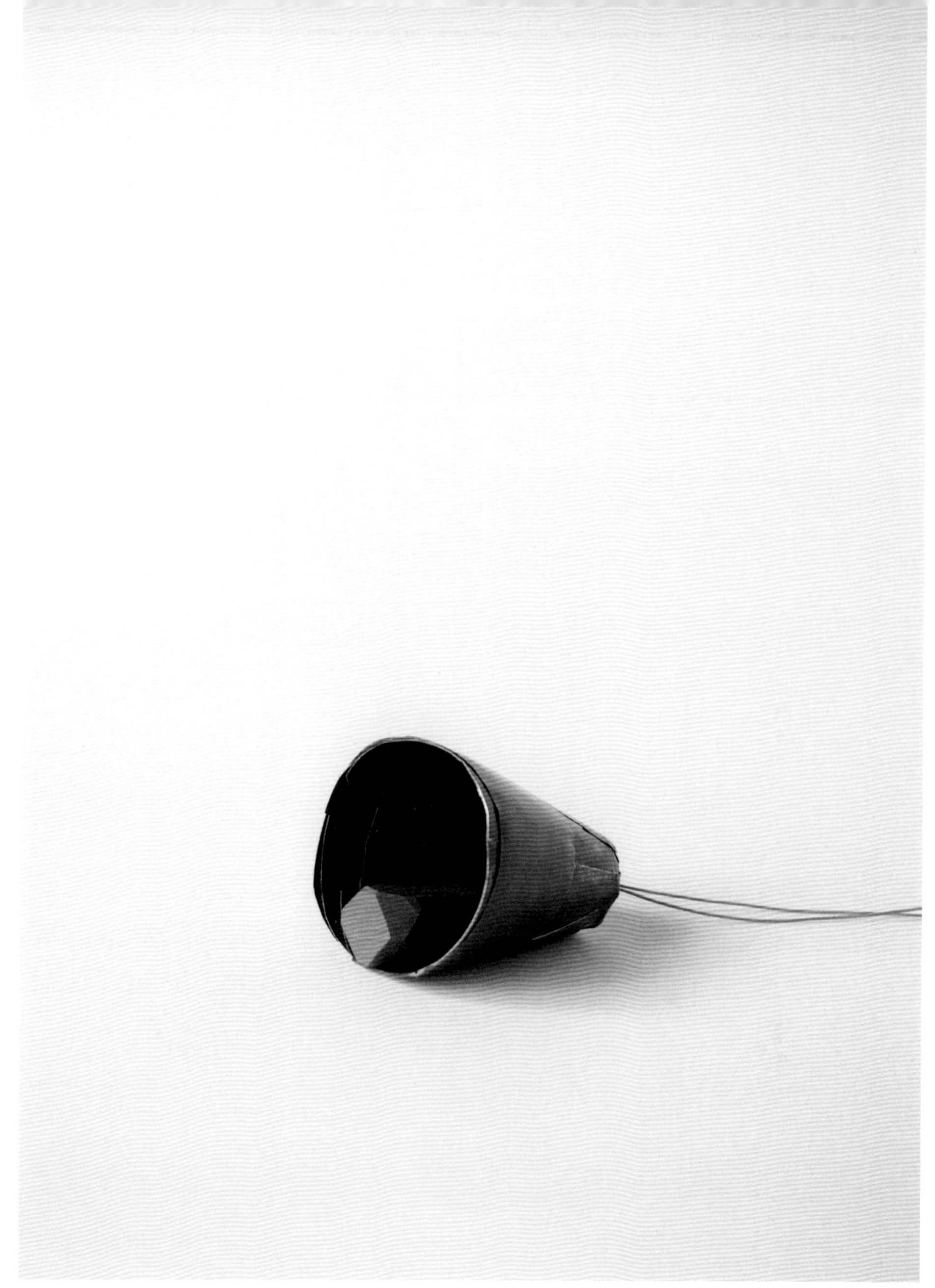

KNELL#1 Anhänger / pendant 2016 Silber / silver Eisen / iron
KNELL#33 Anhänger / pendant 2018 Zinn / tin Silber / silver Graphit / graphite Faden / string

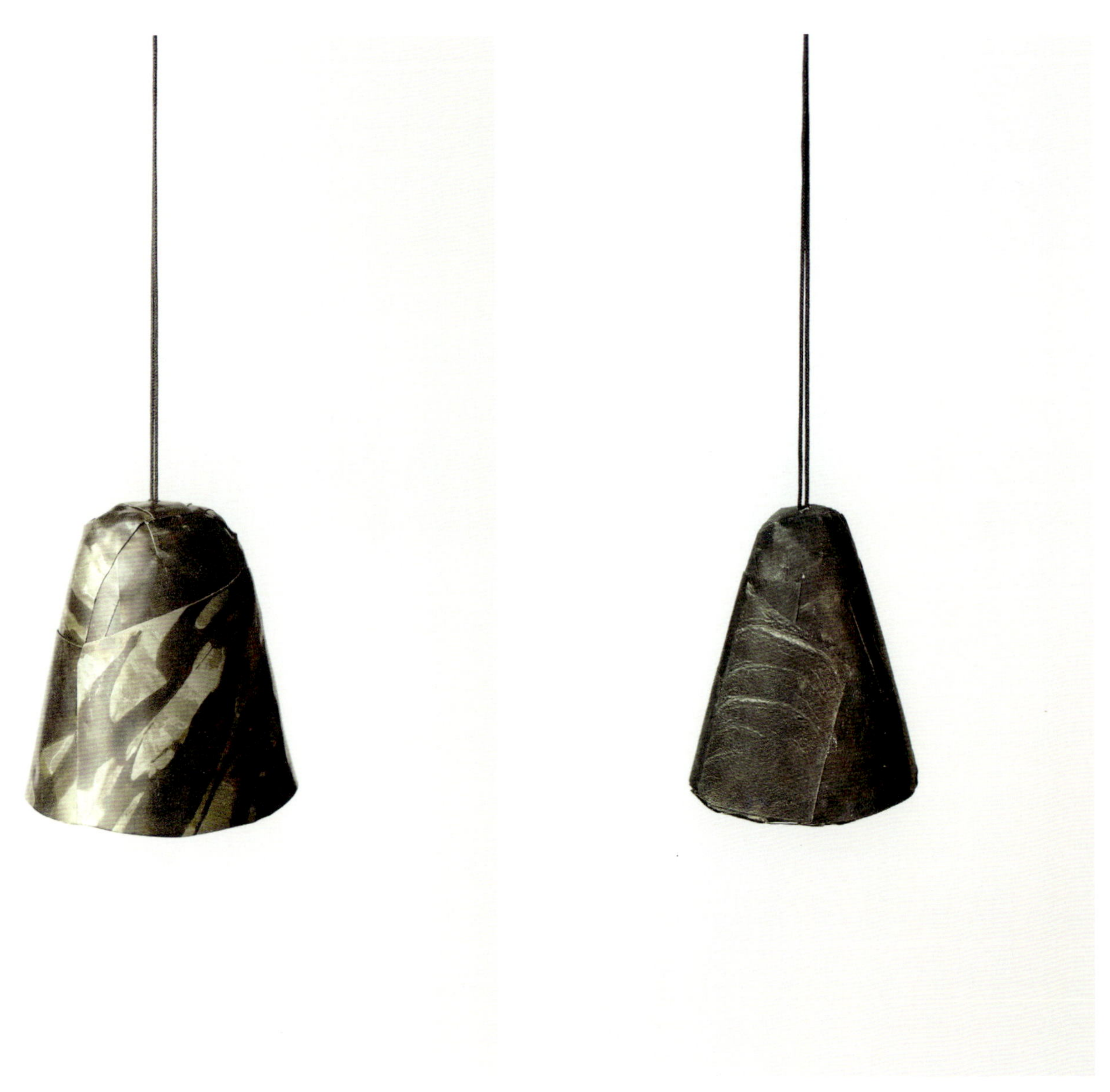

KNELL#29 + #7 + #15 + #4 Anhänger / pendants 2016–2018 Silber / silver Zinn / tin Aluminium / aluminum Schlangenknochen / snake-bones Holz / wood Eisen / iron Faden / string

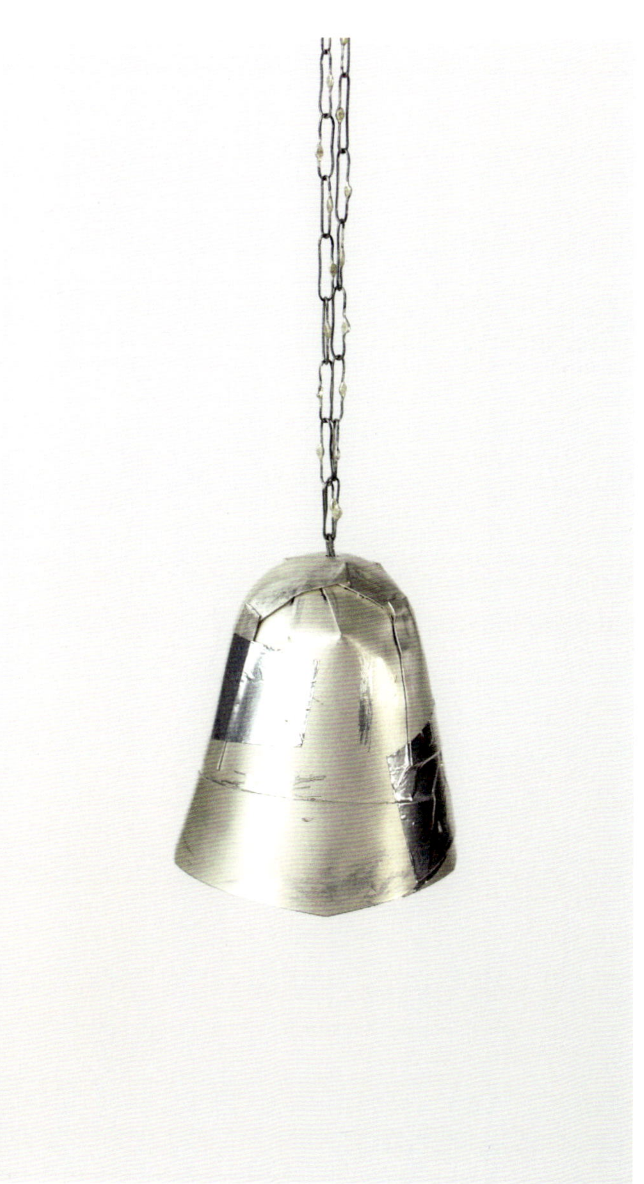

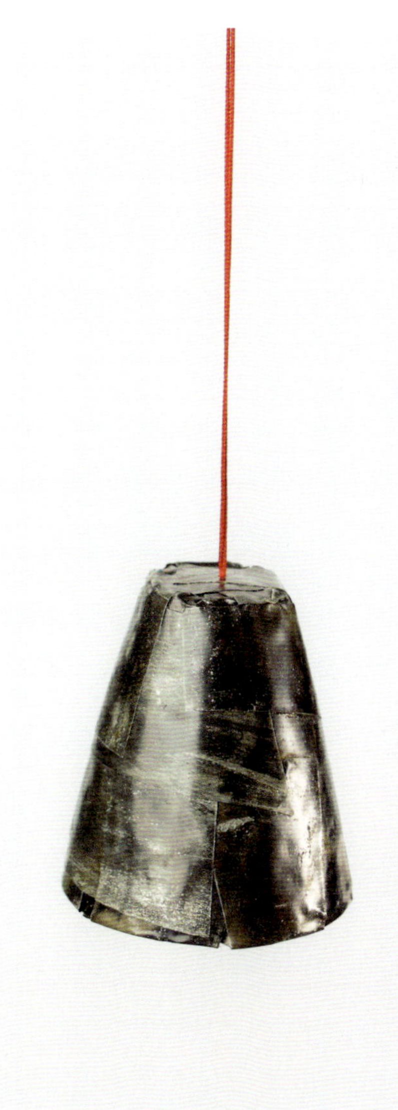

Ein dumpfes Pong statt klarem Klingeln. Diese Glocke um meinen Hals ist irritierend. Sie stört mich und stört mich dann doch nicht. Diese Glocke um meinen Hals tut nicht, was sie soll. Sie soll fein klingen, schön aussehen und mich schön aussehen lassen. Doch bin ich dankbar, dass sie das alles nicht tut, denn sonst wäre ich ein hübsches Schaf und ein potenzieller Schäfer wüsste jederzeit, wo ich bin. Als Frau werde ich stets bemerkt, denn mein Körper wird begutachtet. Mein Körper ist die Glocke, die fein klingen und schön aussehen soll. Wild reiße ich die Zinnglocke hin und her und sie grüßt mich mit ihrem dumpfen Laut.[18]
Jasmin Matzakow

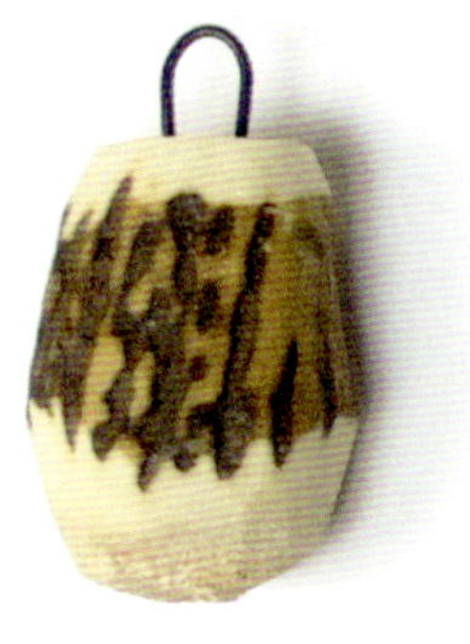

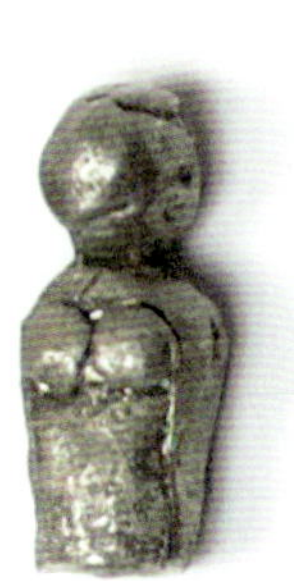

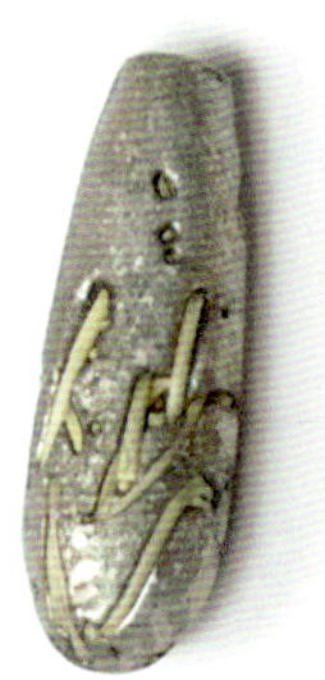

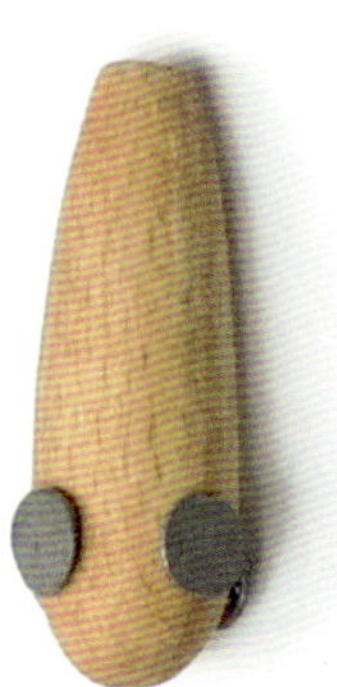

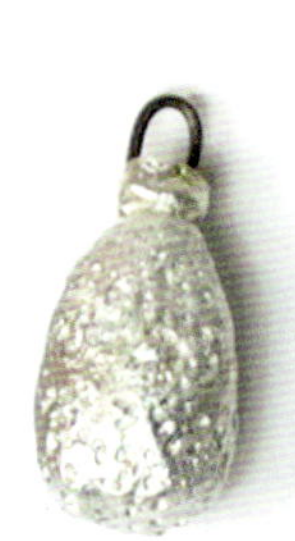

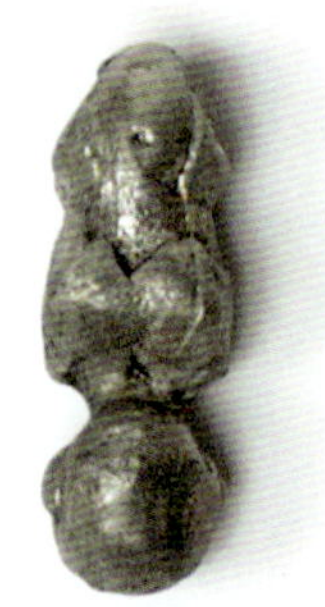

KNELL – The Gender Bell Detail: Klöppel / clapper

A dull thud rather than a clear ring. This bell around my neck is irritating. It disturbs me and then doesn't. This bell around my neck doesn't do what it is supposed to. It should have a delicate ring, look beautiful, and make me look beautiful. Yet I am grateful that it doesn't do any of these, for then I would be a pretty sheep and a prospective shepherd would always know where I am. As a woman, I will always be noticed, because my body is scrutinized. My body is the bell that should ring delicately and look beautiful. I yank the tin bell wildly back and forth and it greets me with its dull sound.[18]
Jasmin Matzakow

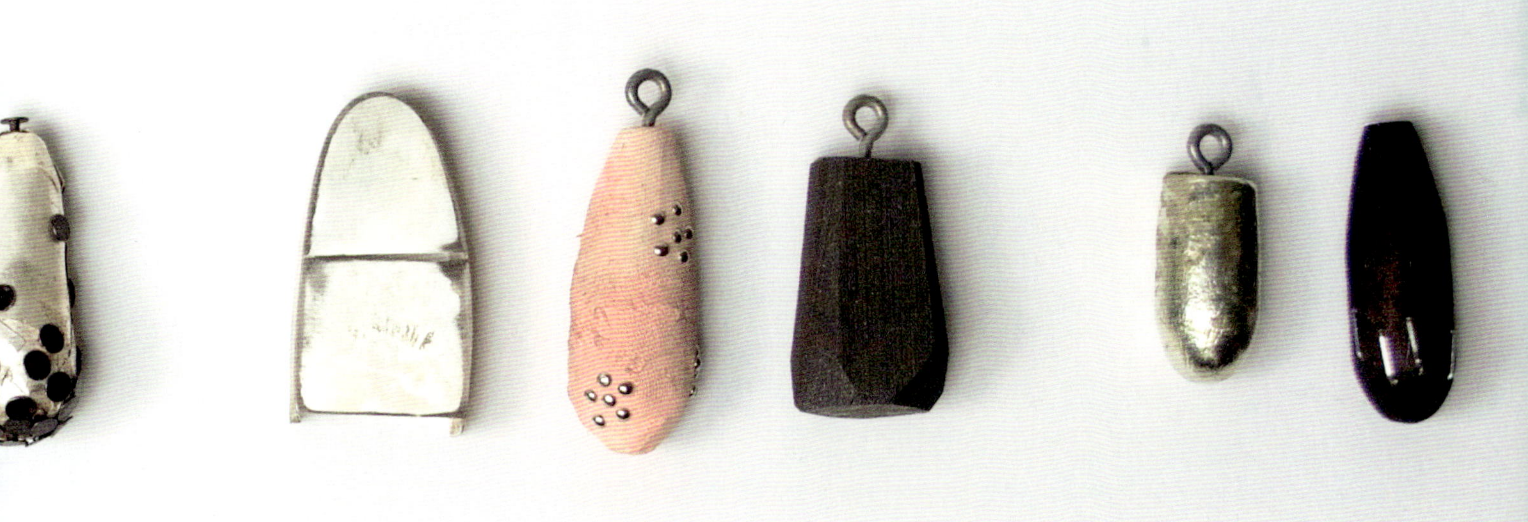

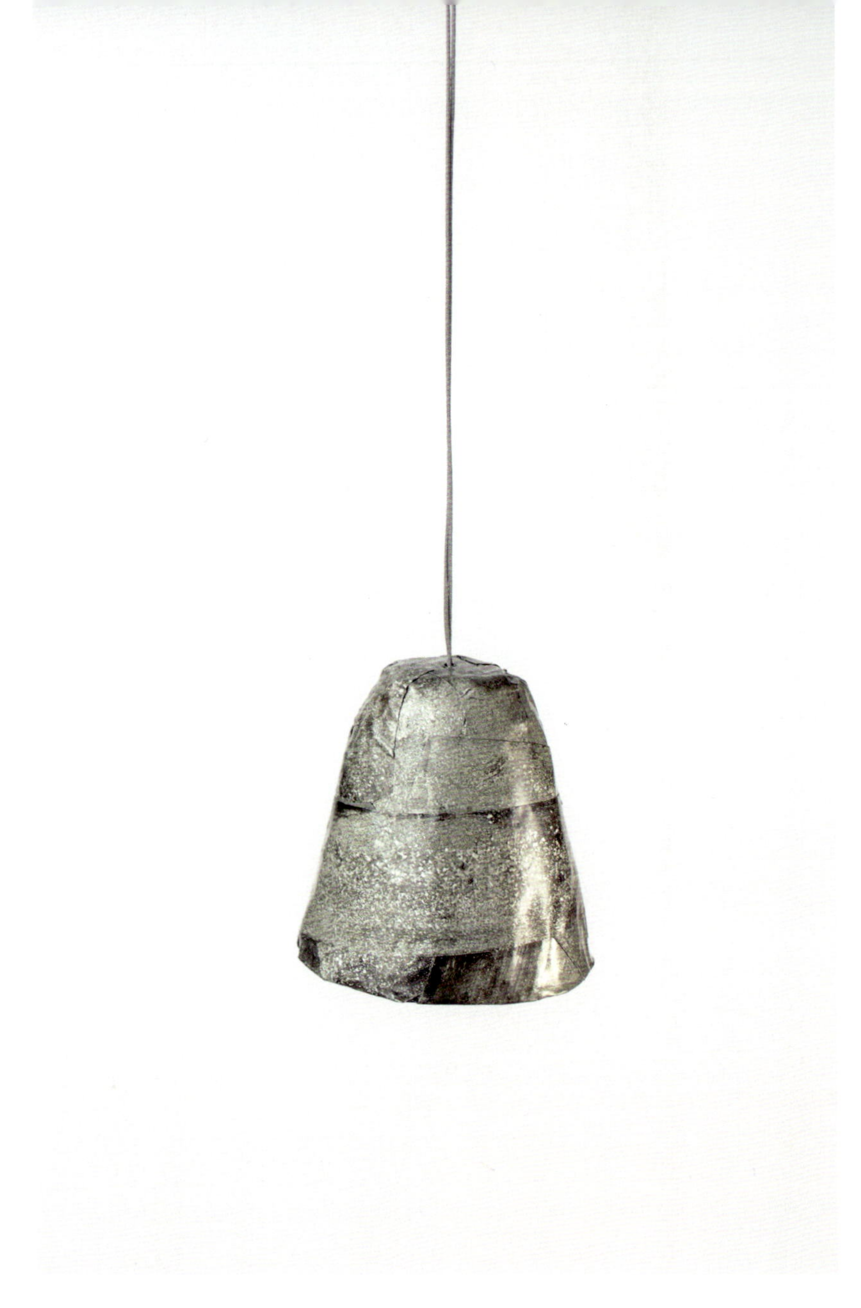

KNELL#11 Anhänger / pendant 2016 Zinn / tin Silber / silver Faden / string
KNELL#15 Anhänger / pendant 2017 Silber / silver Aluminium / aluminum Eisen / iron Zinn / tin

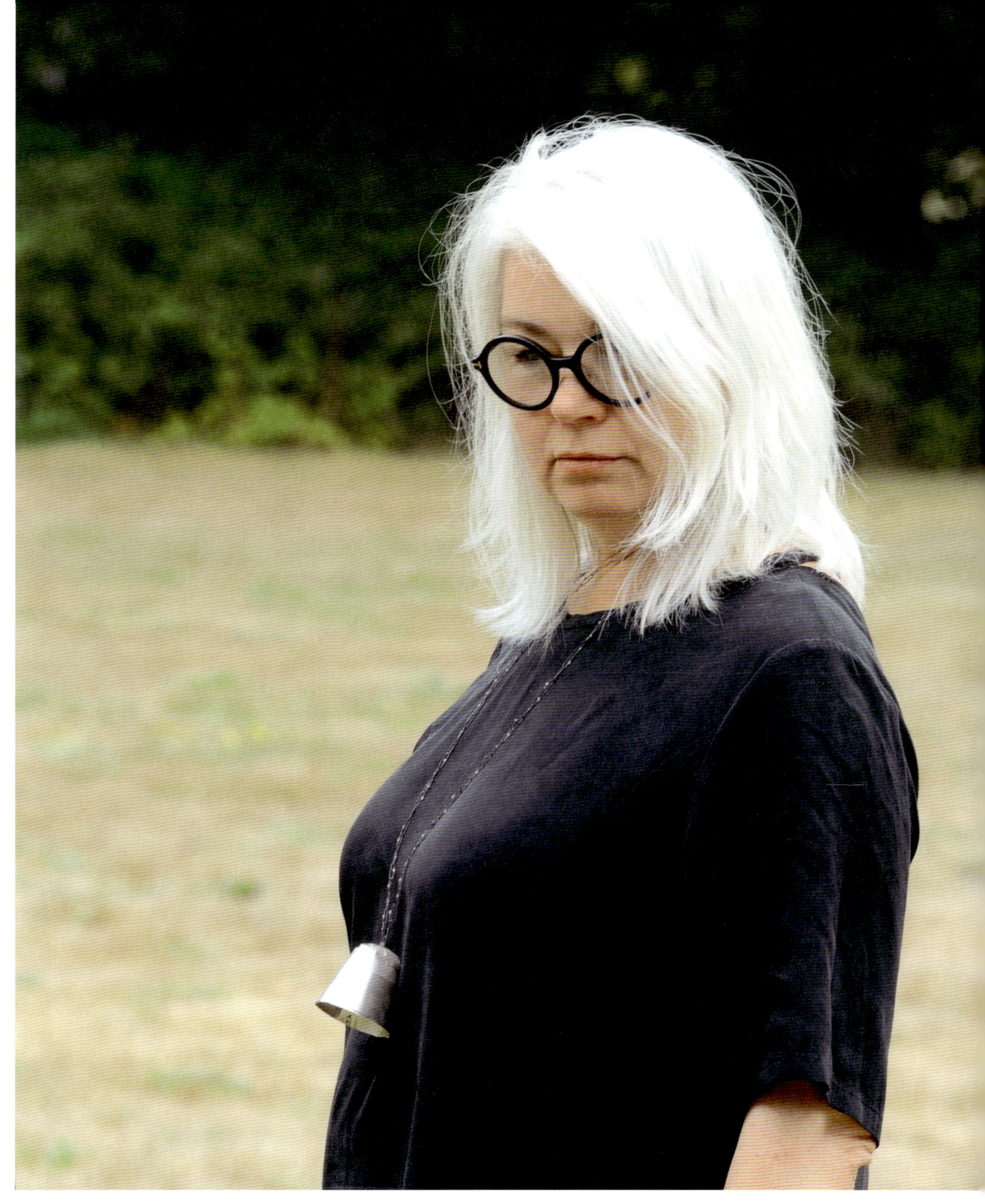

I. D.

Mit dieser Glocke um den Hals macht sich Frau nicht zum behangenen Schmuckstück des Mannes an ihrer Seite. Durch diese Gender Bell wird Schmuck in dieser seiner traditionellen Funktion entblößt. Geschlechterkonstruktion zeigt sich als ein recht und schlecht zusammengestückeltes, einengendes Zwangskorsett. Obwohl sie leicht ist, trägt Frau an ihr schwer. Aber sie schlägt mit jeder Bewegung ihres Körpers gegen das Gendergewicht Krach.[19]
Barbara Vinken

With this bell around her neck, a woman does not make herself the draped piece of jewelry around the man at her side. With this Gender Bell, jewelry is exposed in its traditional function. Gender construction appears as a rough-and-ready pieced together corset of constricting coercion. Even though it is light, the weight of womankind wears heavy. Yet she creates a riot against the weight of gender with every movement of her body.[19]
Barbara Vinken

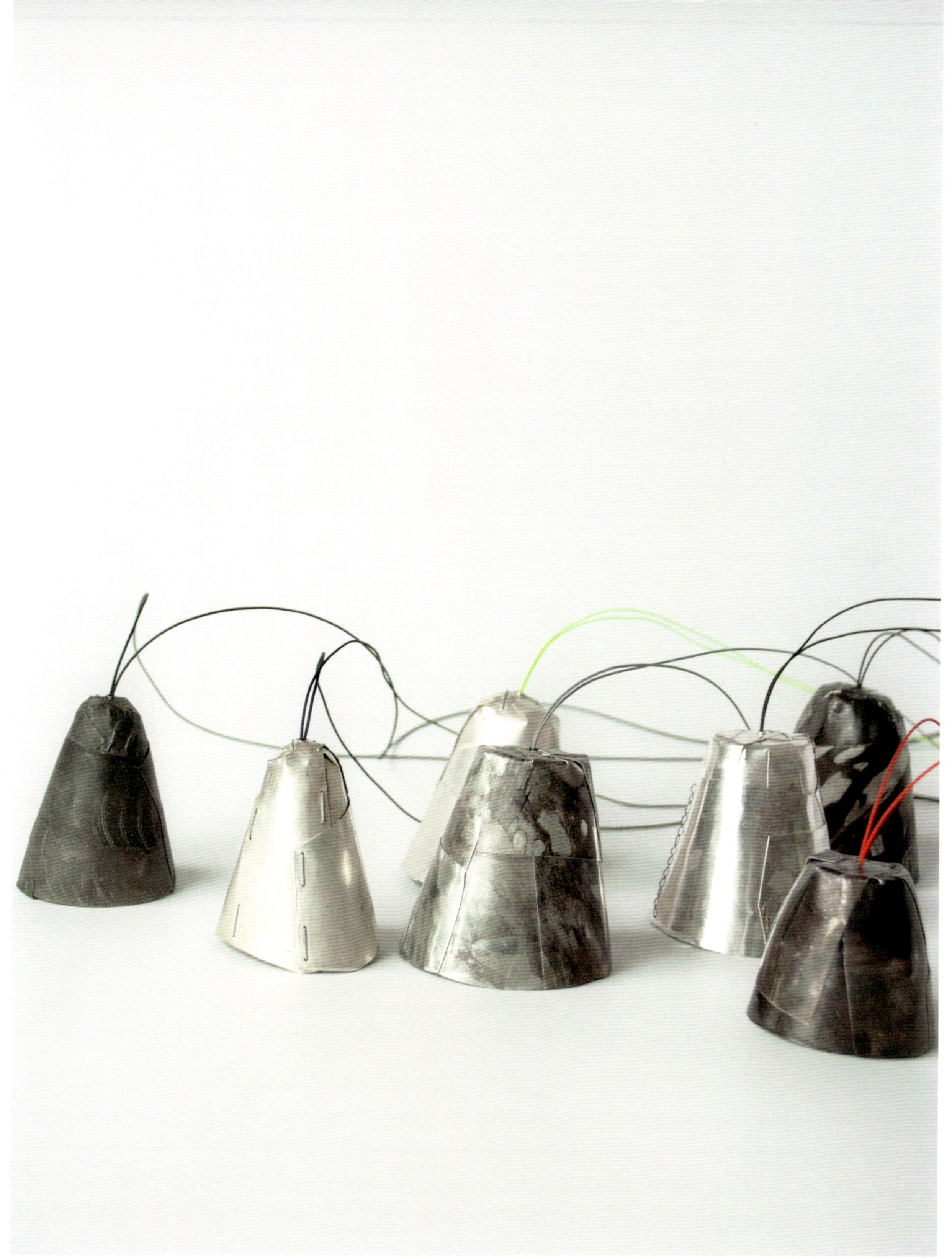

I. D.

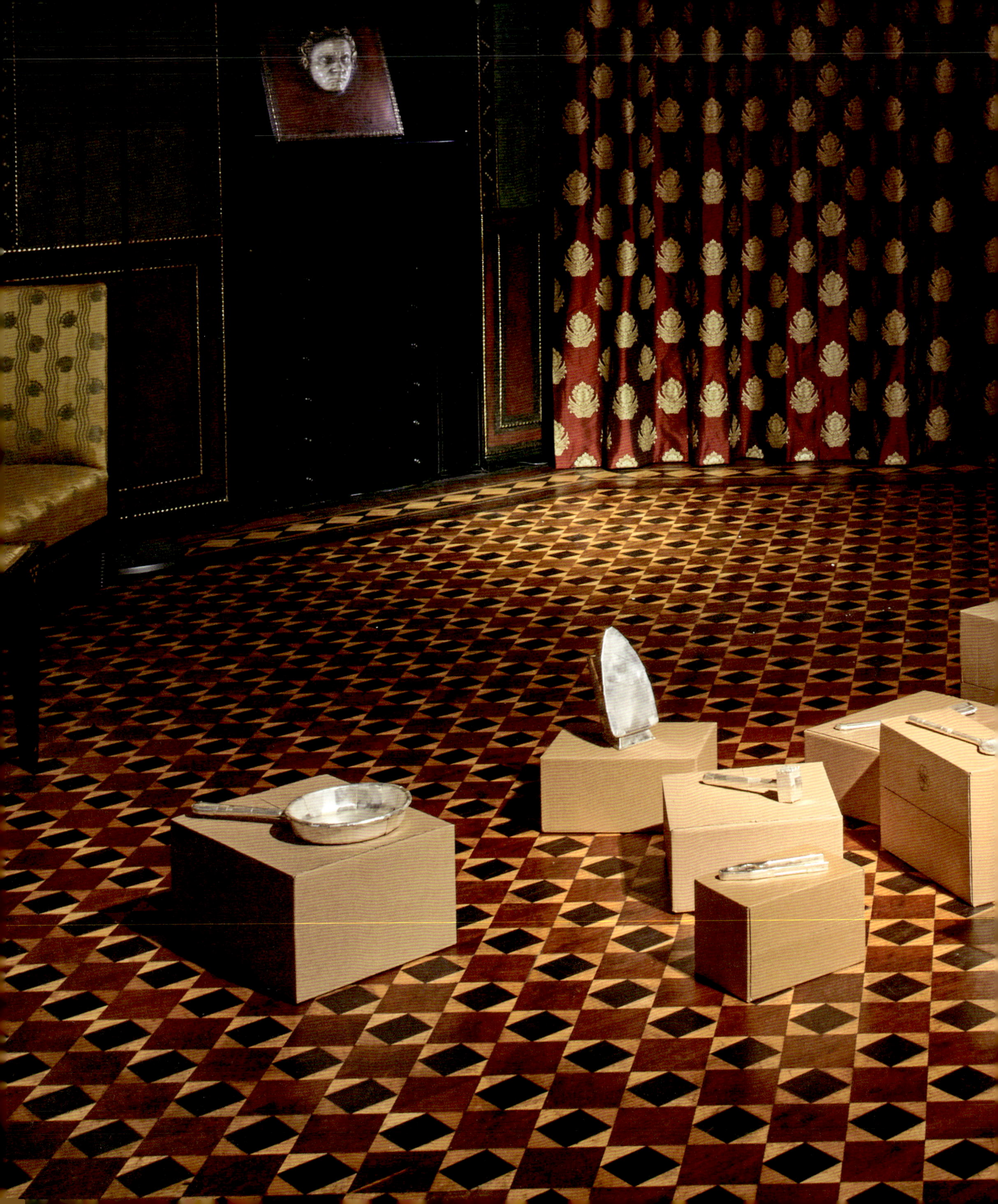

KNELL II

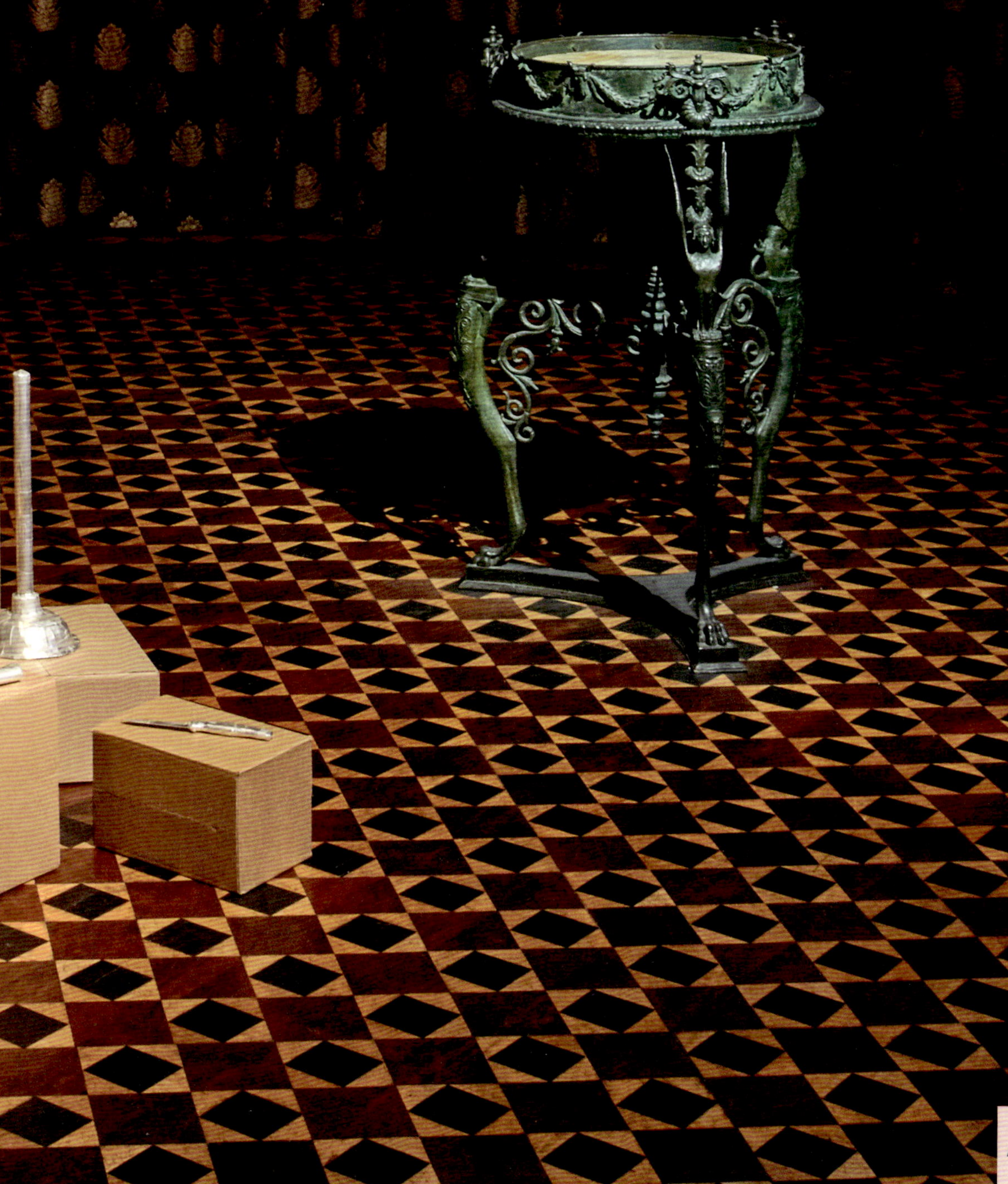

A.N.

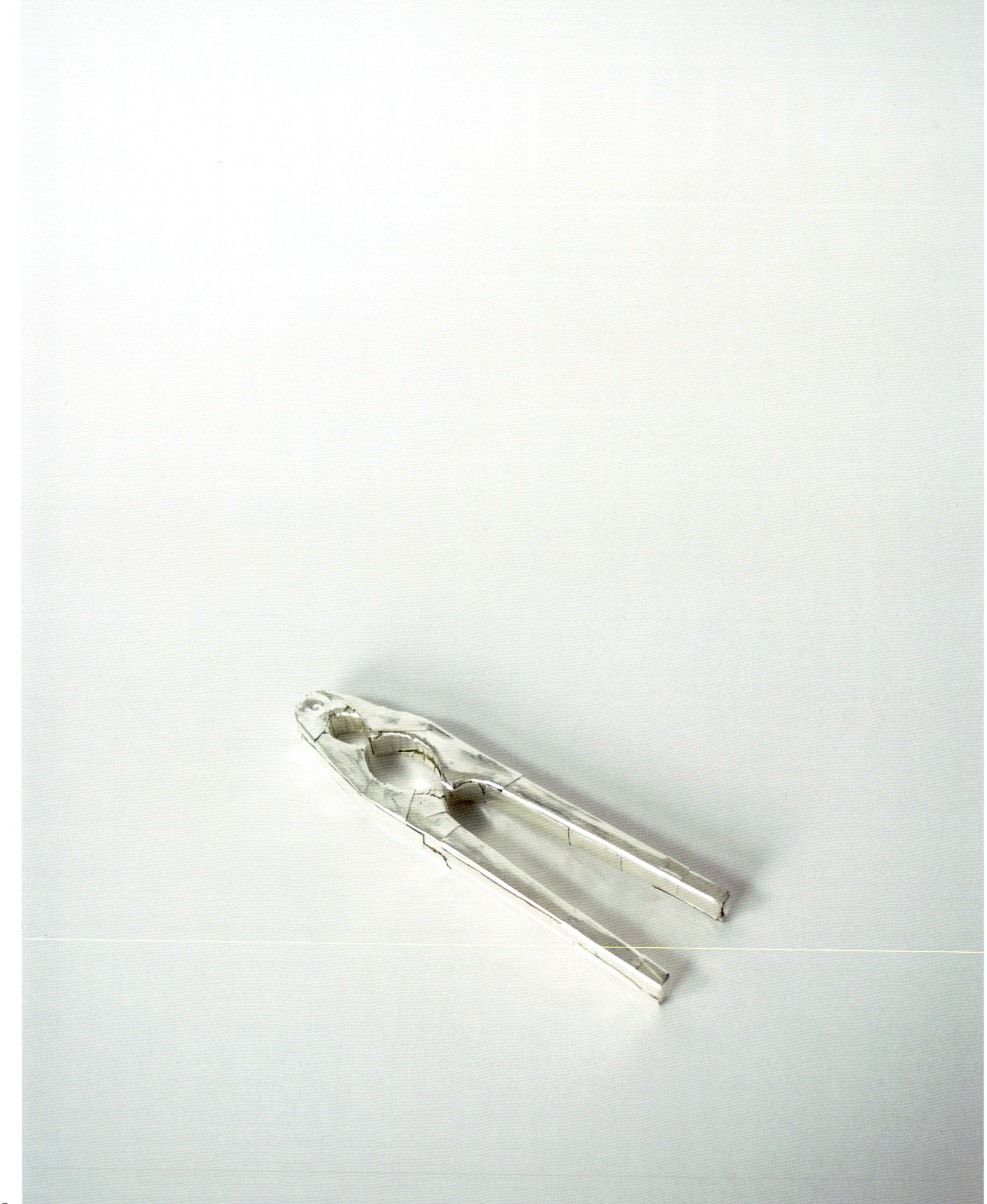

Der Haushalt ist ein naheliegender Schauplatz des Geschlechterkampfs, daher war es nur eine logische Konsequenz, Haushaltsgegenstände als Ansatzpunkt zu wählen. Die filigranen Stücke sind als Ergebnis dieser Arbeit allesamt aus sehr dünnem Silber gefertigt. Sie erfordern ein Maß an Sorgfalt und feinfühliger Handhabung, welches in unserer heutigen Gesellschaft zunehmend verloren zu gehen scheint.[20]
Ward Schrijver

The world of domestic chores is a likely arena for the "battle between the sexes," so it felt only logical to choose household items as a starting point. The delicate objects, which resulted from these endeavors, are also made of very thin silver. They require an attention and care that seems to be getting more and more lost in our contemporary society.[20]
Ward Schrijver

KNELL II Nussknacker (nutcracker) Gerät / hollowware 2018 Silber / silver Klebstoff / glue

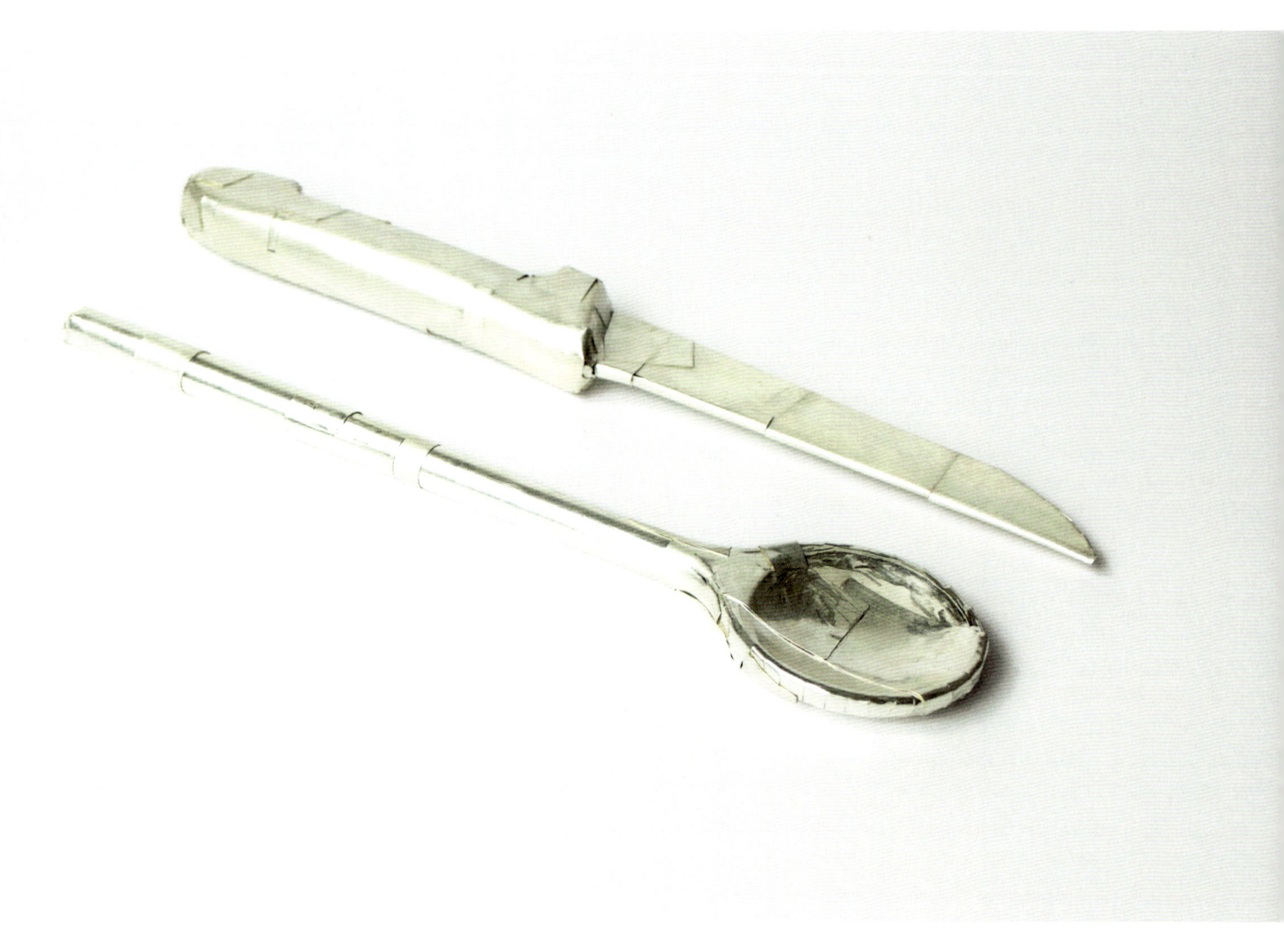

KNELL II Messer (knife) + KNELL II Löffel (spoon) Geräte / hollowware 2017 Silber / silver Klebstoff / glue
KNELL II Hammer (hammer) Gerät / hollowware 2018 Silber / silver Klebstoff / glue

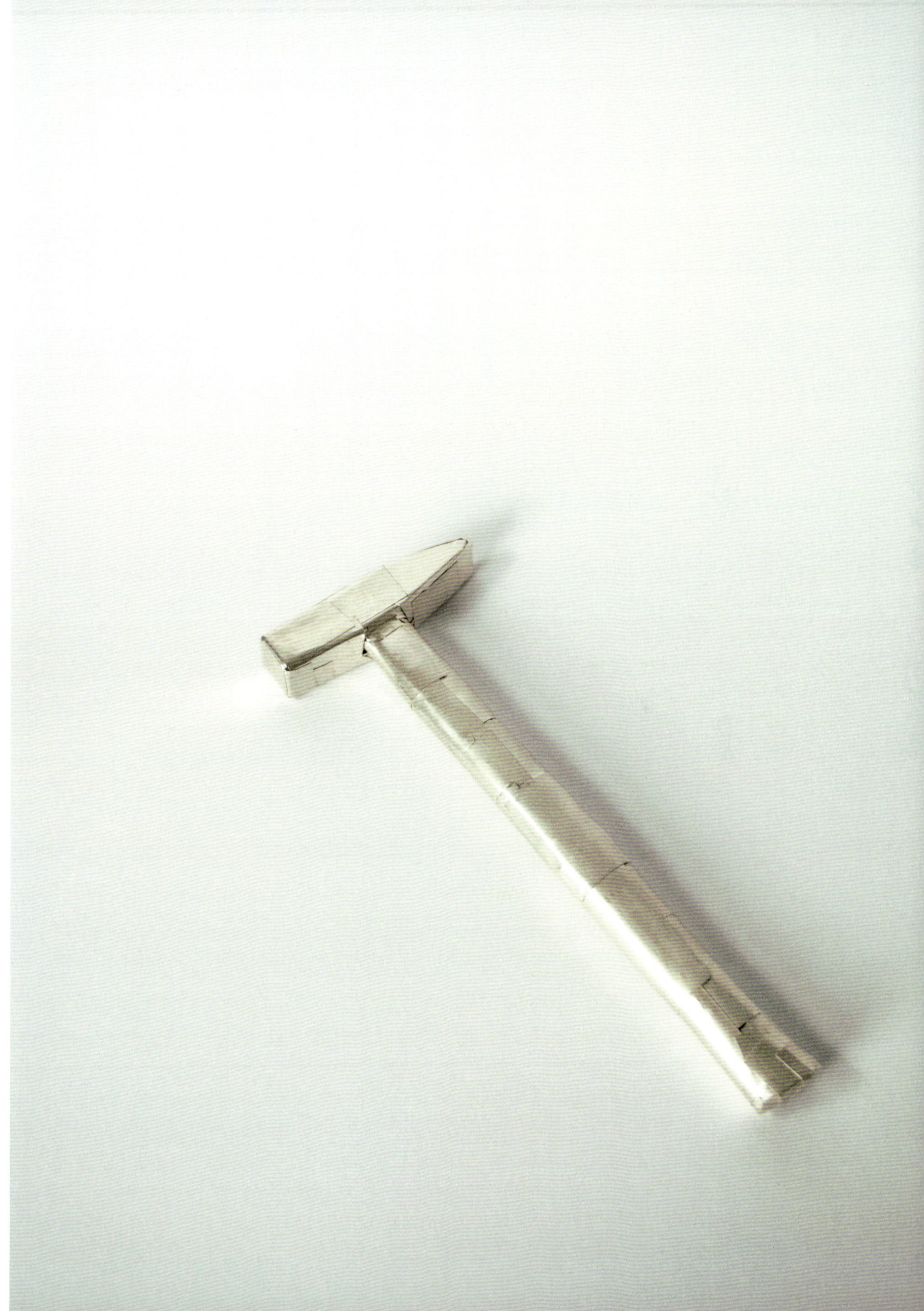

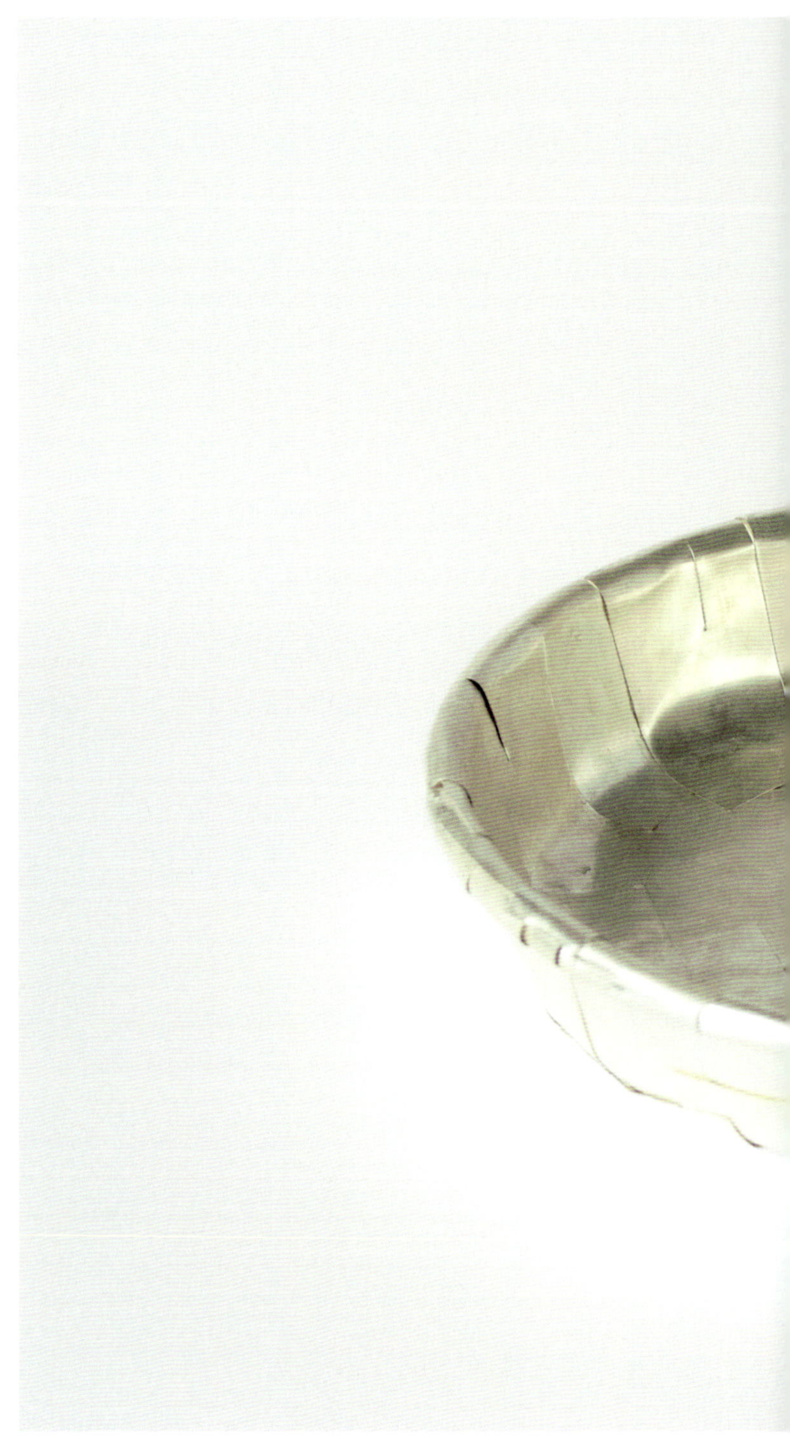

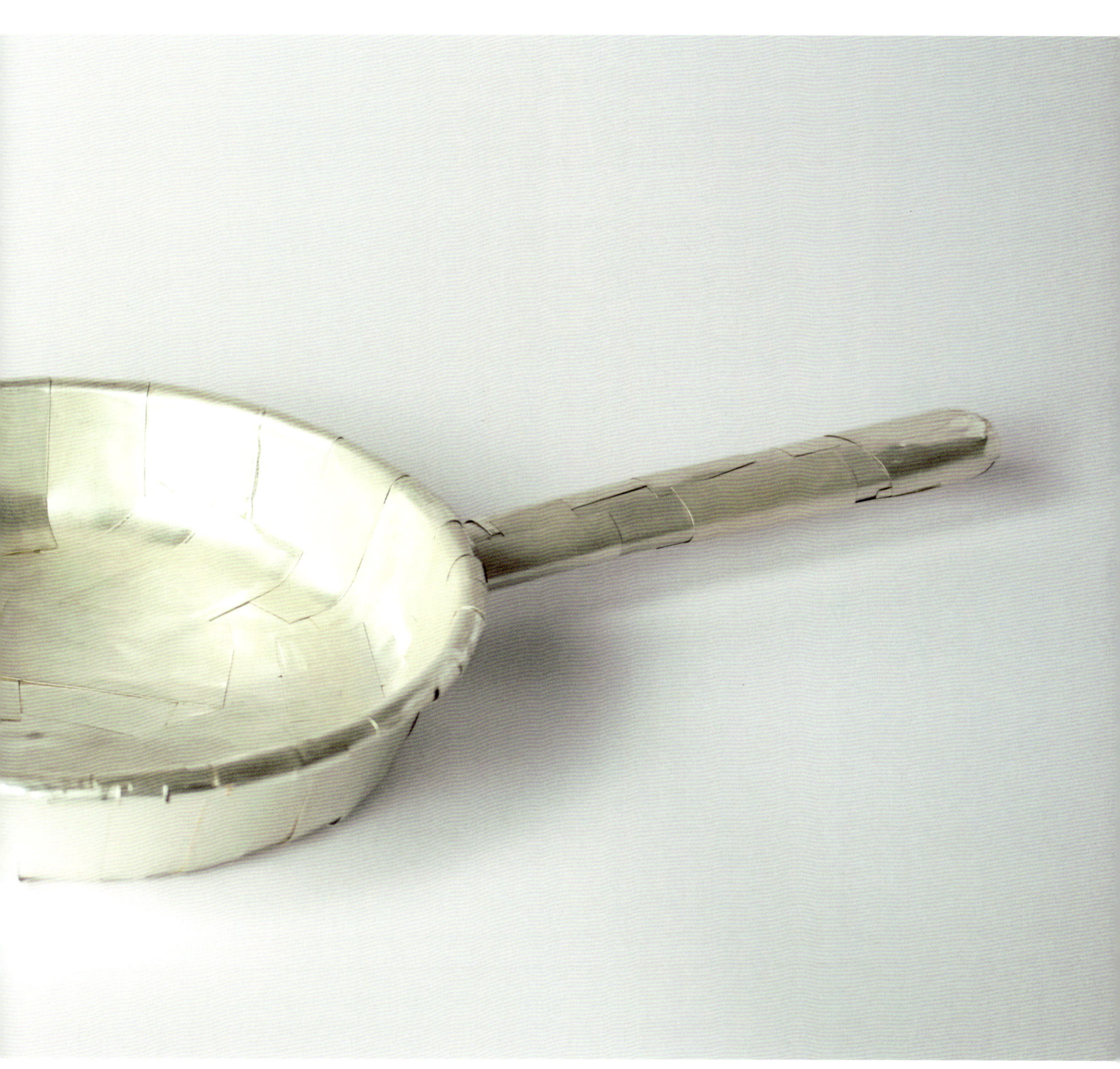

KNELL II Pfanne (frying pan) Gerät / hollowware 2018 Silber / silver Klebstoff / glue

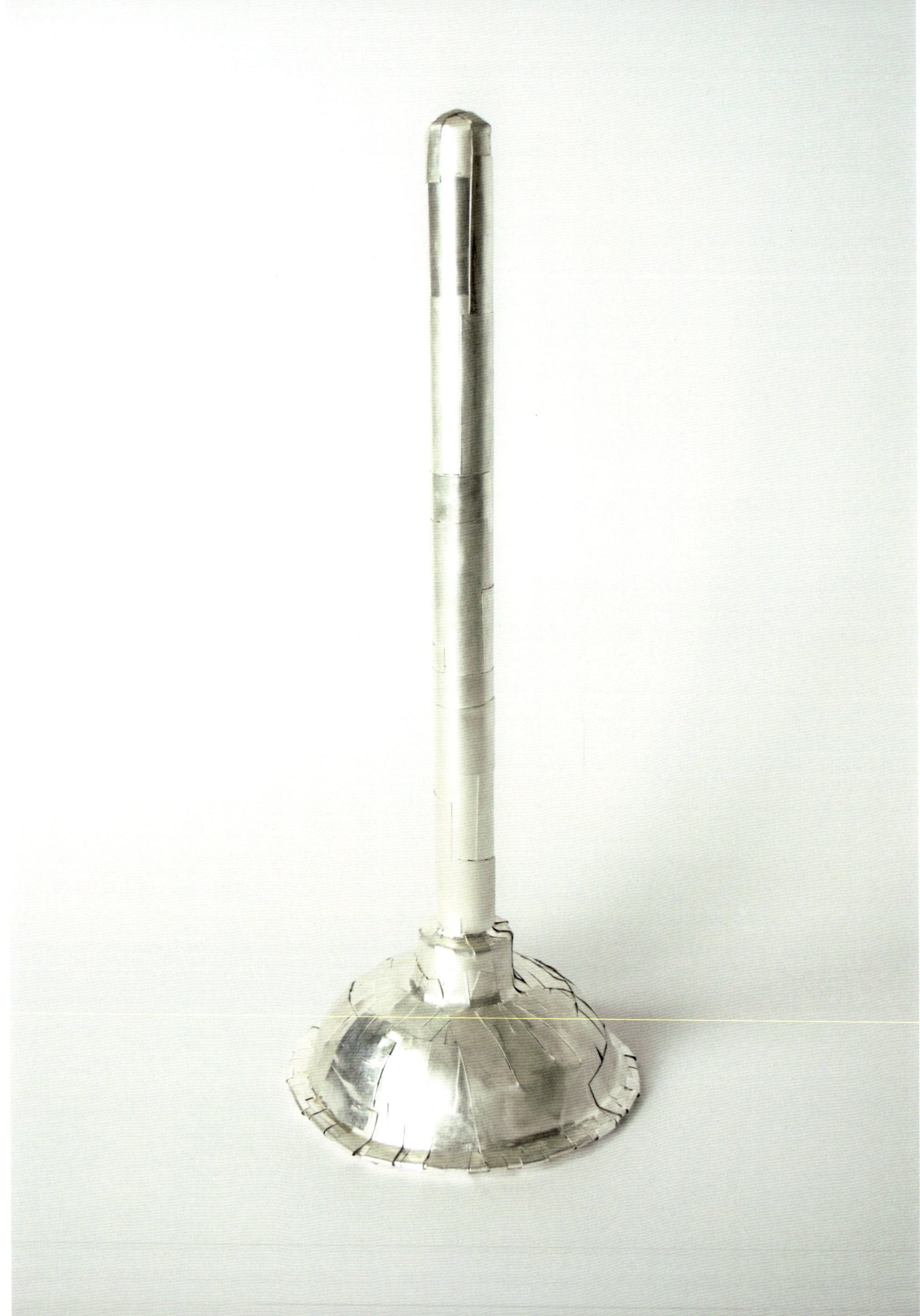

In der heutigen Gesellschaft kann Schmuck weder geschlechtsneutral sein, noch können die Geschlechter schmuckneutral sein.[21]
A.N.

In today's society, it is no longer possible for jewelry to be gender neutral nor is it possible for gender to be jewelry neutral.[21]
A.N.

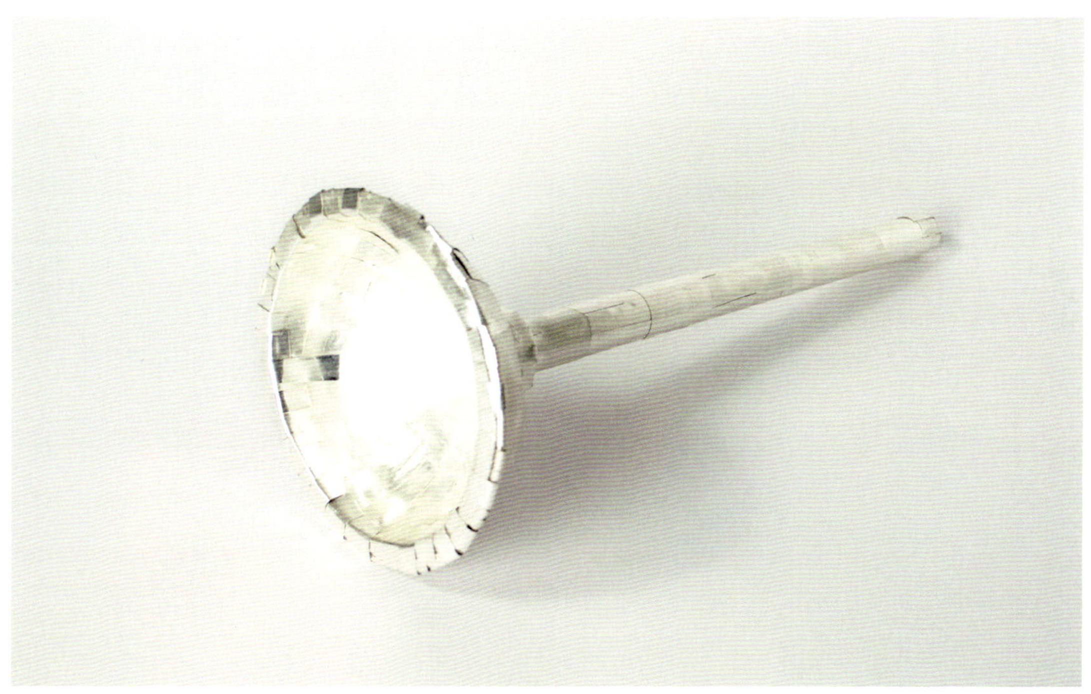

KNELL II Pömpel (plunger) Gerät / hollowware 2018 Silber / silver Klebstoff / glue

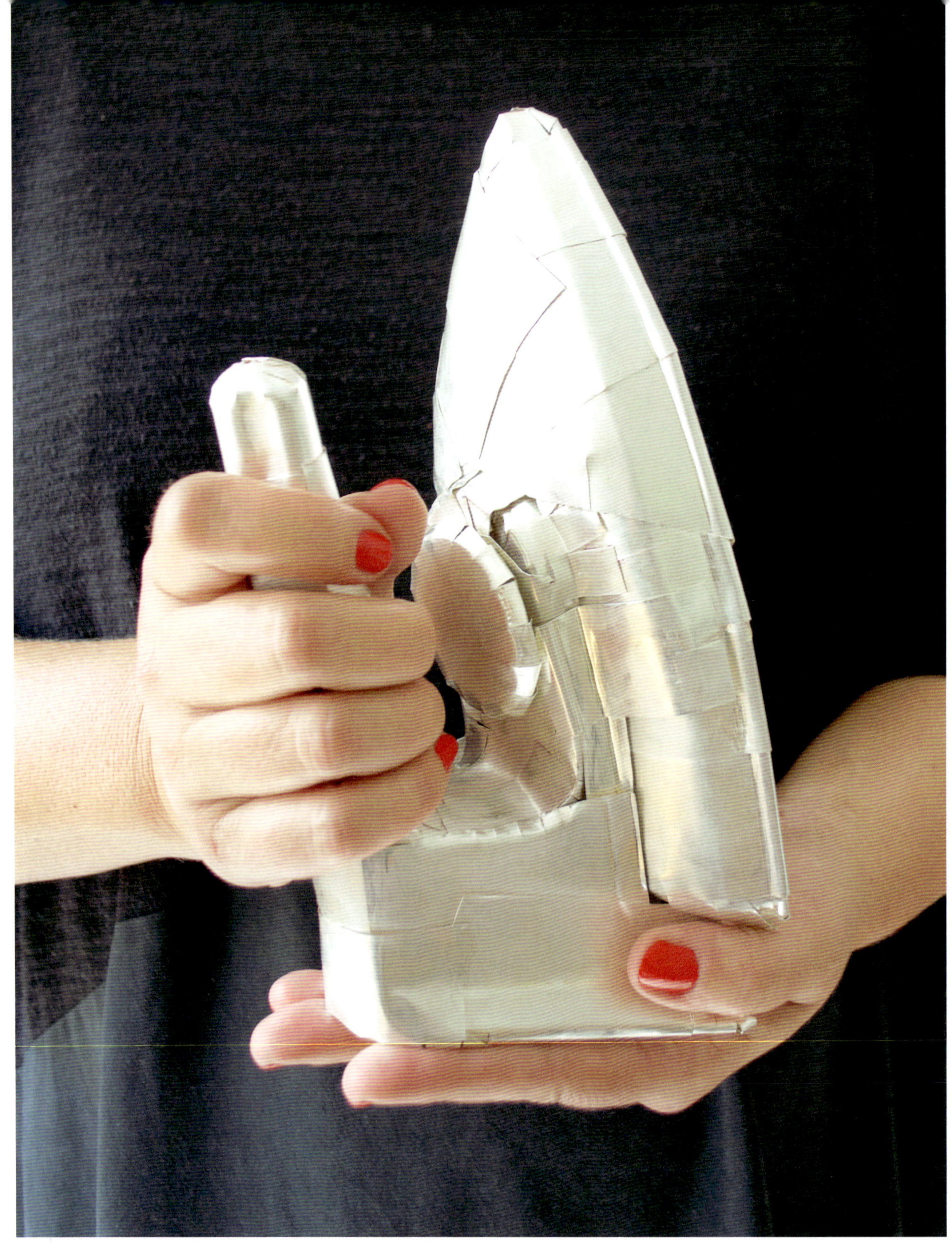

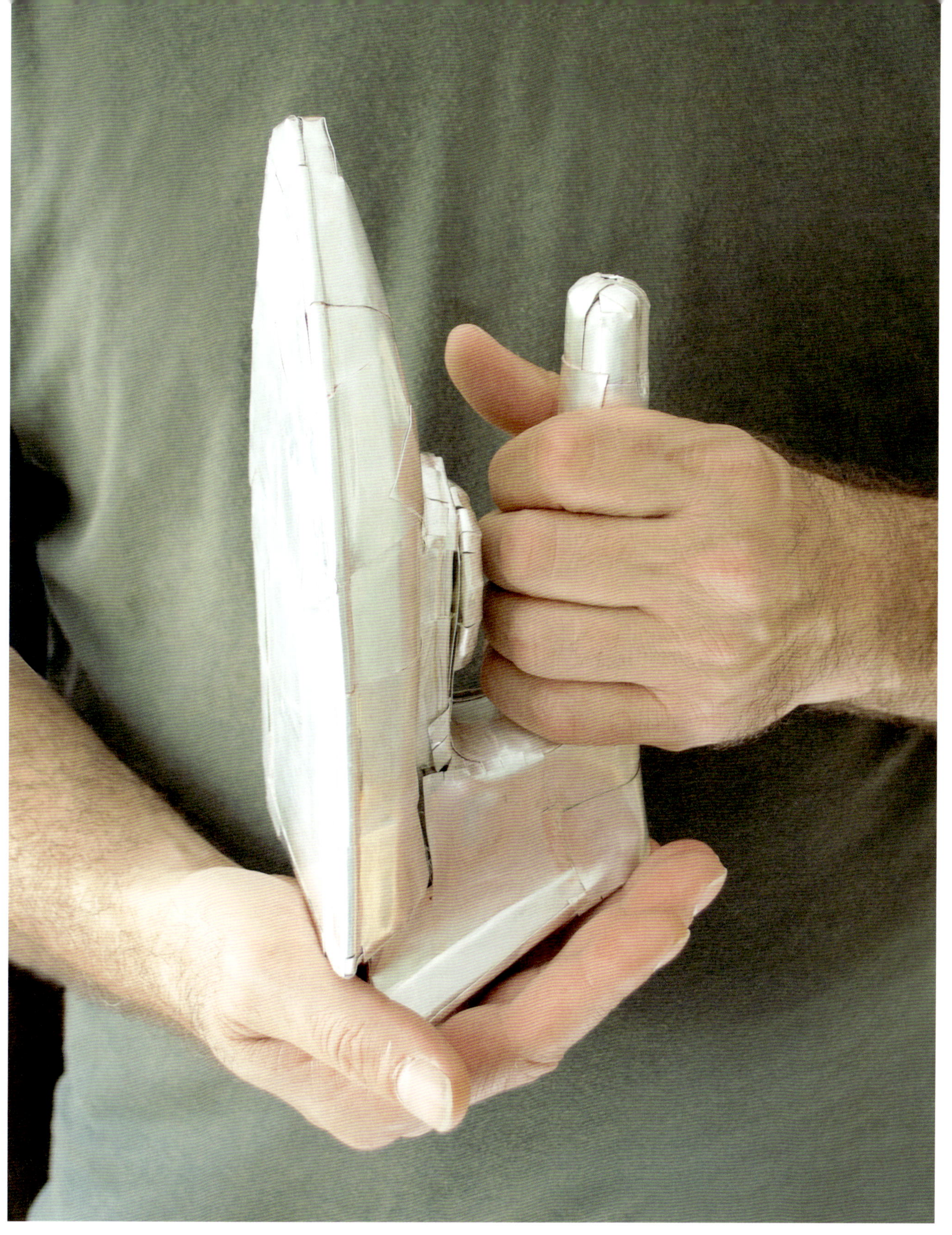

KNELL II Bügeleisen (iron) Gerät / hollowware 2017 Silber / silver Klebstoff / glue

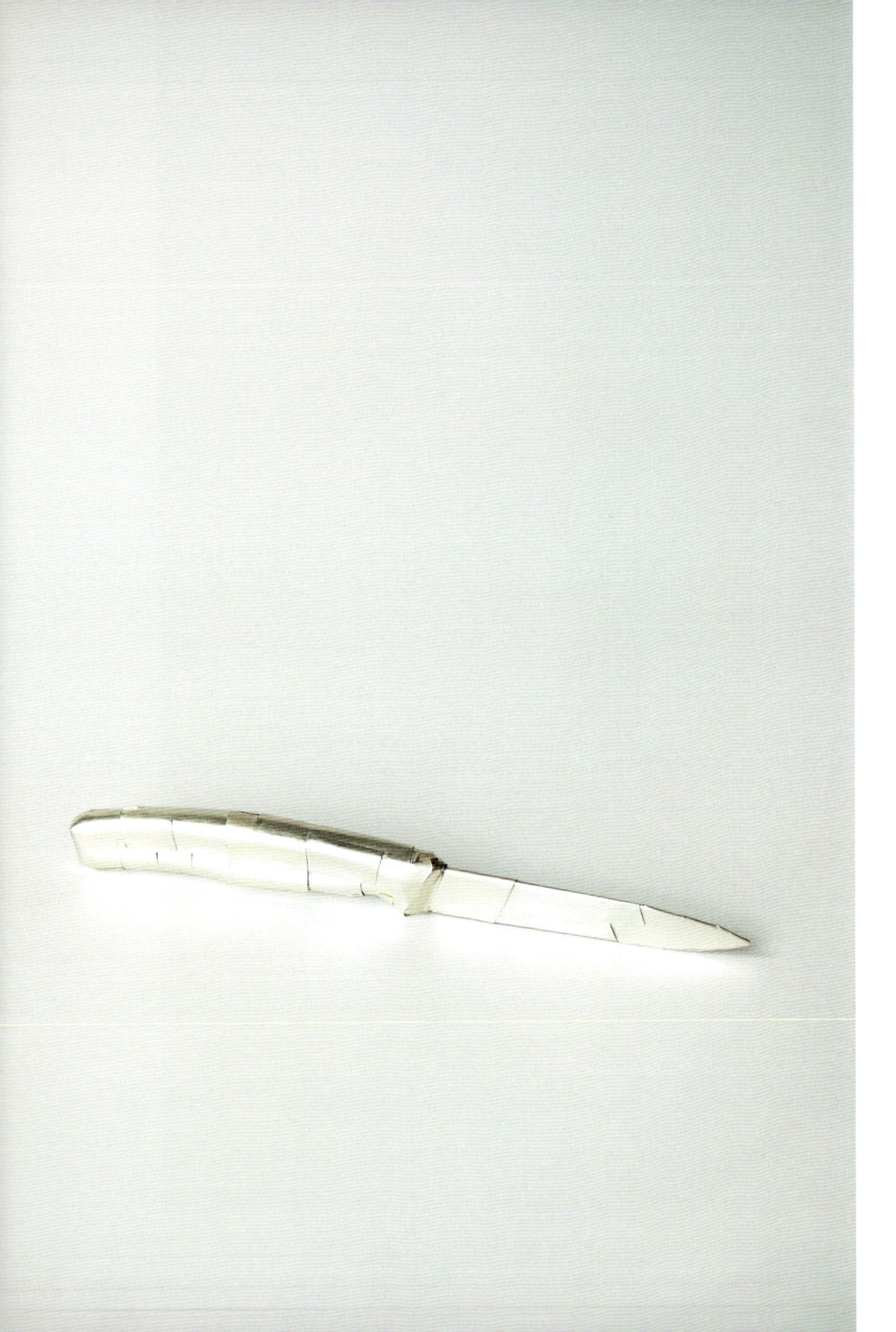

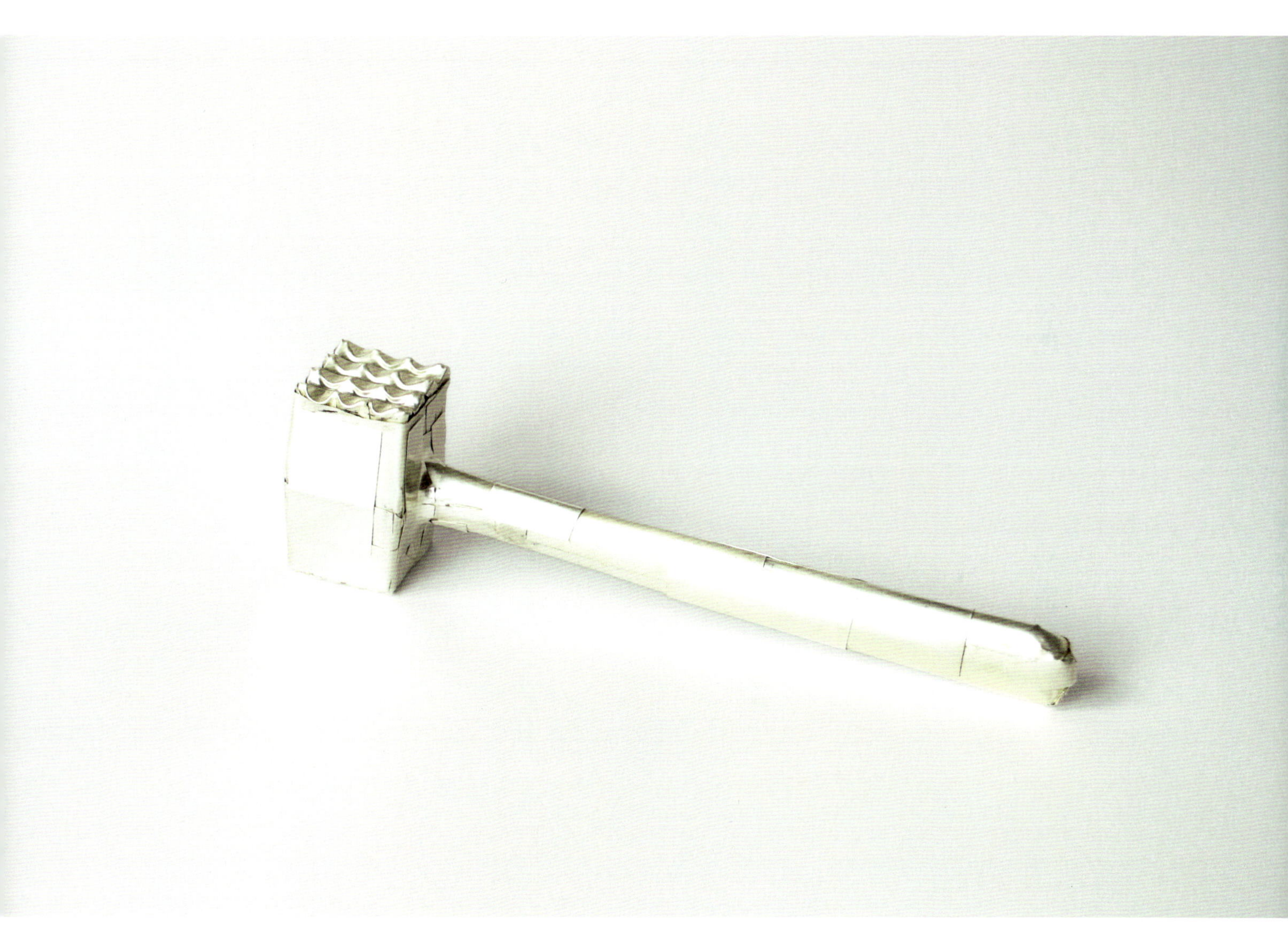

KNELL II Gemüsemesser (vegetable knife) Gerät / hollowware 2018 Silber / silver Klebstoff / glue
KNELL II Fleischhammer (meat tenderizer) Gerät / hollowware 2018 Silber / silver Klebstoff / glue

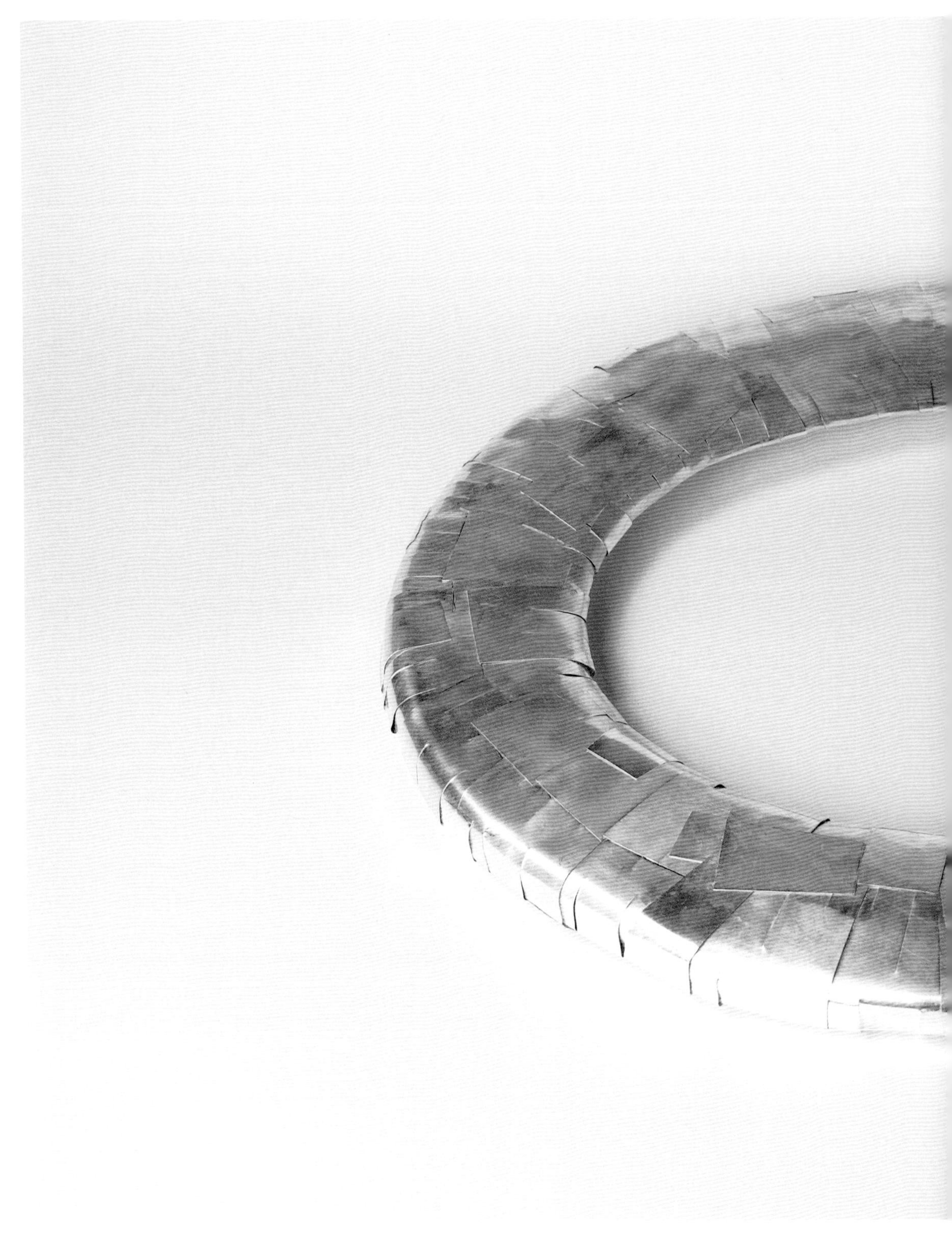

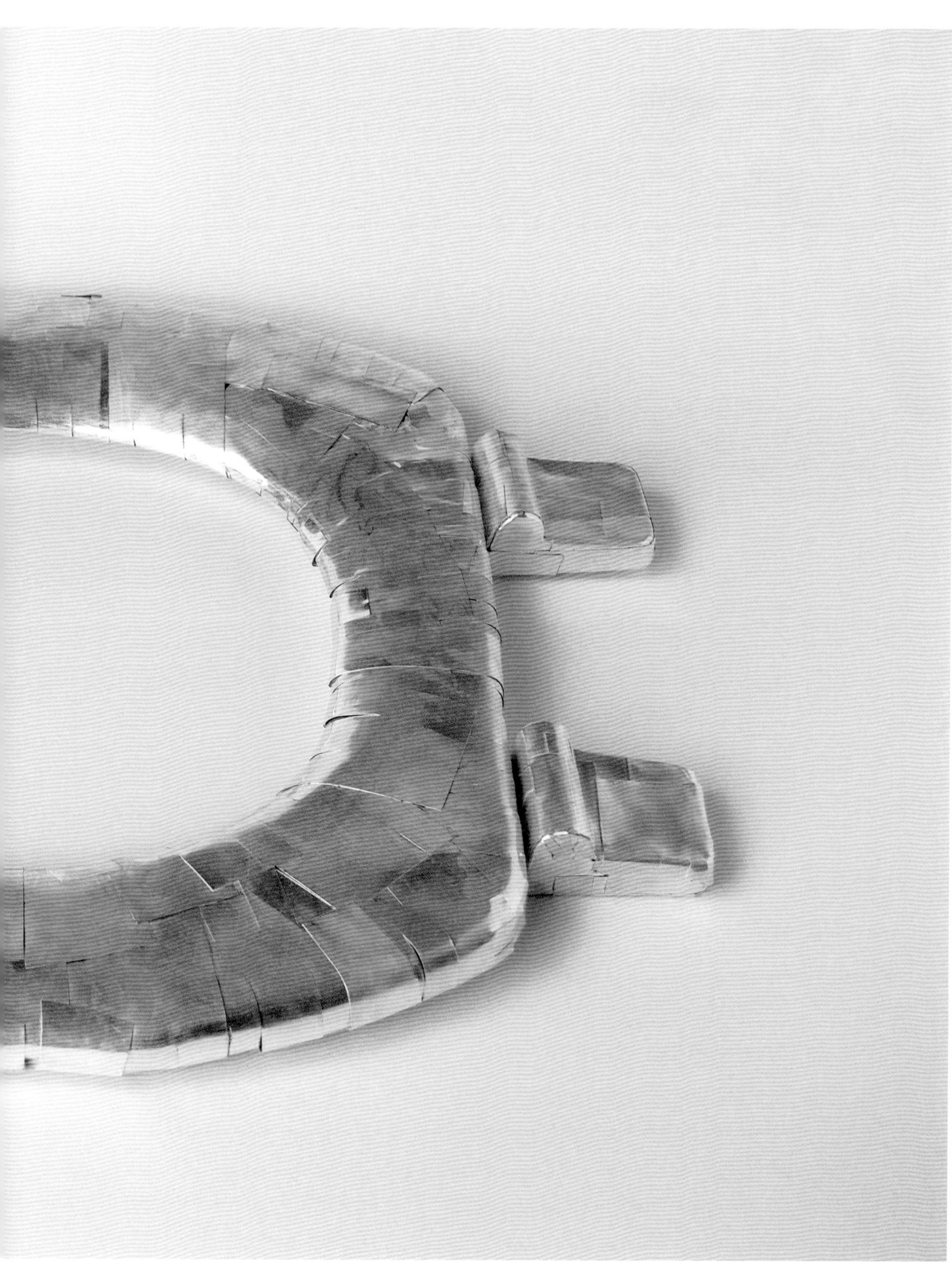

:NELL II Klobrille (toilet seat) Gerät / hollowware 2019 Silber / silver Klebstoff / glue

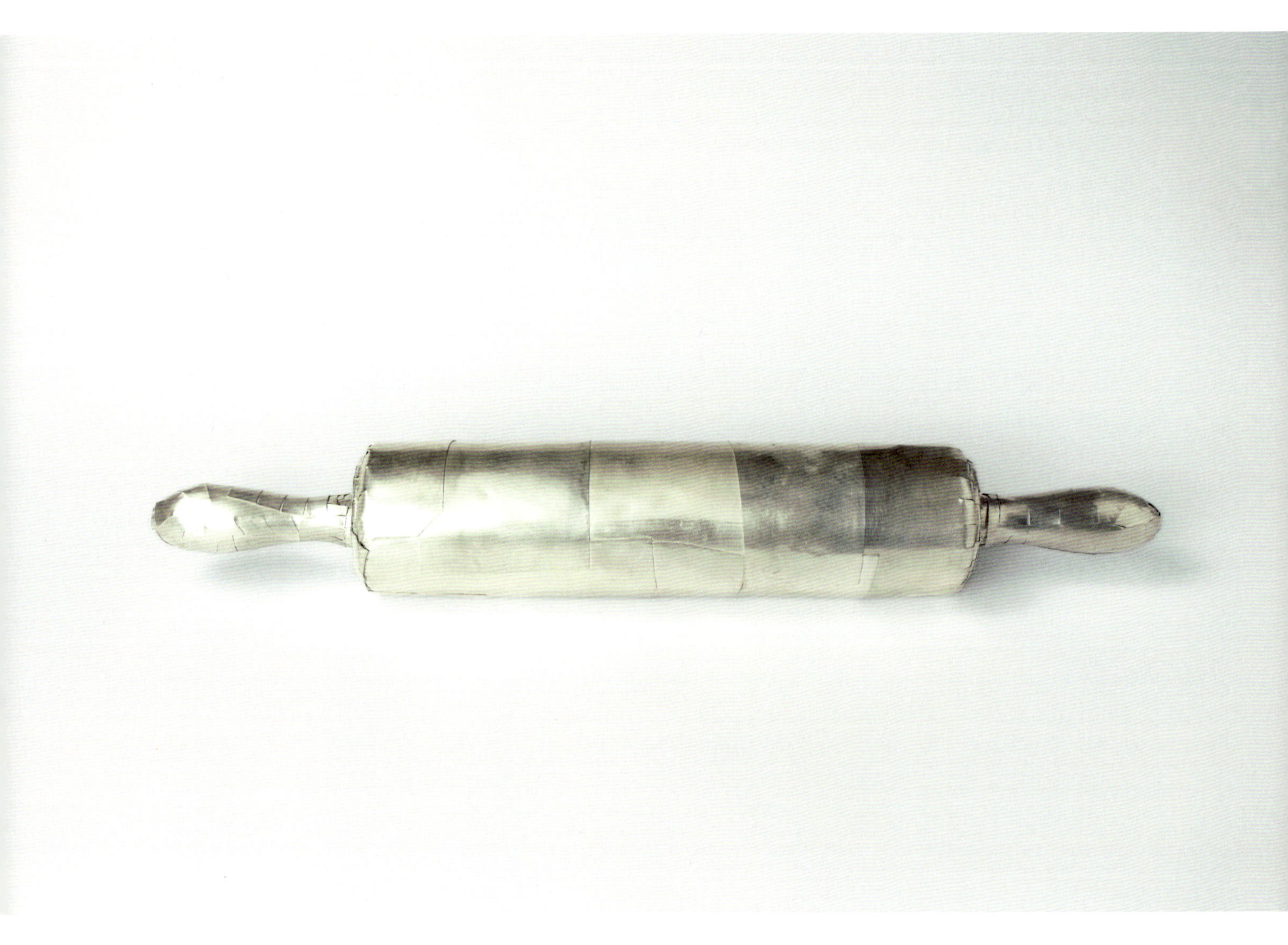

KNELL II Nudelholz (rolling pin) Gerät / hollowware 2019 Silber / silver Klebstoff / glue

Zitate / Quotations

1 Unveröffentlichter Text von Karen Pontoppidan. / Unpublished text by Karen Pontoppidan.
2 Otto Künzli, »Wie wenn ein Kind die Füße in den noch warmen Kuhfladen steckt«, in: Reizstoffe. Positionen zum zeitgenössischen Kunsthandwerk: 75 Jahre Danner-Stiftung, Stuttgart 1995, S. / p. 204 / Übersetzt von / by Wendy Brouwer / Translated von Wendy Brouwer.
3 Barbara Maas, »Vom Schmuck und vom Menschen«, in: Choice, hrsg. v. / eds. Elisabeth Holder und / and Herman Hermsen, Ausst.-Kat. / exh. cat. Museum of Arts and Crafts Itami / JP, Galerie YU, Hiko Mizuno College Tokyo / JP, Schmuckmuseum Pforzheim / DE, Schmuck- und Edelsteinmuseum Turnov / CZ, Düsseldorf 2005/2006, S. / p. 203. / Translated into English by Timothy M. Green.
4 Unveröffentlichter Text von Karen Pontoppidan. / Unpublished text by Karen Pontoppidan.
5 Aus einem unveröffentlichten Text von Carin E.M. Reinders, Apeldoorn 2017. / From an unpublished text by Carin E.M. Reinders, Apeldoorn 2017.
6 Aus einem unveröffentlichten Text von Pravu Mazumdar. / From an unpublished text by Pravu Mazumdar.
7 Ward Schrijver, Karen Pontoppidan FAMILYPORTRAITS, www.galerierobkoudijs.nl, Amsterdam 2009.
8 Unveröffentlichter Text von Karen Pontoppidan. / Unpublished text by Karen Pontoppidan.
9 Ward Schrijver, Karen Pontoppidan CANVAS, www.galerierobkoudijs.nl, Amsterdam 2011.
10 Aus einem unveröffentlichten Text von Karen Pontoppidan. / From an unpublished text by Karen Pontoppidan.
11 Aus einem unveröffentlichten Text von Karen Pontoppidan. / From an unpublished text by Karen Pontoppidan.
12 Ward Schrijver, Karen Pontoppidan CONTEXT, www.galerierobkoudijs.nl, Amsterdam 2013.
13 CURRENT OBSESSION, www.current-obsession.com, 2014.
14 Aus einem unveröffentlichten Text von Carin E.M. Reinders, Apeldoorn 2017. / From an unpublished text by Carin E.M. Reinders, Apeldoorn 2017.
15 Ward Schrijver, Karen Pontoppidan CASH, www.galerierobkoudijs.nl, Amsterdam 2015.
16 CURRENT OBSESSION, www.current-obsession.com, 2014.
17 Angelika Nollert, in: KNELL The Gender Bell, Ausst.-Kat. / exh. cat. Maurer Zilioli – Contemporary Arts München 2017. / Translated into English by Wendy Brouwer.
18 Jasmin Matzakow, in: KNELL The Gender Bell, Ausst.-Kat. / exh. cat. Maurer Zilioli – Contemporary Arts München 2017. / Translated into English by Wendy Brouwer.
19 Barbara Vinken, in: KNELL The Gender Bell, Ausst.-Kat. / exh. cat. Maurer Zilioli – Contemporary Arts München 2017. / Translated into English by Wendy Brouwer.
20 Ward Schrijver, Karen Pontoppidan KNELL, www.galerierobkoudijs.nl, Amsterdam 2018.
21 Unveröffentlichter Text von Karen Pontoppidan. / Unpublished text by Karen Pontoppidan.

Fotonachweise / Photo Credits

Jann Averwerser, S. / pp. 22/23, 34/35, 58/59, 74/75, 90/91, 98/99, 110/111, 124/125
Antje Hanebeck, VG Bild-Kunst, Bonn 2019, S. / pp. 36, 57
Susanne Dell, Hintergrundbild / background photo, S. / pp. 68/69
Oliver Hofmeister, S. / p. 121
Alle anderen Abbildungen von / all other pictures by Karen Pontoppidan.

KAREN
PONTOPPIDAN 29. Februar / February 29, 1968 . Kerteminde . DK

Ausbildung / Education

1986–1988	Praktikum / Internship . Gerda Lynggaard / Monies . Kopenhagen / Copenhagen . DK
1988–1991	Ausbildung zur Formgeberin / Training as jeweler . Berufskolleg für Formgebung Schmuck und Gerät Schwäbisch Gmünd . DE
1991–1997	Studium / Study . Klasse / class Prof Otto Künzli . Akademie der Bildenden Künste / Academy of Fine Arts München / Munich . DE
1995	Meisterschülerin
1998	Diplom / Diploma . Akademie der Bildenden Künste / Academy of Fine Arts . München / Munich . DE
Seit / since 1997	Atelier / studio . München / Munich . DE

Lehrtätigkeit / Teaching Experience

2000–2006	Assistentin / Assistant professor von / by Prof Otto Künzli . Akademie der Bildenden Künste / Academy of Fine Arts . München / Munich . DE
2003–2004	Gastdozentin / Guest professor . Fachhochschule . Düsseldorf . DE
2005–2006	Gastdozentin / Guest professor . Hochschule . Pforzheim . DE
2006–2015	Professorin / professor . Ädellab . Konstfack University of Arts Crafts and Design . Stockholm . SE
seit 2015	Professorin / professor . Akademie der Bildenden Künste / Academy of Fine Arts . München / Munich . DE

Workshops / Tutorials

2003	Jewellery & Taboo . Workshop . Koru 1 Symposium . South Karelia Polytechnic . Lappeenranta . FI
	Jewellery & Taboo . Workshop . Konstfack University of Arts Crafts and Design . Stockholm . SE
2004	Jewellery & Taboo . Workshop . Institutet for Ædelmetal . Kopenhagen / Copenhagen . DK
	From Food to Spoon . Workshop . Hiko Mizuno College of Jewelry . Tokio / Tokyo . JP
2005	Jewellery & Taboo . Workshop . Gerrit Rietveld Academy . Amsterdam . NL
	Externe Examinatorin / Opponent . Institutet for Ædelmetal . Kopenhagen / Copenhagen . DK
2006	Tutorin / tutor . Diplom / diploma . Hochschule . Pforzheim . DE
	Tutorin / tutor . MfA-Examen / MfA exam . Ädellab . Konstfack University of Arts Crafts and Design Stockholm . SE
	Arven . Workshop . Institutet for Ædelmetal . Kopenhagen / Copenhagen . DK
	Enamelmania! . Workshop . Institutet for Ædelmetal . Kopenhagen / Copenhagen . DK
	to use to make to melt to hate to burn for . Workshop . Ecole d'arts appliqués . Genf / Geneva . CH
2007	Enamelmania! . Workshop . South Karelia Polytechnic . Lappeenranta . FI
2008	Enamel is a bitch . Workshop . Akademie der Bildenden Künste / Academy of Fine Arts . München / Munich . DE
	Tutorin / tutor . Diplom / diploma . Hochschule . Pforzheim . DE
2009	Tutorin / tutor . Diplom / diploma . Hochschule . Pforzheim . DE
2010	Enamelmania! . Workshop . Saimaa University of Applied Sciences . Imatra . FI
2011	Externe Examinatorin / Opponent . MfA-Examen / MfA exam . Bezalel Academy of Art and Design . Jerusalem . IL
2017	Finishing Jewellery . Workshop . China Academy of Art . Hangzhou . CN

Vorträge / Lectures

2000 Karen Pontoppidan . Zimmerhof Symposium . Bad Rappenau . DE
2001 Karen Pontoppidan . Institutet for Ædelmetal . Kopenhagen / Copenhagen . DK
2002 Das Tier in Mir . Galerie V+V . Wien / Vienna . AT
2003 Karen Pontoppidan . Koru 1 . Symposium . South Karelia Polytechnic . Lappeenranta . FI
Thinking Jewellery . Hochschule für angewandte Wissenschaft und Kunst . Hildesheim . DE
Thinking Jewellery . Galerie Platina . Stockholm . SE
2004 Smykker . Holbæk Kunsthøjskole . Holbæk . DK
Smykker . Institutet for Ædelmetal . Kopenhagen / Copenhagen . DK
2005 Schmück Dich! . Hochschule . Pforzheim . DE
Schmück Dich! . Gerrit Rietveld Academy . Amsterdam . NL
2006 Talking Jewellery . Rhode Island School of Design . Providence . USA
Talking Jewellery . Rhode Island College . Providence . USA
Talking Jewellery . Konstfack University College of Arts Crafts and Design . Stockholm . SE
Schmück Dich! . Akademie der Bildenden Künste . München / Munich . DE
Talking Jewellery . Ecole d'arts appliqués . Genf / Geneva . CH
Talking Jewellery . Institutet for Ædelmetal . Kopenhagen / Copenhagen . DK
2007 Talking Jewellery . South Karelia Polytechnic . Lappeenranta . FI
2008 Educating Artists . Palazzo Vecchio . Florenz / Florence . IT
Educating Artists . MUDAC . Lausanne . CH
Why I do What I do . Konstfack University College of Arts Crafts and Design . Stockholm . SE
2011 Ramble . The Spirit of Stones . Symposium . Lappeenranta . FI
Why I do What I do. Bezalel Academy of Art and Design . Jerusalem . IL
2013 The State of Things . From The Coolest Corner Symposium . KHIO . NO
2014 Jewellery & Gender . WCC-BF . Mons . BE
2015 Jewellery & Gender . KORU 5 . Imatra . FI
Jewellery & Society . Denmarks Design Museum . Kopenhagen / Copenhagen . DK
2016 Why Jewellery? . Samia University . Imatra . FI
2017 Why I Love Jewellery . China Academy of Art . Hangzhou . CN
A Very Rough Guide to Jewellery History and Why It Matters! . Ädellab . Konstfack University College of Arts Crafts and Design . Stockholm . SE

Weitere Tätigkeiten / Further Activities

1994	Herausgeberin / Publisher . [ʃmΔk] Magazin . München / Munich . DE
2002	Teilnehmerin / Participant . Erfurter Schmuck Symposium . Erfurt . DE
	Artist in Residence . Gallery V+V . Wien / Vienna . AT
2006	Jurymitglied / Member of the jury . Scandal . Legnica Silver Competition . Legnica . PL
2007	Kuratorin der Ausstellung / Curator of the exhibition . Konnti . Helsinki . FI
2008	Jurymitglied / Member of the jury . Krawatte . Handwerks Museum . Deggendorf . DE
	Podiumsdiskutantin / Podium-discourse . Salone de' Cinquecento . Palazzo Vecchio . Florenz / Florence . IT
2009	Eröffnungsrede / Opening Speech . Nothing in Common . Kunstarkaden . München / Munich . DE
2010	Jurymitglied / Member of the jury . Talente . IHM . München / Munich . DE
	Jurymitglied / Member of the jury . Oberbayerischer Förderpreis für Angewandte Kunst . Freising . DE
2011	Jurymitglied / Member of the jury . Talente . IHM . München / Munich . DE
	Jurymitglied / Member of the jury . Oberbayerischer Förderpreis für Angewandte Kunst . München / Munich . DE
2012	Kuratorin der Ausstellung / Curator of the exhibition . Ädellab – The State of Things . Die Neue Sammlung – International Design Museum . Pinakothek der Moderne . München / Munich . DE
2013	Jurymitglied / Member of the jury . Talente . IHM . München / Munich . DE
	Podiumsdiskutantin / Podium-discourse . From The Coolest Corner Symposium . KHIO . NO
	Eröffnungsrede / Opening Speech . SUBSTANCE . Gustavsberg Konsthall . Gustavsberg . SE
seit 2013	Mitglied der Ankaufskommission der Dannerstiftung / Member of the jewellery committee of the Danner Foundation . München / Munich . DE
2014	Kuratorin der Ausstellung / Curator of the exhibition . The Talking Table . Galerie Rossana Orlandi . Mailand / Milan . IT
2015	Kuratorin der Ausstellung / Curator of the exhibition . LAGOMLAND . Galerie für Angewandte Kunst München / Munich . DE
2016	Jurymitglied / Member of the jury . Grassi Messe . Grassi Museum . Leipzig . DE
seit / since 2016	Vizepräsidentin / Vice President . Akademie der Bildenden Künste / Academy of Fine Arts . München / Munich . DE
2019	Kuratorin der Ausstellung / Curator of the exhibition . SCHMUCKISMUS . Die Neue Sammlung – International Design Museum . Pinakothek der Moderne . München / Munich . DE

Arbeiten in öffentlichen Sammlungen / Works in Public Collections

CODA Museum . Apeldoorn . NL
Cooper Hewitt . Smithsonian National Design Museum . New York . USA
Die Neue Sammlung – The Design Museum . München / Munich
Grassi Museum . Leipzig . DE
Hiko Mizuno College of Jewelry . Tokio / Tokyo . JP
Alice and Louis Koch Collection . National Museum . Zürich / Zurich . CH
Københavns Kunstforeningen . Kopenhagen / Copenhagen . DK
Marzee Collection . Nijmegen . NL
Nasjonalmuseet for Kunst Arkitektur og Design . Oslo . NO
Röhsska Museum . Göteburg / Gothenborg . SE
Schmuckmuseum Pforzheim . Pforzheim . DE

Einzelausstellungen / Solo Exhibitions

2019	THE ONE WOMAN GROUP EXHIBITION . Museum Villa Stuck . München / Munich . DE (K)
2018	KNELL . Galerie Rob Koudijs . Amsterdam . NL
2017	KNELL – The Gender Bell . Maurer Zilioli – Contemporary Arts . München / Munich . DE (K)
	WOMEN . Galerie Platina . Stockholm . SE (mit / with B. Speckner J. Yang)
2015	CASH . Galerie Rob Koudijs . Amsterdam . NL
2014	CANVAS_CONTEXT_CASH . Maurer Zilioli – Contemporary Arts . München / Munich . DE (K)
2013	CONTEXT . Galerie Rob Koudijs . Amsterdam . NL
	CONTEXT . Galerie Spektrum . München / Munich . DE
2012	Besser Mit Als Ohne . Event . München / Munich . DE
2011	CANVAS . Galerie Rob Koudijs . Amsterdam . NL
	CANVAS . Galerie Spektrum . München / Munich . DE (K)
	ADAPTATION . Galerie V+V . Wien / Vienna . AT
2010	Teach Us To Outgrow Our Madness . Galerie Platina . Stockholm . SE (mit / with M. Sadiz)
2009	FAMILY PORTRAIT . Galerie Rob Koudijs . Amsterdam . NL
2008	FAMILY PORTRAIT . Ø 12.714 . Galerie Spektrum . München / Munich . DE (K)
	FAMILY PORTRAIT . Villa Bengel . Idar-Oberstein . DE
	FAMILY PORTRAIT . Galerie Jewelers'Werk . Washington DC . USA
2007	Welcome To My World . Galerie Konsthantverkarna . Stockholm . SE
2006	Ebb and Flow . Maurer Zilioli – Contemporary Arts . Desenzano . IT (mit / with A. Hanebeck)
	Strangely Familiar . Galerie Jewelers'Werk . Washington DC . USA
	An dich gedacht . Galerie V+V . Wien / Vienna . AT
2005	Maniacal Botanical . Galerie Louise Smit . Amsterdam . NL
	Strangely Familiar . Galerie Verzameld Werk . Gent / Ghent . BE
2004	Anima . Galerie Hnoss . Göteborg / Gothenburg . SE
2003	It Takes Two to Tango . Galerie Louise Smit . Amsterdam . NL . (mit / with D. Betz)
	Das Tier in Mir . Galerie Spektrum . München / Munich . DE (K)
2002	A Twist of Beauty . Galerie Jewelers'Werk . Washington DC . USA
	Das Tier in Mir . Galerie V+V . Wien / Vienna . AT
	Chiffre / Dechiffre . Galerie Hermsen . Wiesbaden . DE
2001	Tankevækker . Gladsaxe Hovedbibliotek . Kopenhagen / Copenhagen . DK
2000	Småting og Mirakler
	Galerie Metal . Kopenhagen / Copenhagen . DK
	Schöne Aussichten . Galerie Spektrum . München / Munich . DE (K)
1999	Anatomie und Entomologie . Galerie Francoise Heitsch . München / Munich . DE (mit / with M. Harvey)
1997	Karen Pontoppidan . Galerie Neuer Schmuck . Hannover . DE
	Täglich Neu: Kennerüberraschung . Ausstellungsraum Balanstrasse . München / Munich . DE
1996	H. and P. Fine Jewellery . U Bahn Galerie . München / Munich . DE (mit / with M. Harvey)

Gruppenausstellungen (Auswahl) / Group Exhibitions (selection)

2018 50 Jahre Galerie Handwerk . Galerie Handwerk . München / Munich . DE
Made in Denmark . Grassi Museum für Angewandte Kunst Leipzig . DE (K)
2017 CHROMA . Toldboden . Kerteminde . DK
Private Confessions . Museum Villa Stuck . München / Munich . DE (K); CODA Museum . Apeldoorn . NL (K)
2016 Open Space – Mind Maps . National Museum Design / Kulturhuset . Stockholm . SE (K)
2015 ANSWERING PRAVU . Private Räume / Private Spaces . München / Munich . DE
2014 Platina – 15 Years of Jewellery Art . Färgfabriken . Stockholm . SE
2013 Det Unikke Danske Smykke . Kunstetagerne . Hobro . DK (K)
2012 BACULUM . Jagd- und Fischereimuseum . München / Munich . DE
From Mouth to Mouth . Vitahavet . Konstfack University College . Stockholm . SE
Schmuck . IHM . München / Munich . DE (K)
2011 Embraced . Gustavsbergs Konsthal . Gustavsberg . SE (K)
Värksted . Johannes Larsen Museet . Kerteminde . DK (K)
Castelli Miniature Astri ed Alchimia . Oratorio di San Rocco . Padua / Padova . IT (K)
Fortellinger I Sölv . Kunstnerforbundet . Oslo . NO (K)
2010 Nicht dass Du mir von der Bluse fällst . Galerie für Angewandte Kunst . München / Munich . DE
Schmuck . IHM . München / Munich . DE (K)
2009 Sieren met Dieren . CODA Museum . Apeldoorn . NL
KORU 3 . Imatra Art Museum . Imatra . FI (K)
2008 Des Wahnsinns Fette Beute . Die Neue Sammlung – International Design Museum . Pinakothek der Moderne München / Munich . DE (K)
Framing–The Art of Jewelry . Museum of Contemporary Craft . Portland . USA
De Main à Main . MUDAC . Lausanne . CH (K)
New Play in Art . Heller Garden . Gardone Riviera . IT (K)
All-Ready-Made . Galerie Koppe . Kopenhagen / Copenhagen . DK
Winter . Galerie Platina . Stockholm . SE
2007 Springtime in the Zoo . Galerie Beatrice Lang . Bern . CH
Animal . Galerie Platina . Stockholm . SE
Hnoss . Röhsska Museum . Göteborg / Gothenburg . SE (K)
Schmuck . IHM . München / Munich . DE (K)
2006 Mehr Schmuck! . Schmuckmuseum . Pforzheim . DE
Bijoux et objets émaillés . Galerie Helene Porée . Paris . FR
Schmuck . IHM . München / Munich . DE (K)
Skandal! . Galeria Sztuki . w Legnica . PL (K)
Plus 5 . Galerie Spektrum . München / Munich . DE
Choice . Schmuckmuseum . Pforzheim . DE (K) . Deutsches Goldschmiedehaus . Hanau . DE
Villa Bengel . Idar-Oberstein . DE
2005 Pensieri Preziosi . Oratorio di San Rocco . Padua / Padova . IT (K)
Nomad Room . Centro Cultural de Belém . Lissabon . PT
Choice . Museum of Arts and Crafts . Itami . JP . Galerie YU . Hiko Mizuno Jewelry College . Tokio / Tokyo . JP
CODA Museum . Apeldoorn . NL

2004 Valuable Links . Museum für Völkerkunde . Wien / Vienna . AT (K)
Centre Céramique . Maastricht . BE
Ringe i dialog . National Museum . Kopenhagen / Copenhagen . DK (K)
Gioelleria contemporanea . Studio GR20 . Padua / Padova . IT (K)
Schmuck macht munter . Galerie Detailzwo . Düsseldorf . DE
2003 Experiment Schmuck . Schmuckmuseum . Pforzheim . DE (K)
Schmuck . IHM . München / Munich . DE (K)
Koru 1 . South Karelia Museum . Lappeenranta . FI (K)
2002 Natur und Zeit . Goldschmiedehaus . Hanau . DE (K)
Experiment Schmuck . Angermuseum . Erfurt . DE (K)
2001 Schmuck . IHM . München / Munich . DE (K)
Avantgarde im neuen Jahrtausend . W. W. Haus . Bremen . DE
Von Wegen . Goldschmiedehaus . Hanau . DE (K)
Bijou noir . Galerie Hélène Porée . Paris . FR
Schmuck lebt! . Schmuckmuseum . Pforzheim . DE (K)
20 Jahre Galerie Spektrum . Galerie Spektrum . München / Munich . DE (K)
Mikromegas . Galerie für Angewandte Kunst . München / Munich . DE (K)
American Craft Museum . New York . USA; Musee de l'horlogerie et de l'emaillerie . Genf / Geneva . CH; Galerie YU . Tokio / Tokyo . JP; Powerhouse Museum . Sydney . AU; John Curtis Gallery . Curtis University . Perth . AU; Oratorio di San Rocco . Padua . IT
2000 Vier junge Schmuckkünstlerinnen . Galerie Stühler . Berlin . DE
Schönmachen . Kunsthaus . Kaufbeuren . DE
The Ego Adorned . Koningin Fabiolazaal . Antwerpen / Antwerp . BE (K)
München presenteert . Galerie Louise Smit . Amsterdam . NL
1998 Micro Organism . Galerie Wooster Gardens . New York . USA
Wo anders ist es auch schön . Orangerie . München / Munich . DE
1997 Amsterdam München-Tokyo . Galerie für Angewandte Kunst . München / Munich . DE (K)
The Pavilion of the Gerrit Rietveld Academie . Amsterdam . NL; Gallery YU . Tokio / Tokyo . JP
1996 Schmuck . IHM . München / Munich . DE (K)
Student work . Galerie Jewelers'Werk . Washington DC . USA
Student work . Galerie Mari Funaki . Melbourne . AU
1995 Smykker mod år 2000 . Vejle Fair . Vejle . DK
4th Generation . Woods Gerry Gallery . Providence . USA
Guest Stars . Galerie Wittenbrink . München / Munich . DE
1994 Schmuck . IHM . München / Munich . DE (K)

(K) = Katalog / Catalogue

Publikationsverzeichnis / List of Publications

Ausst.-Kat. / Exh. cat. THE ONE WOMAN GROUP EXHIBITION . Museum Villa Stuck, München / Munich . DE
RIAN Design Museum Falkenberg SE 2019
Ausst.-Kat. / Exh. cat. Made in Denmark . Grassi Museum für Angewandte Kunst, Leipzig 2018 . DE
Ausst.-Kat. / Exh. cat. Private Confessions . Zeichnung & Schmuck . Museum Villa Stuck, München / Munich . DE
CODA Museum Apeldoorn . NL 2017
Ausst.-Kat. / Exh. cat. KNELL – The Gender Bell . Maurer Zilioli – Contemporary Arts, München / Munich 2017 . DE
Und Magazin / magazine Nr. 62, München / Munich 2017 . DE
NOOVO . digitales Magazin / digital magazine Februar / February 2017 . ES
Ausst.-Kat. / Exh. cat. Open Spaces – Mind Maps . Positions in Contemporary Jewellery . Nationalmuseum Kulturhuset
Stockholm 2016 . SE
Art Jewelry Forum (Interview mit Benjamin Lignel) . digitales Magazin / digital magazine 19.10.2016 . USA
Ausst.-Kat. / Exh. cat. Platina – 15 Years of Jewellery Art . Gallery Platina, Färgfabriken Stockholm 2014 . SE
Ausst.-Kat. / Exh. cat. CANVAS CONTEXT CASH . Maurer Zilioli – Contemporary Arts, München / Munich 2014 . DE
Current Obsession. Magazin / magazine März / March, Amsterdam 2014 / NL
Art Jewelry Forum (Interview mit Susan Cummins) . digitales Magazin / digital magazine 6.2.2014 . USA
Ausst.-Kat. / Exh. cat. Det Unikke Danske Smykke . Kunstetagerne, Hobro 2013 . DK
Ausst.-Kat. / Exh. cat. Sonderschau Schmuck . IHM (Internationale Handwerksmesse) München / Munich 2012 . DE
Ausst.-Kat. / Exh. cat. Embraced – Jewellery Sites, Gustavsbergs Konsthall 2011 . SE
Ausst.-Kat. / Exh. cat. Värksted . Johannes Larsen Museet, Kerteminde 2011 . DK
Ausst.-Kat. / Exh. cat. CANVAS . Galerie Spektrum, München / Munich 2011 . DE
Ausst.-Kat. / Exh. cat. Fortellinger I Sölv . Kunstnerforbundet, Oslo 2011 . NO
Ausst.-Kat. / Exh. cat. Omaggio a Guariento . Studio GR 20, Padua / Padova 2011 . IT
Ausst.-Kat. / Exh. cat. Sonderschau Schmuck 2010. IHM (Internationale Handwerksmesse) München / Munich 2010 . DE
Ausst.-Kat. / Exh. cat. KORU 3 . Imatra Art Museum, Imatra 2009 . FI
Ausst.-Kat. / Exh. cat. Room For New . Galerie Rob Koudijs, Amsterdam 2009 . NL
Ausst.-Kat. / Exh. cat. Des Wahnsinns Fette Beute . Die Neue Sammlung – Staatliches Museum für angewandte Kunst /
Design in der Pinakothek der Moderne, München . Munich 2008 . DE
Ausst.-Kat. / Exh. cat. De Main à Main . MUDAC (Museum of Contemporary Design and Applied Arts), Lausanne 2008 . CH
Ausst.-Kat. / Exh. cat. Golden Rain . MOCA (Museum of Contemporary Art), London 2008 . GB
Ausst.-Kat. / Exh. cat. FAMILYPORTRAITS . Galerie Spektrum, München / Munich 2008 . DE
Ausst.-Kat. / Exh. cat. New Play in Art . Fondazione Giardino André Heller, Gardone / Riviera 2008 . IT
Ausst.-Kat. / Exh. cat. Hnoss Depended . Hnoss Gallery . Röhsska Museum, Göteborg / Gothenburg 2007 . SE
Svenska Dagbladet . Zeitung / newspaper 21.4.2007 . SE
Ausst.-Kat. / Exh. cat. Sonderschau Schmuck . IHM (Internationale Handwerksmesse) München / Munich 2007 . DE
Ausst.-Kat. / Exh. cat. Sonderschau Schmuck 2006 . IHM (Internationale Handwerksmesse) München / Munich 2006 . DE
Ausst.-Kat. / Exh. cat. Collect . Galerie Louise Smit, Saatchi Gallery, London 2006 . GB
Ausst.-Kat. / Exh. cat. Skandal! Galeria Sztuki w Legnica, Legnica 2006 . PL
Ausst.-Kat. / Exh. cat. Pensieri Preziosi. Scuola di San Rocco, Padua / Padova 2005 . IT
Ausst.-Kat. / Exh. cat. Choice . Itami Museum of Arts and Crafts / JP . Galerie YU Hiko Mizuno College Tokio / Tokyo . JP
CODA Museum Apeldoorn . NL 2005
Ausst.-Kat. / Exh. cat. Valuable Links . Österreichisches Museum für Volkskunde, Wien / Vienna . AT
Centre Céramique, Maastricht 2004 . NL

Ausst.-Kat. / Exh. cat. Ringe i dialog . Nationalmuseum, Kopenhagen / Copenhagen 2004 . DK
Christianne Weber – Stöber, Schnellkurs Schmuck . Köln / Cologne . 2004 . DE
Ausst.-Kat. / Exh. cat. Gioelleria contemporanea . Studio GR20, Padua / Padova 2004 . IT
Peter Skubic, Christianne Weber-Stöber, Karola Weidemüller, Peter Egli, Experiment Schmuck
Das Erfurter Schmucksymposium 1984–2002 . Angermuseum Erfurt 2002, Schmuckmuseum Pforzheim 2003 . DE
Ausst.-Kat. / Exh. cat. Das Tier in Mir . Galerie Spektrum, München / Munich 2003 . DE
Ausst.-Kat. / Exh. cat. Sonderschau Schmuck . IHM (Internationale Handwerksmesse) München / Munich 2003 . DE
Ausst.-Kat. / Exh. cat. KORU 1 . South Karelia Museum, Lappenranta 2003 . FI
Kunsthandwerk und Design . Magazin / magazine 1/2003 . DE
PS van de week . Magazin / magazine 9.8.2003 . NL
Helsingin Sanomat . Zeitung / newspaper 19.7.2003 . FI
Etelä-Saimaa . Zeitung / newspaper 10.6.2003 . FI
Ausst.-Kat. / Exh. cat. Natur und Zeit . Deutsches Goldschmiedehaus, Hanau 2002 . DE
Kunsthandwerk und Design . Magazin / magazine 4/2002 . DE
Ausst.-Kat. / Exh. cat. 10. Erfurter Schmucksymposium . Erfurt 2002 . DE
Wiener Bezirks Blatt . Zeitung / newspaper 10/2002 . AT
Washington Post . Zeitung / newspaper 21.3.2002 . USA
Ausst.-Kat. / Exh. cat. Sonderschau Schmuck . IHM (Internationale Handwerksmesse), München / Munich 2001 . DE
Ausst.-Kat. / Exh. cat. Von Wegen . Deutsches Goldschmiedehaus Hanau 2001 . DE
Ausst.-Kat. / Exh. cat. Schmuck lebt! Schmuckmuseum Pforzheim 2001 . DE
Ausst.-Kat. / Exh. cat. 20 Jahre . Galerie Spektrum, München / Munich 2001 . DE
Ausst.-Kat. / Exh. cat. 100 Schmuckstücke. Schmuckmuseum Pforzheim 2001 . DE
Süddeutsche Zeitung . Zeitung / newspaper 1.3.2001 . DE
Ausst.-Kat. / Exh. cat. Mikromegas . Galerie für angewandte Kunst München / Munich . DE; American Craft Museum, New York . USA; Musée de l'horlogerie e de l'emaillerie, Genf / Geneva . CH; Galerie YU Hiko Mizuno College Tokio / Tokyo . JP; Powerhouse Museum, Sydney . AU; John Curtis Gallery, Curtis University, Perth . AU; Scuola di San Rocco, Padua / Padova 2001 . IT
Ausst.-Kat. / Exh. cat. The Ego Adorned . Koningin Fabiolazaal, Antwerpen / Antwerp . 2000 . BE
Ausst.-Kat. / Exh. cat. Schöne Aussichten . Galerie Spektrum, München / Munich 2000 . DE
Politiken . Zeitung / newspaper 15.3.2000 . DK
Politiken . Zeitung / newspaper 10.9.2000 . DK
Kerteminde Avis . Zeitung / newspaper 29.2.2000 . DK
Jyllands-Posten . Zeitung / newspaper 17.3.2000 . DK
JP København . Zeitung / newspaper 23.3.2000 . Herausgeber / Editor: JP København . DK
Ausst.-Kat. / Exh. cat. Sierraden Jewellery Zwolle's Choice . Galerie Marzee 1999 . NL
Abendzeitung München . Zeitung / newspaper 13.11.1998 . DE
Ausst.-Kat. / Exh. cat. Amsterdam München-Tokyo . Galerie für Angewandte Kunst, München / Munich . DE;
The Pavillon of the Gerrit Rietveld Academy, Amsterdam . NL; Gallery YU Hiko Mizuno College, Tokio / Tokyo . JP 1997
X-Ray . Magazin / magazine Juli 1997 . DE
Ausst.-Kat. / Exh. cat. Sonderschau Schmuck . IHM (Internationale Handwerksmesse) München / Munich 1996 . DE
Reizstoffe: 75 Jahre Danner-Stiftung . Positionen zum zeitgenössischer Kunsthandwerk . Stuttgart 1995 . DE
Ausst.-Kat. / Exh. cat. Sonderschau Schmuck . IHM (Internationale Handwerksmesse) München / Munich 1994 . DE

Impressum / Colophon

Dieser Katalog erscheint anlässlich der Ausstellung /
This catalogue is published on the occasion of the exhibition
THE ONE WOMAN GROUP EXHIBITION . KAREN PONTOPPIDAN

Museum Villa Stuck, München / Munich
14. Februar – 5. Mai 2019 / February 14 – May 5, 2019
RIAN Design Museum
25. Mai – 25. August 2019 / May 25 – August 25, 2019

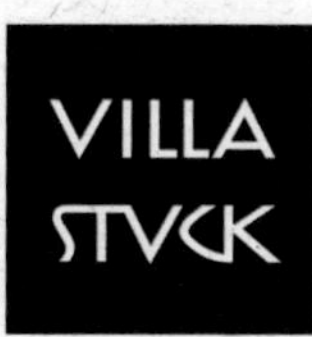

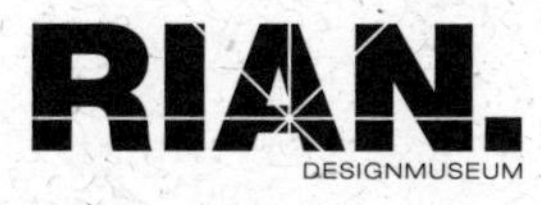

Katalog / Catalogue

Herausgeber*innen / Editors: Michael Buhrs, Ellen Maurer Zilioli
Redaktion / Editing: Josepha Brich, Sara Kühner,
Ellen Maurer Zilioli, Karen Pontoppidan
Lektorat / Copyediting: Tina Rausch (dt.), Sarah Trenker (engl.)
Übersetzung / Translation: Wendy Brouwer (engl.)
Gestaltung / Design: Susanne Dell
Installationsansichten / Installation Views: Jann Averwerser
Lithografie / Image Editing: Marc Teipel
Druck und Bindung / Printing and Binding: Gutenberg Beuys
Feindruckerei GmbH, Langenhagen
Produktion / Production Management: DISTANZ Verlag

Vertrieb / Distribution
edel Germany GmbH
www.edel.com
international-books@edel.com

ISBN 978-3-95476-279-8
Printed in Germany

Erschienen im / Published by
DISTANZ Verlag
www.distanz.de

Museum Villa Stuck
Prinzregentenstraße 60
D-81675 München
www.villastuck.de

Ausstellung / Exhibition

Kuratorin / Curator: Dr. Ellen Maurer Zilioli
Projektkoordinatorin / Project Coordination: Sara Kühner
Restauratorische Betreuung / Conservation: Susanne Eid
Ausstellungstechnik / Installation: Christian Reinhard und / and
Danni Chen, Michael Grudziecki, Johee Han, Johannes Koch,
Nadine Kuffner, Patrick Matthews, Robert Matthews, Kerol
Montagna

Direktor / Director: Michael Buhrs
Wissenschaftlicher Mitarbeiter / Research Associate:
Roland Wenninger
Leitung Sammlungen Franz von Stuck/Jugendstil / Head of
Franz von Stuck/Jugendstil Collections:
Margot Th. Brandlhuber
Volontärin / Trainee: Josepha Brich
Ausstellungskoordination / Exhibition Coordinators:
Nadja Henle, Sara Kühner, Dr. Sabine Schmid
Leitung Vermittlung / Head of Art Education: Anne Marr
FRÄNZCHEN. Kinder- und Jugendprogramm / Art Education:
Johanna Berüter
Ausstellungstechnik / Chief Preparator: Christian Reinhardt
Presse- und Öffentlichkeitsarbeit / Press and Public Relations:
Birgit Harlander, Anja Schneider
Verwaltungsleitung / Administration Officer: Gudrun Gaschler,
Annette Schier
Buchhaltung / Accounting: Sylvia Obermeier, Isabella Schleich
Verwaltungsmitarbeit / Administrative Assistant: Ruzica Bagaric
Technischer Dienst / Facility Management: Wolfgang Leipold
Leitung Aufsichtsdienst / Head of Security:
Georgios Sidiropulos, Erwin Richter

Leihgeber / Lenders

Schmuckmuseum Pforzheim
Die Neue Sammlung – The Design Museum, München / Munich (Sammlung / Collection Katrin Basiner)
Die Neue Sammlung – The Design Museum, München / Munich (Dauerleihgabe der / Permanent loan of the Danner-Stiftung)
Catherine Rose / Dallas, TX USA
Collection CODA Museum, Apeldoorn, Niederlande / The Netherlands
Sammlung / Collection Koudijs / Schrijver, Amsterdam
Sammlung / Collection Maurer Zilioli, München / Munich

Dank / Acknowledgments

Großen Dank an / A large word of thanks to:
Wolfgang, Jens, Frederik, Jörg, Susanne, Dagny, Sabine, Jasmin, Bobby, Oliver, Else, Martin, Regine, Maja, Marlene, Su

Fotograf*innen / Photographers: Antje und Oliver
Helferinnen / Assistants: Nadine, Danni, Joohee

Besonderen Dank für ihre Unterstützung an / For their support, special thanks go to:
Jasmin Matzakow und / and Matthias Mönnich

Ich danke der Zusammenarbeit mit / I am grateful for the help of:
Galerie Koudijs, Amsterdam
Maurer Zilioli – Contemporary Arts, München / Munich

K.A.R.E.N.P.O.N.T.O.P.P.I.D.A.N.